Charles Honorton and the
Impoverished State of Skepticism

CHARLES HONORTON
(1946–1992)

Charles Honorton and the Impoverished State of Skepticism

Essays on a Parapsychological Pioneer

Edited by
K. Ramakrishna Rao

McFarland & Company, Inc., Publishers
Jefferson, North Carolina, and London

British Library Cataloguing-in-Publication data are available

Library of Congress Cataloguing-in-Publication Data

Charles Honorton and the impoverished state of skepticism : essays on a parapsychological pioneer / edited by K. Ramakrishna Rao.
   p. cm.
Includes bibliographical references.
ISBN 0-7864-0003-X (lib. bdg. : 50# alk. paper) ∞
   1. Honorton, Charles, 1946- . 2. Parapsychologists—United States. 3. Parapsychology—United States—History—20th century.
I. Ramakrishna Rao, K.
BF1027.H66C48 1994
133.8′092—dc20   94-9066
                                             CIP

Manufactured in the United States of America

McFarland & Company, Inc., Publishers
 Box 611, Jefferson, North Carolina 28640

TABLE OF CONTENTS

PREFACE

The untimely death of Charles Honorton on November 4, 1992, shocked the parapsychological community as no other event has in recent years. He was only forty-six years old and had just moved to Edinburgh "to begin a new phase in his life." His considerable research accomplishments and his outstanding skills in debating and dealing with the skeptics and detractors of the field placed him in a leadership role. The expectations were high that Honorton was close to knocking on the doorsteps of the hall of science with a message that could no longer be ignored. All this came to an abrupt and unexpected end.

Several of us at the FRNM discussed what would be the most fitting tribute to Honorton that we could offer. We all agreed that a commemorative issue of the *Journal of Parapsychology* devoted to a discussion of Honorton's contributions to the field dating from his early days at the FRNM to his most recent activities in Scotland would be most appropriate. As I planned the issue and the possible contributions, it became clear that a single issue could not cover all that we wanted; we had enough material for two issues. Accordingly, the March and April 1993 numbers of the *Journal of Parapsychology* were devoted to the Honorton articles.

Once we had the manuscripts, I felt that the articles would have interest to many others besides the *Journal of Parapsychology* subscribers. Robbie Franklin, a friend of Chuck and of parapsychology, agreed; and the result is this book.

Almost everyone I approached to contribute to this volume agreed to the arrangement. They had short notice, but they met the deadline and provided articles that not only describe and assess Honorton's contributions to parapsychology but also give us the inspiration and direction for future research. I am grateful to all the contributors to this volume for their cooperation.

Mrs. Dorothy Pope did much of the editorial work with the assistance of Ms. Patricia Spivey. I acknowledge my indebtedness to them.

K.R. Rao
Durham, N.C.
May 1994

INTRODUCTION

By K. Ramakrishna Rao

Charles Honorton, "Chuck" to many of us, was a man of many talents. He was a natural leader, an outstanding researcher, a gifted experimenter, and an excellent communicator. To lead came naturally to him. He organized research even while he was in school and college, and he was a leader even when he was an apprentice under another powerful leader. He received no college degrees; yet, his guidance was sought by several who had PhD degrees. Holding no university appointments, he attracted tenured professors to his lab and impressed them with his knowledge and skills.

None of Chuck's talents, however, were apparent to a casual observer. In many ways he did not fit the conventional descriptions and stereotypes of "great men." In a sense, he was as anomalous as the phenomena he studied. Who would imagine that within that short and somewhat disproportionate physical frame was a powerful person, a born leader? Who would suspect that behind the childish face that exuded innocence rather than mature confidence, there was hidden such a seriousness of purpose and unshakable resolve? Again, who would have thought that this man, who spurned formal education, would make some of the most significant contributions for advancing parapsychology since the days of the Rhines? Chuck was simply a savant of his own kind.

Charles Honorton was born on February 5, 1946, in a small Minnesota town. His interest in parapsychology dates back to childhood. While in high school he corresponded with J. B. Rhine and spent summer months at the Parapsychology Laboratory of Duke University. He was enrolled at the University of Minnesota, but his intense and irresistible interest in psi research led him to leave the university before completing his undergraduate studies and to join Rhine at the newly established Institute for Parapsychology of the Foundation for Research on the Nature of Man. Chuck needed only a few years of apprenticeship with Rhine before maturing into a full-fledged parapsychologist.

Leaving the FRNM in 1967, Honorton joined Stanley Krippner and Montague Ullman at Maimonides Medical Center in Brooklyn and later became the Director of its Division of Parapsychology and Psychophysics. After the "Dream Lab" at Maimonides closed in 1979, Chuck obtained the support of James McDonnell and founded the Psychophysical Research Laboratories (PRL) in Princeton, NJ. PRL closed in 1989, and Chuck then moved on to Edinburgh, Scotland, in 1991, where he died on November 4, 1992.

The relationship between Chuck and the FRNM was very special. Chuck's professional career started there with J. B. Rhine as his mentor. Chuck was a regular contributor to the *Journal of Parapsychology*. When the PRL closed, he donated a good deal of PRL equipment, including the auto-ganzfeld, to the FRNM. Chuck admired and respected Rhine as a pioneer. His admiration was genuine; he named his only son Joseph Rhine. Rhine recognized Chuck's potential at an early stage and did what he could to nurture it. To be sure, there was disappointment and disenchantment on both sides, which culminated in Chuck's leaving the FRNM in 1967. Rhine and Honorton were two strong persons, each with his own agenda. They were like two swords that could not fit into a single sheath.

With Chuck's premature demise, the field of parapsychology lost one of its most productive and influential investigators. We at the FRNM considered a number of ways we could pay homage to this remarkable man. It was agreed that the best way we could do this would be to publish a series of articles on his life and work. Such a collection would not only be a fitting memorial tribute to him, but also an occasion to place his research and ideas in their most appropriate perspective so that they might inspire the future course of parapsychology. All the articles in this series are invited contributions.

We are glad that Don McCarthy, one of Chuck's close friends, has contributed the special article with which we begin this series. In his article, McCarthy focuses on more personal aspects of Chuck's life. As he points out, Chuck's "commitment to parapsychological investigation was absolute; his life was his work."

Chuck's professional life falls into four distinct epochs: (1) The preparatory period, which lasted until he left FRNM in 1967; (2) the stay at Maimonides from 1967–1978; (3) the PRL years, 1979–1989; and (4) the post-PRL days, including those at Edinburgh.

James C. Carpenter, who knew Chuck from his first Duke visit in 1962, describes the early period in his article. Drawing not only from Chuck's publications in the mainstream parapsychology journals, but also from such little known sources as *The Psi Worker's Newsletter*, Carpenter sketches the formative years of "the parapsychologist's parapsychologist" with a great deal of sensitivity, professional esteem, and personal affection for Chuck.

The Maimonides period is covered in the articles by Stanley Krippner and Mario Varvoglis. Both Krippner and Varvoglis were Honorton's colleagues at Maimonides and collaborated with him in some of his research. Reviewing Chuck's early ganzfeld experiments and the ESP-dream studies, Krippner concludes: "The ganzfeld work will stand as Charles Honorton's most important contribution to parapsychological research."

In his paper, Varvoglis, who worked with Chuck for about ten years, discusses the research during the latter part of Chuck's stay at Maimonides. This included the ganzfeld as well as RNG research. According to Varvoglis, Honorton considered his RNG study in which significant results were obtained in alpha-gated trials during feedback periods as one of his most promising lines of research.

Ephraim Schechter, who was at PRL from 1981 to 1986, describes in summary form the different projects carried out at PRL and the various people who were associated with Chuck. "PRL," writes Schechter, "was a combination of people and projects. So is its legacy. Chuck's vision and forcefulness attracted people to work with him on his projects and incorporate the energy and shared information as they pursued their own."

The final phase, which sadly was a very brief one, is discussed in the article by Robert Morris. Morris had been a friend of Chuck's since the Duke days, and it was at his home that Chuck breathed his last.

We conclude the first part of the memorial series, which sketches the progress of Chuck's work in its chronological order, with the paper Chuck completed just before his death for publication in *Scienza & Paranormale*, the journal of the Comitato Italiano per il Controllo delle Aftermazioni sul Paranormale, the Italian counterpart of CSICOP. This paper succinctly defines Chuck's final position as a psi researcher and the reason why he had such scant respect for the "self-appointed protectors" of science. "True skepticism," wrote Honorton, "involves the suspension of belief, not disbelief." He felt that the description of psi as paranormal has outlived its utility and that a more fruitful conceptualization is that psi involves anomalous processes, anomalous because they are "unexplained," and not "unexplainable."

The second part of the memorial series, which will follow in the next number, contains evaluations of Chuck's five major areas of contribution for advancing parapsychology: (1) the ESP-ganzfeld studies; (2) theoretical and conceptual advances; (3) use of meta-analyses in evaluating psi results; (4) development of special techniques for psi testing; and (5) dialogues with critics. These five areas are to be discussed in the articles by Daryl Bem, Rex Stanford, Jessica Utts, Richard Broughton, and John Palmer, respectively.

Chuck played many roles: administrator, fund raiser, public relations man, advocate of the case for psi, and so on; he was, however, primarily a research scientist. Clearly, his contributions to psi research are substantial and lasting. The ESP-ganzfeld studies he championed constitute one of the most important segments of parapsychology's credible database today. I think it most appropriate that Daryl Bem, who coauthored with Chuck the paper on ganzfeld experiments which will appear in the *Psychological Bulletin*, is the one to contribute the article dealing with Chuck's ganzfeld research. In this paper, specially written for this series, Bem summarizes the history of Honorton's ganzfeld work and describes in more personal terms their collaborative efforts to bring ESP-ganzfeld research to the attention of mainstream psychology.

Chuck's research effort was not expended for the purpose of reinventing the wheel or of merely amassing additional empirical data. He was a synthesizer and a system builder. His research focused on progressive research programs characterized by conceptual clarity, methodological rigor, and a well-thought-out theoretical framework. His emphasis on internal attention states as a means of reducing sensory noise and enhancing psi receptivity is based on his understanding of Patanjali's *Yoga Sutras*, and it is clearly the leading paradigm that guides much of current psi research. Rex Stanford, himself a highly regarded contributor to the theoretical domain of parapsychology, writes at some length in his article about the many facets of Honorton's contributions in dealing with perplexing empirical data. He points out that a common conceptual thread runs throughout much of Chuck's work. It is that sensitivity to internal cues is an important factor in successful psi. Stanford also believes that Honorton's goal was to obtain replicable evidence through process-oriented research that he could place before a broader scientific community.

As a researcher, Chuck was not a loner. His research was built on the achievements of the past research efforts, and he carefully blended his results with those of others for a maximum cumulative effect. He made full use of powerful analytical tools such as effect size and meta-analysis in forcefully presenting the case for psi. In so doing, not only did he achieve greater credibility for his own work, but he also brought about a fresh measure of confidence in earlier research results which might have been too weak to stand on their own. This aspect of Chuck's contribution is covered in the article by Jessica Utts, a statistician at the University of California, Davis. Utts provides an interesting outline of the development of meta-analysis as an evaluation tool in psi research and illustrates how it played an increasingly important role in the final decade of Chuck's life.

Honorton belonged to a small and select group of successful psi experimenters who obtained significant results with relative ease. For this reason he is regarded by some as a gifted experimenter. Perhaps he was. Experimental data are unambiguous in support of experimenter effects in psi research. Whether these effects are due to the exercise of psi by the experimenter is arguable, however. In the case of Chuck, it seems that his success was in no small part due to the attention he gave to providing the necessary psychosocial atmosphere in which subjects would feel at home and be at ease without being threatened in any way. Parapsychologists have known for many years that a warm, supportive, nonthreatening, and motivating environment is important for eliciting psi in the laboratory. Yet it is not uncommon to find a parapsychology test situation no different from what we would find in a physics or animal lab, with little attention given to the human side of testing. Chuck was different. He understood, more than anyone I know, the importance of the ecological validity of the tests we administer. It is therefore not surprising that those who visited his lab were uniformly impressed by the human side of his highly sophisticated technological set-up, one that was carefully crafted so as not to offend any of the subject's sensibilities but to maximize his/her involvement in the experiment. The unfailing warmth and cordiality with which subjects were greeted and treated, the subject-friendly experimental set-up, and the relaxing and yet highly motivating test environment that Chuck helped to create in his lab are likely to have been the main reasons for his experimental success.

Richard Broughton is one of those who was totally taken by Honorton's attention to detail in making his test techniques and equipment subject-friendly. In his article entitled "Chuck Honorton and the New Technology: A Craftsman and His Tools," Broughton, who shares Chuck's enthusiasm for high-tech gadgetry, describes in some detail the auto-ganzfeld set-up and several of the computer games crafted by Honorton, and he makes it easy for us to see why Chuck was such a successful psi experimenter.

Finally, Chuck was one of the more effective spokespersons and defenders of the case for parapsychology. He relentlessly endeavored to present his results to mainstream science. His early failures to publish in *Science* did not deter him from continuing that course. It is therefore highly significant that his last published paper will be in the *Psychological Bulletin*, a prestigious mainstream psychology journal. Chuck did not hesitate to defend parapsychology when it was unfairly attacked. He took Hansel head-on in his forthright 1965 review of the latter's book *ESP: A Scientific Evaluation*. He debated with Hyman in conferences and in journal articles. In his final response to psi critics, which is printed in this series, Honorton shows "the impoverished state of skepticism." John Palmer, who himself has had his own share of encounters with skeptics, brings out in his article the nuances of Chuck's critique of the critics, his logic, and his compelling arguments for taking psi research seriously.

The final piece in this collection is a bibliography of Honorton's writings by Carlos Alvarado and Rhea White, prominent bibliophiles among parapsychologists.

It is not easy for many of us to write about Chuck. Doing so has brought back many memories and deep sorrow at the realization that Chuck is no more. The field of parapsychology will miss him for more than one reason. He will be missed as a highly productive and ingenious experimental scientist; he will be missed as an effective spokesperson and a tireless champion of parapsychology's case; he will be missed as a leader to guide the course of psi research; and he will be missed as an affectionate friend and a valued colleague.

TO BOLDLY GO: AN APPRECIATION OF CHARLES HONORTON

By Donald McCarthy

It is not possible to describe Chuck Honorton meaningfully without also commenting on his work, but this will be primarily a subjective narrative. Chuck was a sufficiently complex person that it is unlikely any one individual can claim to offer a definitive view of the "real" Chuck Honorton; and while I have included anecdotes and comments from a number of people, the view presented here is of Chuck as I saw him. Making myself visible in this account may render it easier for others to filter me out and recognize the Chuck they knew.

Sometimes a more complete understanding of another person follows from knowledge of key aspects of that person's early, formative years. That certainly seems to be the case here. Chuck suffered from a congenital disease known as *osteogenesis imperfecta*. I once mentioned to a physician that I had a friend with this condition, and he asked if my friend was short, round, with a large head and a powerful intellect. He interpreted my startled glance as an affirmative and then asked if my friend had experienced heart problems, since the cardiac valves in such a person were likely to be prone to viral attack. After another nod, he conjectured that this friend almost certainly had experienced broken bones in childhood, because having weak, brittle bones was a major symptom of the disease. Right. In fact, Chuck had broken his legs at least nine times, and after each break, was immobilized in a full body cast for a period of months. I never appreciated what that entailed until one of my own children was in a similar cast for a short period of time; the degree of discomfort and confinement was truly impressive. Some of the personal qualities that might enable one to survive such a recurring traumatic ordeal were evident in Chuck as an adult: tremendous determination, genuine courage, and a robust sense of humor. It is

While the opinions expressed in this article are my own, I had input from many others, to whom I extend gratitude; special thanks go to Chuck's cousin, Gloria Brownlee, for clarifying some early history and to Ephraim Schechter for helpful comments on preliminary versions of this paper.

easy to conjecture that such childhood experience might enhance either a pragmatic willingness to deal unflinchingly with harsh reality, or a powerful ability to escape into the realm of the mind; these seemingly contradictory tendencies were both strongly evident in Chuck, in a very special blend. Bob Morris remarked that Chuck once told him how much he hated the feeling of being powerless and at the mercy of others that he had experienced while in those body casts; perhaps that contributed to a desire to maintain control and not relinquish power over himself to others. In any case, Chuck liked to be in charge of situations and to do things in his own way.

Chuck always seemed to rely on his own inner resources. He had no siblings and lived alone with his parents, Henry and Emma, in St. Paul during the school year, spending summers with his mother's family in Grand Rapids, where several cousins lived nearby. There Chuck stayed with his grandmother and his Uncle Ed, who was deaf. This last is significant, for Chuck told me that his interest in parapsychology really grew out of early speculations that arose from time spent with his uncle, who clearly inhabited a different perceptual world.

For reasons I can only speculate on, Chuck also developed an early interest in hypnosis; he once described a typical Honorton family scene: a young lad bidding an early good night to his parents and then going up to his room to stare at a candle for long periods as an autohypnosis exercise. By all accounts, Chuck enjoyed some success as a stage hypnotist while in high school, but eventually gave up hypnosis because he was uncomfortable with the power over others it could confer. In connection with this, he mentioned an incident later in life that involved his reluctant use of hypnosis to relieve the pain of someone close to him who was dying of cancer, and his distress in playing this role. I thought, incorrectly as it turned out, that this story involved his mother, but in fact she died of a heart attack as did many members of her family, including Chuck. His father had died earlier, when Chuck was a teenager, as the result of a fall from a low building where he was working as a window washer—a fall that was witnessed by Chuck, who had gone to meet his father after work. Chuck's cousin Gloria said this experience affected him profoundly and led to his giving up on religion; Chuck was unwilling to accept the existence of a personal God who could allow his father to die in such a pointless accident.

On matters of religion I always found Chuck to be a thoughtful agnostic, and if he had a hidden spiritual agenda, as certain critics seem to suspect of parapsychologists, it was very well hidden. He had no doubts whatsoever about the reality of psi phenomena, but this was based on evidence rather than on unshakable prior commitment; Chuck asserted bluntly that he had no interest in wasting his time, and his life's work, by fooling himself. He acknowledged that the statistical evidence for psi, while very strong, was not compelling, but he had witnessed far too many powerful examples of nonsensory communication under carefully controlled laboratory conditions to maintain personal disbelief. Yes, the phenomena were genuine, but he felt that the nature of psi was still unknown, and he remained largely unwilling to speculate. Chuck had no personal conflict with the possibility that psi phenomena might ultimately be accounted for in some manner that extended, rather than disrupted, the formulations of contemporary physics; but he was also willing to acknowledge that adequate understanding of psi might well require a drastic revision in our concept of the nature of physical reality. While he seemed equally open to either possibility, he recognized that others might not be, and his immediate concern was to gain acknowledgment of the legitimacy of scientific investigation of psi and to stimulate interest in pursuing such investigation. He told me, not long ago, that in designing the ganzfeld procedure, a primary reason for his choosing a telepathy protocol was that it might lead to more ready acceptance, since people seemed less threatened by the idea of "mental radio" than by other ways of conceptualizing psi.

Whatever Chuck's personal motivation for getting into parapsychology, it was a passionate pursuit, and all other aspects of his life assumed supporting roles. In attending the University of Minnesota, he eagerly took those courses that seemed relevant to the career he had already decided to pursue; but when it appeared that continuing in college would advance his objectives more slowly than full-time investigation, he dropped out of school and went to work for J. B. Rhine. While he remained a ferocious learner all his life, Chuck did not formally return to school until he enrolled in a doctoral program at the University of Edinburgh; and his chief motivation in relocating to Scotland was not to earn a degree, but rather to have an opportunity to pursue research again after his own laboratory closed. Chuck deeply admired his mentor, Dr. Rhine, but truly envied him for one thing: his good fortune in having a lifelong colleague and intellectual companion in his wife, Louisa. Many years after Chuck's own marriage ended in divorce, he continued to express a deep yearning for such a comrade, but I suspect it would have taken someone of the stature and dedication of Louisa Rhine to pull it off; for he was not only married to his work, but deeply in love with it. I've never seen anything quite comparable to the undiluted joy Chuck brought to the analysis of fresh experimental data. His commitment to parapsychological investigation was absolute; his life was his work.

My own involvement with parapsychology began almost accidentally. In 1974, part of my teaching duties at St. John's University was in a special undergraduate program that was interdisciplinary and somewhat unorthodox. I usually taught mathematics, but that year I wound up running a seminar in "Unexplained Phenomena" as a replacement for an anticipated course in parapsychology that was to have been conducted by Rex Stanford. When it turned out that Rex would not be available, I agreed to try to put something together for the Fall semester that would address several topics, including parapsychology, in the broad context of philosophy of science. That seemed feasible on paper, but knowing nothing of the current state of parapsychology, I made desperate contact with Rex that summer, and he served as a gracious and stimulating mentor. I read a lot, we talked a lot, and I had a wonderful opportunity to see a lot of parapsychologists up close, for the annual convention of the Parapsychological Association was to take place that August right on the St. John's campus. That convention was dubbed by some as "the year of the ganzfeld"; thus, my first exposure to Chuck Honorton was, appropriately enough, in the context of the experimental paradigm that became the focus of his finest work.

Actually, my strongest recollections of my first PA conference are of a post-convention party, held at Chuck's apartment in Brooklyn, and of a conversation we had that did not seem to end much before dawn—a precursor of many late-night discourses we would share over the years. However, those were well into the future; I actually had little personal contact with Chuck during the next year and a half, as my interest in parapsychology was still being piqued and fed by Rex Stanford, who was close at hand. That situation was due to change, for Rex was planning to leave St. John's for a full-time research opportunity in Texas. Thus, in the Spring of 1976, accompanied by Rex, I paid my first visit to Chuck's lab in the Maimonides Medical Center in Brooklyn, and a wonderful period of my life began. It was a casual association at first, but eventually Chuck became my closest personal friend and remained so for more than a decade.

The Maimonides lab is worth describing. Located in the basement of the Community Mental Health Center in the hospital complex, it was still known to most of the hospital locals as "The Dream Lab" despite the sign beside the door that proclaimed it to be the Division of Parapsychology and Psychophysics, a name that must surely have been chosen by Chuck. The basic decor of the lab was that of the surrounding basement: institutional cinderblock. This, together with the underground location and the absence of windows, led to its more familiar designation by lab staff as "The Bunker." Despite the stark surroundings and the presence of special equipment that gave some of the rooms a distinctly technical flavor, the atmosphere that greeted a visitor was warm and friendly. That is certainly how it seemed to me when I first visited, and I subsequently realized that lab personnel made a special effort to create just that atmosphere.

Indeed, Chuck made sure that everyone working in the lab agreed on one fundamental policy: People who came to participate in an experiment were to be given warm attention and made to feel welcome and at ease. "Look," he often said, "if we want to encourage someone to let us see what's going on inside their head, or to do things that are out of the ordinary, then they need to feel comfortable with us and with the situation." This was something he never let co-workers lose sight of; there was little chance that a subject in one of Chuck's studies would be handled like a rat in a maze. This was especially true of "special subjects," who are sometimes treated by experimenters with remarkable insensitivity. Despite the fact that much of the focus of his research was on developing replicable procedures that other investigators could employ to obtain comparable results without the need for access to subjects with special talents, Chuck was delighted by the opportunity to work with gifted people like Malcolm Bessent and Felicia Parise, and he treated them as collaborators and friends. He gave them the attention they deserved and took special pains to develop procedures in which the experimental controls were unobtrusive and the psi tasks tailored to suit their personal styles. Of course the ultimate motivation was to maximize results, but the feelings were genuine, and Chuck had warm, long-term relationships with Malcolm and Felicia, and with Ellen Messer, his first ganzfeld superstar. To Chuck, these were not special subjects, they were very special friends.

At any rate, I liked the atmosphere at the Maimonides lab, felt welcome, and eagerly signed on as a volunteer. I spent several full days there each month, soaking up information, learning the ropes, and trying to find ways to be helpful. Initially I served as a critical reader/listener, and as a foil for new ideas; at times I played the role of subject or experimenter in working the kinks out of a new procedure; mostly I asked a lot of questions. I learned a great deal about parapsychology and about how to be an experimental investigator; my training was in theoretical mathematics, and I had quite a lot to learn about dealing with key aspects of experimental life: equipment, data, people. So I learned! Chuck expected his lab personnel to learn, to master whatever was needed to get the job done properly. Sometimes this was a definite challenge; for example, when a battery of fancy new biofeedback equipment arrived, Chuck insisted that all the regular staff learn to use each of the devices— a formidable task, since the equipment manuals were filled with technical jargon and written in the literary style of an apartment lease. At one point a frustrated volunteer, struggling unsuccessfully to program the skin temperature device so that it would sample at specified intervals, suggested that it was impossible to figure out how to work the thing and that it was unreasonable for Chuck to dump this task on her. Chuck just stepped over and unhestitatingly showed her how to do it. No one knew when he had deciphered the manuals and acquired expertise in using the equipment, but he had, and he expected them to do the same. Similarly, Chuck wanted everyone in the lab to acquire reasonable proficiency at statistical analysis; he could easily have done all the analyses himself more quickly and reliably, but the goal was not simply to get the job done, but to develop personal competence and understanding. Gradually it dawned on me that in Chuck's view the business of the lab was not just to conduct research, but to advance the field by developing competent experimenters.

Slowly I came to appreciate what an incredible apprenticeship I had fallen into, almost by walking in off the street! Chuck made such opportunities available freely; if you were interested and capable and willing to learn, you were welcome. At that time the lab was staffed almost entirely by young volunteers; a small core of regulars was augmented by a transient flow of eager newcomers who contributed their energy and assistance. Chuck welcomed them and encouraged them to find their niche; self-starters were especially welcome and their creative input was solicited. Those who came up with good ideas for projects received initial praise and encouragement followed by probing criticism and, if they could take the heat, a round of additional encouragement and more challenging criticism. Those who couldn't handle it dropped out or fell into disfavor; and over time there were quite a few of the latter.

Chuck was willing to play the heavy: the tough, unrelenting, exacting Master Craftsman. In restrospect I came to see him in the role of a potter or perhaps a smith, shaping raw materials, seeking and developing inherent good features, gauging potential, testing strength, firing/tempering the best pieces in his kiln/forge, admiring the finished products that met his expectations and discarding those he found flawed. To one of these human products such treatment could be unpredictable, confusing, and threatening: today he might be the well-turned urn, but tomorrow he could be just another shard on the scrap heap. Thus the behind-the-scenes atmosphere in the lab was not always as pleasant and relaxed for the staff as it was for subjects and visitors. Chuck was a tough man to work for. Long-term survival required a favorable balance between one's potential and limitations—as seen by Chuck. All this was only dimly perceived at the time, and not everyone may agree with my interpretation. I cannot recall that Chuck ever explained this apprentice system and his role as master/teacher explicitly to anyone; perhaps this was something else he expected people to figure out on their own. Few of us did so to our satisfaction—or his. During my Maimonides apprenticeship I was mildly perplexed by the tacit rules of the game, but I was treated very well personally. Although we weren't close friends as yet, my relations with Chuck were very amiable, and I felt I was held in high regard. This may have been due, at least in part, to the simple fact that I was not on the scene on a daily basis, so that my limitations were not as evident as my potential; and before the balance could shift, my potential soared, for the lab acquired a computer. Here at last was an area where I had some relevant expertise; not a great deal, actually, but I was at the least an advanced learner.

That first computer provided quite a learning experience for all of us. A Cromemco System III, it was one of the most powerful microcomputers available at the time, which was early 1978. It followed the leading industry standard: a Z-80 CPU with an S-100 bus; running under CP/M, the Cromemco had dual (8-inch) floppy disk drives and a huge 64K of RAM. Anyone familiar with the current generation of microcomputers should find these specifications amusing, although all that technical jargon made as little sense to us initially as it would to a complete computerphobe today. However, we learned quickly, and Chuck was certainly not phobic about computers; indeed, he was captivated by their potential. From the outset, his view of the role of the lab computer went far beyond the possibilities for mechanized collection and analysis of experimental data. He envisioned a situation in which computers were used to manage all the details of an experiment, maintaining precautions against sensory leakage and data corruption while presenting the subject with an entertaining and engaging task, and at the same time leaving the experimenter free to create optimal interpersonal conditions.

During the next few years, a lot of brainstorming took place in Chuck's lab about the kinds of things that might be done. The fact that the same underlying psi task could be presented to the subject in a variety of different guises led to the idea of a super-experiment that could be personalized for individual subjects. The computer would select from a pool of apparent tasks one that was optimally suited to the subject's personality and mood; optimality would be determined by consulting an on-going database that would keep track of past performance correlated with a variety of factors. In addition to choosing the style of the experimental task, it would be possible for the computer to manipulate other aspects of the experimental environment as well, such as lighting or music. All this was pie-in-the-sky, of course, but it suggests the way in which the mere presence of the computer stimulated our thinking and raised the level of excitement in the lab. Chuck was certainly stimulated, and while he never implemented the truly grand schemes we conjured up (the above scenario was just one of many), a few ambitious computer projects were brought to fruition, most notably the Psi Lab package, which included several computer psi games that could be distributed to other laboratories, and the automated ganzfeld experiment. But all that occurred well after the lab had ceased to exist at Maimonides and was reincarnated in new improved form as the Psychophysical Research Laboratories (PRL) in the fall of 1979.

In terms of improvement, the most significant aspects of PRL were a much greater degree of autonomy and funding stability than was the case at Maimonides, but the physical environment was noteworthy as well. In sharp contrast to The Bunker, not only was the new lab rather spacious, but most of the offices had a wall of windows. Chuck's corner office had two such walls, and he worked in sunlight for the first time in many years. Located in a research park just outside Princeton, PRL was considerably less accessible than its metropolitan predecessor, hence less densely populated by the accustomed stream of volunteer workers and interested subjects. I continued my involvement by making monthly pilgrimages, staying for several days during each visit. My friendship with Chuck had blossomed by this point, partly as a result of sharing an unpleasant ordeal shortly before leaving Maimonides. One of the lab workers, concerned about the fact that funding for PRL was to come from a source he perceived as an agent of the military-industrial complex, decided to uphold the purity and integrity of the lab by taking into his personal custody all the computer disks, which represented a year's collection of data and programs. He craftily safeguarded all the back-up copies as well. While Chuck was quite capable of great diplomacy, he did not often exercise it, even under ordinary circumstances. In this situation he was simply furious, and having the culprit thrown in jail was one of the milder alternatives he considered. However, because this person was someone who had been a valuable worker and a good friend for many years, and since he did in fact have all those fragile floppy disks, several of us were able to persuade Chuck to approach the problem with more finesse. It was sticky for awhile, and banding together to provide counsel and emotional support led to deeper bonds of friendship. In time the disks were recovered and the Cromemco continued running experiments smoothly at PRL.

Soon after this, Chuck purchased a small personal computer of his own so that he could increase his programming skills (and thereby be less dependent on others), and also have something to work on when the lab computer was in use. That machine was a Radio Shack TRS-80 with 16K of RAM, and it stored data on audio cassettes. I mention this to indicate the primitive state of microcomputer technology at the time Chuck began to be actively involved. He followed the computer literature closely, and when funds became available for additional equipment, he was able to make a shrewd decision. Rather than duplicate the Cromemco system, he decided to obtain a battery of less expensive Apple II computers, which were then emerging as ideal laboratory machines. The Apples were also ideal game machines and easier to program than the aging Cromemco.

In a reasonably short time Chuck had preliminary versions of some interesting psi games up and running—not bad for someone who knew absolutely nothing about programming only a short time before. Chuck was an impressive learner. The microcomputer field skyrocketed, with new developments occurring at a breathtaking pace; Chuck stayed at the cutting edge. I made a sharp upward revision of my already high impression of his intellectual abilities. Here we were, learning about microcomputers together, although not quite starting on equal footing, as I had a tremendous initial advantage, being a professional mathematician and having taught programming courses; but soon Chuck had far outstripped me in terms of his knowledge of computer hardware and mastery of software tools. Anything that would be useful in his work he learned in depth and with lightning speed. He upgraded to more powerful computers several times and acquired great proficiency with an impressive variety of software packages for database manipulation, statistical analysis, word processing, desktop publishing, as well as programming. Chuck and I were equally inspired by the incredible capabilities of these wonderful computers, but while I was enamored of the possibilities almost for their own sake, he always had a bottom line: "How can I use this in parapsychology?" He viewed everything with that objective in mind.

Still, Chuck did get hooked on computers. I remember an incident when he wanted to leave a phone number with his son Joe; characteristically, he entered the number in the dialing directory on his home computer, and was attempting to explain how to access it in his absence. When Joe said "Gee, Dad, why don't you just write it on a piece of paper?" Chuck seemed genuinely startled and complied only with obvious reluctance. In later years, when Joe himself discovered the joys of computing via electronic bulletin boards, Chuck was deeply pleased. Not long ago, in a visit to my home, he noticed how I had collected all the assorted games and novelties on my own computer into a folder I'd labelled "FUN"; he commented how that was a good idea, but it wouldn't work for him, since to him it was all fun. How true. Quite apart from computers, Chuck had a long-standing fondness for high-tech devices. He had been a ham radio operator as a kid, and as an adult always had first-rate stereo equipment at home. He was particularly happy with the new audio system he had purchased in Scotland; and when I visited, he proudly demonstrated to me how the sound envelope on the compact disk player could be selected from a menu of options or could even be custom tailored, all using a remote controller; Chuck really enjoyed showing off sophisticated gadgetry and his mastery of it. But good audio and good music served a useful purpose as well in helping him work more effectively; he often listened via a headset when laboring at his computer in the office. He had strong preferences in music, but his tastes were varied; recent favorites ranged from Segovia classic guitar, to Cowboy Junkies rock, to Enya New Age pop, to Rimsky-Korsakov's *Scheherazade*. Sometimes he worked for days in silence, but more often, not.

Chuck's work habits are worth commenting on. I recall one time when a call arrived at PRL from someone at the primary funding source; it was about 11:00 a.m. and Chuck was not yet at the lab. The caller, doubtless working a variant of a nine-to-five schedule, found this most peculiar and probably wondered what sort of unprofessional goof-off was being funded. The basic fact is that Chuck was a night person by preference. The habit dated back at least as far as the early days of the Maimonides dream experiments when working through the night made it natural to sleep through the morning. Long after this justification had expired, Chuck resisted early rising; often he would not begin work until well after noon. John Palmer, visiting from the West Coast, once commented how he enjoyed staying with Chuck when he came east, since that way his body could remain on California time. But while he typically got a late start, Chuck usually continued working long after everyone else had gone home. Ellen Messer recounted leaving him hard at work in The Bunker late one afternoon and returning the next day to find him sitting at his desk in exactly the same position, under what looked like the same aromatic cloud of Captain Black pipe tobacco. She wondered if he'd been there the whole time; quite possibly. There were periods at Maimonides when, for various reasons, Chuck did not go home at all but slept at the lab, close to the work. It took a lot to pry him from it. On one occasion, Pat Barker, making a trek to the administrative offices to pick up her paycheck, asked Chuck if he'd like her to get his as well; having gotten a nod of assent, she found he had three checks waiting unclaimed! In a real sense his work was its own reward. At PRL, he no longer slept in the lab, but it was not unusual for him to put in ten hours a day, seven days a week.

What does a workaholic do for recreation? Usually more work, but Chuck had other outlets as well. In addition to listening to music, he read voraciously, usually for several hours each night before sleeping. The shelves behind his bed were filled with partially read books, folded open to mark his place; he might easily have five or six going at a time. He enjoyed mysteries and science fiction, as well as a variety of non-fiction, especially biography and solid popular science writing; and he devoured computer magazines. He had a lingering interest in tales of the Old West, dating back to childhood periods of confinement, when he had read original accounts of the bad old days in the archives of the *Tombstone Gazette*. Chuck followed political events closely and, among all my knowledgeable acquaintances, was easily the most astute; having him provide an insightful commentary on the Sunday morning TV analyses of national affairs was often an educational experience. Apart from news shows, he didn't watch a great deal of television, except for a few favorite dramatic series that he followed avidly; *China Beach, LA Law,* and *Crime Story* were high on his list. Chuck was also a big movie fan. During my monthly visits to PRL we usually saw at least one film, if anything good was playing in the area; and what we missed in the theaters, he caught later on videotape (this was especially true during the period after the lab closed its doors and he was working at home). Good science fiction movies were his particular favorites and he habitually organized (and funded at his personal expense) special expeditions of lab staff to see film like *Star Wars*, or the latest Indiana Jones adventure. The hands-down winner of the Chuck Honorton award for best movie of the year was *Close Encounters of the Third Kind*. Chuck must have seen that film well over a dozen times, taking various groups of friends; Ellen Messer said jokingly that he was the only person she knew who thought it was a documentary— or wished it were.

In this context, it is worth pointing out that Chuck was an ardent *Star Trek* fan. Like many of us who were captured by the wonder of that remarkable 1960s television series, he had seen each of the episodes many times. In the Princeton area, rebroadcasts of the original shows were commonly available during the evening on several cable channels, and in flipping the dials to see what was on TV, Chuck's son Joe would often stumble on a *Star Trek* in progress; at this point he and Chuck would match wits to see who would be first to identify the episode. Chuck once commented with a wry smile that having *Star Trek* playing unattended in the background was rather comforting, and had for him many of the same qualities as a fire burning on an open hearth. I feel that some of Chuck's deepest qualities are epitomized in the *Star Trek* theme: "to explore strange new worlds... to boldly go where no man has gone before."

In a memorial gathering after Chuck's death, Ruth Reinsel made some cogent remarks about parapsychologists and science fiction. She observed that her own interest in parapsychology had grown from reading science fiction since childhood, for it was this genre that suggested most strongly that there is more to life than meets the eye, that the mind is capable of wondrous things, that there is a veil that clouds our vision of reality and that we can learn to pierce that veil and see what lies beyond, whatever it may be. This may sound like religious motivation to some, but it really springs from a different source. Ruth commented that among her scientific acquaintances, parapsychologists seemed to include a higher percentage of science fiction buffs, and speculated that those drawn to parapsychology were often the ones willing to investigate questions that were taboo in other disciplines, and eager to confront the boundaries of our understanding of nature, of reality, and of mind.

Thus it may be natural for parapsychology to attract those willing to explore strange new words...to boldly go....

At any rate, *Star Trek* found a responsive chord in Chuck that was revealed in some of his work. The first computerized psi task developed at Maimonides was called "Psi Trek" and had an explicit *Star Trek* theme; and more than a few people commented on how the experimenter's console for the autoganzfeld set-up at PRL reminded them of the bridge of the starship "Enterprise." This should be viewed, not as a personal indulgence in fantasy, but rather an explicit attempt to tap into a rich theme that resonated deeply in many of those likely to volunteer as subjects in parapsychology. More generally, it was an effort to create an experimental environment that provided subtle encouragement to suspend the psychological restrictions of mundane consensus reality. The lab atmosphere was one of benign high technology with futuristic overtones, gently inviting participation in exploring a scientific understanding of the world of tomorrow. Besides, anyone exposed to *Star Trek* knew that in that future setting a form of telepathy (at least among Vulcans) was accepted as scientific fact; permission was tacitly being given for psi to be manifested.

There is another level on which I strongly associate Chuck with *Star Trek*. Friends who worked with J. B. Rhine have often commented on the extent to which Chuck seems to have modelled his professional style after Rhine's. I can only accept their judgment on this, but it always seemed to me that Chuck was a representative of the James T. Kirk school of executive management. For non-trekers, Kirk was the fictional captain of the starship "Enterprise," who ran his ship with absolute authority. Honorton often reminded me of Kirk in the way he managed his staff; but the heroic Captain had the advantage of years of sophisticated Starfleet training in decision-making skills, as well as a highly trained crew raised in a semimilitary tradition of unquestioning obedience to authority. Even Kirk made mistakes. George Hansen, who was the last crew member still on board when PRL was decommissioned, and who had not always enjoyed being subject to the Captain's stern authority, made an insightful observation. He commented that Chuck had absolutely no lust for personal power or high position, but sometimes he needed power to achieve his goals, so he used it.

Chuck did indeed have goals, far-reaching, visionary goals, that he reviewed continually in his own mind but did not always elaborate on to others. Unfortunately, he sometimes imposed these goals on his lab workers without inviting collaborative input or evaluation;

and there were times when critical feedback would have been very helpful. At PRL, in considering prospective staff members with special skills, Chuck often envisioned the wonderful potential they had for contributing to fulfillment of his goals, and during the early phases of employment, he gave new workers enthusiastic encouragement. Typically this was followed by a period of disenchantment as he came to see that his great expectations were unrealistic; even when the potential was there in principle, the time frame was usually off by at least an order of magnitude. The less desirable aspects of the Maimonides apprenticeship program were still operative at PRL, with the effects exaggerated now that the stream of expendable volunteers had been replaced by a more permanent group of paid employees. When Chuck's estimate of the potential for attaining his goals crashed, it often led to reassignment of a worker from personal creative projects to more mundane aspects of lab activities on the grounds that this was necessary to achieve the overall objectives of PRL ("That's what you're being paid to do, Mister"). Honorton ran his ship with a heavy hand, sometimes provoking mutinous sentiments in the crew.

Perhaps some of this could have been avoided if Chuck had made his goals more explicit and had submitted them to the sort of collegial review that might lead to more realistic initial expectations or alternative objectives. On occasion he did do this, but generally he seemed reluctant to air his deeper views before thinking them through to his satisfaction; and there were some areas in which he simply had no interest in modifying, or even discussing, his plans. I suspect there were times when Chuck assumed that what was evident to him should also be clear—and desirable—to anyone who took the trouble to think about it. In this I think he underestimated both the power of his own intellect and the diversity of alternative viewpoints. He deliberately avoided peer review by anyone he did not fully accept as a peer and sometimes appeared tremendously stubborn in resisting good ideas that didn't fit in with his plans. Even when he had strong reasons for resisting, he often would not bother to explain his thinking. This somewhat arbitrary, authoritarian stance contributed to problems in management and staff morale.

Yet, when I think of Chuck as a friend, it is clear that his most salient personal characteristics bore little trace of such autocratic privacy, but involved a potent blend of openness and honesty. Indeed, our friendship rested on a base of brutal candor, a prime ingredient being self-honesty. Chuck was not strong on pretense; he was quick to point out the faults of others, but subjected himself to the same critical appraisal. In private he acknowledged his lack of effective executive skills, but had no remedy for it. He looked forward with pleasure to a time when he might have the opportunity to pursue research without the burdens of running the entire show.

Chuck wore a number of hats. One of them was that of single parent. His marriage had dissolved in the early Maimonides years, and for almost ten years he lived alone as a bachelor, except when young Joey came to visit for a few weeks during summer; then, a year after PRL opened, a fourteen-year-old Joe came to live with him permanently. Chuck struggled with the complexities of raising a teenager, often resorting to the familiar methods of Captain Kirk. At times it wasn't easy for either of them, but having Joe around enriched Chuck's life enormously.

Meanwhile, back at the lab, Chuck juggled careers in administration, fund raising, and public relations, to balance his activities as experimenter, computer expert, and meta-analyst, all the while engaging in an intense dialog with critics. With the exception of administration, he did a magnificent job. He had many talents; he was a very fine writer, an excellent public speaker, and a superb debater. Chuck worked hard to get the most out of himself; he could type about as fast as I could read, he was himself a speed reader, and he had truly impressive learning skills. The goals he set himself were enormous, and he was frustrated by the need to play so many roles. His greatest frustrations, though, came from failure to win the attention of the scientific community, at being unable to publish in mainstream journals, or gain the thoughtful evaluation his work, and the field, deserved.

Over the years, it was driven home forcefully to me that life as a parapsychologist is often filled with frustration. From my own experiences as a mathematician, I was familiar with some of the personal difficulties to be expected in pursuing a research career, but I could not have imagined the special hardships most workers in parapsychology endure, not the least of which is the skepticism and ridicule provided by colleagues in other scientific disciplines. Chuck once commented with some bitterness that one of the rewards of obtaining strong positive psi results seemed to be that often skeptics would question one's competence, and then one's integrity. Yet, because scientific acceptance was such an important goal, he exerted strenuous efforts to maintain a dialog with those critical of the field.

Another eye-opener for me was the tremendous difficulty in obtaining funding for research in parapsychology. Chuck did much better than most, partly because he won the interest and regular financial support of James McDonnell, but even that was precarious at times. At Maimonides, the funding from Mr. Mac was provided one year at a time, and each year the decision to renew support was pushed back later and later. At one point, a commitment for the coming year was not obtained until several months after the previous funding period had expired. There were times when the continued existence of the Maimonides laboratory was in serious doubt. I recall one meeting when Chuck informed the staff that it was unclear if they would be able to continue for more than another week or two, and if anyone was in serious financial difficulty, well, he had a few thousand dollars in personal savings he could make available in an emergency. When PRL was established with funding supplied by the McDonnell Foundation, Chuck insisted that they be given a five-year commitment. At the end of that period, funds were committed for an additional five years, but toward the end, some of that money was diverted from PRL to other projects. Efforts to secure alternative long-term funding proved fruitless, and the lab went out of business. In parapsychology, being absolutely top notch is not enough to assure survival. Chuck was fond of citing the impressive work done at PRL as evidence of what could be accomplished with adequate long-term financial support. His point is a good one, but the success of PRL should be properly attributed to the superb job done by Chuck and a dedicated team of gifted researchers.

The closing of PRL was a personal ordeal for Chuck, with the final weeks brightened only by the spectacular results being obtained with the Juilliard students in a series of truly exceptional ganzfeld sessions. After the lab finally closed, Chuck was essentially unemployed for two years; but he worked at home on a number of projects, chiefly the analysis of the ganzfeld data and the writing of some of his best papers. When the time came to leave for Edinburgh, he was eager to get back to experimental work, although he regretted leaving Joe; and he had some concerns about how well his arthritic body would handle the Scottish clime. In fact Chuck did very well physically in the new location and was deeply satisfied at being reunited with Bob and Joanna Morris. He enjoyed the research team at Edinburgh, and things were progressing nicely. The set-up for the new autoganzfeld experiment was finally near completion, and soon he could start collecting data. He told me, via electronic mail, of his recent activities: He had finished his article evaluating contemporary criticism of the field and was looking forward to a long period of focusing on other areas. He was about to deliver a presentation at the Cavendish Lab that promised to be very rewarding; and that important paper with Daryl Bem had been submitted to *Psychological Bulletin*—access to an influential mainstream journal at last! In addition to all this professional satisfaction, Chuck had found someone to love; all in all, I'd say he seemed as happy as at any time since I'd known him. The icing on the cake must have been his watching the election returns in the wee hours and having things turn out just as he'd hoped. Then he died.

Chuck was a good friend, and I miss him sorely. It seems fitting to close with the comments of a mutual friend, Norman Herzberg. A mathematician living in the Princeton area, Norman was a frequent visitor at PRL; his initial interest involved computers, but he was curious about just what it was that Chuck was up to in that lab. A true iconoclast, Norman generally offered probing observations from a unique and valuable perspective. Upon learning of Chuck's death he had this to say: "Chuck was one of the brightest and most honest men I knew. It was never a secret that I did not share Chuck's enthusiasm for parapsychology. But he was someone who clearly was searching for the truth and was willing to see where that would lead him. One had to take him seriously, and so in the end, to reconsider the whole field as well. I will miss him as a friend, but parapsychology, I think, will miss him more." Just so.

THE EARLY PARAPSYCHOLOGICAL CONTRIBUTIONS

By James C. Carpenter

Charles ("Chuck") Honorton, the parapsychologist, was born in 1946 in Deer River, Minnesota. Did he begin his research career *in utero*, as the speed of his development suggests? Perhaps the floaty, altered state of consciousness there helped develop some prescient guesses about life after birth. Still, he could not yet have known about statistics, the published literature of parapsychology, the philosophy of science, and the politics of scientific controversy. He may not have rounded out his knowledge of these things until age 16 or so, when he first carried out a well-grounded, elaborate piece of research and interpreted it in a way that placed it sharply in the center of the issues swirling about the field. He was a rocket—speed and flare. While his peers were dawdling through high-school assignments, he was avidly corresponding with a famous scientist, envisioning remarkable vistas of discovery; while they were trying to find the way from college dormitory to cafeteria, he was organizing and running a scientific society, debating professors, and carrying out research in several settings; as they began to worry about choosing a major he was setting up shop for full-time research with a ferocious band of collaborators. The rest of his career developed apace. And now suddenly he is dead.

My topic is Honorton's professional contributions up to the moment that he left the Foundation for Research on the Nature of Man at age 21. It is not for the work of this period that he will be remembered, although it was well done, and if we knew no more about the nature of psi than what he had discovered by then, we would still have some very good leads. His activities during this period suggest the dimensions his career would take: an omnivorous student of the field, a bold, persistent apologist for it with the larger world of mainstream science, a tireless contributor to its body of knowledge, and a molder of its strategies, methods, and questions.

I want to thank the following people for their helpful reminiscences: Robert Flint, H. Kanthamani, Robert Joesting, Donald McCarthy, Paul Meehl, David Rogers, and Rex Stanford; and also Carlos Alvarado and Robert Joesting for providing copies of the *Newsletter of the Minnesota Society for Psychical Research*.

Can we account for the early development of Honorton's career in parapsychology, his intense focus and interest? If he ever speculated aloud about such matters, it was not to me. He was too committed to the present and future to look back a great deal. Still, we know that he was dealt a weak hand in the physical side of life, and perhaps wanted to optimize the mental. Born with serious orthopedic and cardiovascular problems, he had long bouts of forced inactivity as a child and surely longed for a mind with the power to soar beyond the prison of casts, pain, and boredom. I know that he expected to die young. Whatever he was to do would be done quickly.

J. B. Rhine, the founder of modern experimental parapsychology, had been corresponding with the boy for some time when he invited him to spend the summer of 1962 studying at the Duke Parapsychology Laboratory. This was before Honorton's junior year in high school. Rhine described him to his staff as a remarkable young man, whose intense interest should be encouraged. From the icy outposts of Minnesota, Honorton arrived at the sunny hub of the universe of parapsychology. He ate it up. He stayed in the library until all hours, buttonholed his elders relentlessly, and pondered the future destiny of this field with the Rhines. He absorbed statistics and methods at the side of Gaither Pratt with his calculator whirring and clacking, studied personality tests and theories with John Freeman and Winifred Nielsen, and delved into the powers of yoga and mystical experience with Wadih Saleh. He arrived already devoted to this group and their work, and became more so. He had no doubt that this field was incredibly important, was convinced that the existence of psi had been demonstrated, believed that experimental methods were the best approach to developing knowledge, thought that critics in mainstream science could be educated and converted, and could see no reason for doing anything else besides pursuing all of this as quickly as possible.

Surely Rhine would never find another disciple so precocious, so devoted to the master's methods, so aggressively intelligent in absorbing it all, so whole-hearted in his commitment to helping. Rhine, with his own fierce commitment to developing and defending his young field, welcomed the help. It was a remarkable relationship. Returning to Minnesota for Honorton was exile back to the snowy frontier. A few years later he would name his only child Joseph Rhine Honorton.

After his first summer at Duke, Honorton returned to high school and carried out a well-conceived, appropriately analyzed study on a complex topic (Honorton, 1964). He had steeped himself in the research literature relating hypnosis to ESP performance, as well as the studies that attempted to discriminate psi-hitting from psi-missing subjects. He reasoned that the imperfect replicability of both lines of work could be improved by combining them. At this very beginning of his published work, he showed interest in an issue that would continue to preoccupy him: the distinction between methods that merely predict scoring direction and methods that enhance the strength of the psi effect that is shown. In a hunch that shaped his work until his death, he chose the state of the subject as the variable that might affect the latter. As a good bet for a discriminator of hitters and missers, he selected the Humphrey modification of an interest scale used earlier by Stuart. Somehow he acquired the skills of hypnotic induction and set out to use Casler's (1962) hypnosis protocol as the means of increasing the subjects' ability to perform the ESP task. His six subjects (fellow high-school students) completed 88 runs, half in the waking and half in the hypnotic state, with the order controlled. His hypothesis was confirmed in that the predicted hitters and missers produced a significant difference in scoring, but only in the hypnotic condition. He later replicated these results successfully (Honorton, 1966b) using more subjects and more sophisticated wrinkles to his methods, including elaborate controls about target randomness and security, a standardized assessment of depth of hypnotic state, and manipulation checks on the efficacy of his hypnotic suggestions. In these studies, he helped establish a fact which meta-analysis would later underscore (Schechter, 1984): that hypnosis is a powerful tool for enhancing the expression of ESP; and he added the important point that subject differences must also be taken into account.

Honorton returned to Durham for a second summer of study in 1963. He fell into the rhythm of laboratory life happily, picking up on the relationships with staff that he had formed before, assisting in many studies, full of questions and ideas. He especially loved to talk with Rhine, and spent long hours on the other side of Rhine's desk. The depth and breadth of his reading gave his questions an extraordinary pertinence, and Rhine responded by pouring forth his answers, hopes, and visions. That world-famous founder of parapsychology liked Honorton and took time with him. During these talks their two lives became linked down somewhere deep within the Psyche that they wished to study.

At the same time, other relationships were also forming that would have a lasting importance for Honorton. Before those sweaty months had passed, he had bonded with a group of fellow-travellers, all only a few years older than he, and all almost as devoted to parapsychology. This unnamed, unofficial in-group was a remarkable phenomenon, a nucleus of zealots touched in the head by destiny. This young group (henceforth called YG) would grow a few in numbers and a hundredfold in commitment over the next few years. It had gathered around Rhine and was nourished by him. He flattered, scolded, anointed, and inspired them. He also gave some financial support to the destitute band (all graduate students in psychology at various universities, except for Honorton), held regular conferences in which they were urged to participate, and hosted them again each summer for further study. Beginning with this summer of 1963, and continuing over the next three, these happy fanatics worked seven days a week, discussed sometimes through the night, and conducted farcical and riotous "psychic healings" at parties. Every minute they coaxed the coming breakthroughs out of the cards and calculators. They seemed to own a piece of history unfolding. Each new study whispered the promise: a bit of the map of the Mind's New World. There was remarkably little competition and lots of love and fun. The research of each one of this group came to show a mutual contagion of ideas. When apart during the school months, the group published a newsletter for its own consumption. It was a many-headed beast, and Honorton was its heart.

In 1964 Honorton enrolled at the University of Minnesota. He was already largely self-educated in many areas, and full of the questions and mission of parapsychology. Perhaps he expected to find in the Psychology Department an academy of scholars committed to empirical truth and dedicated to pursuing profound questions about human nature. He got an icy reception. Dust-bowl empiricism reigned, with professors isolated from one another in little enclaves of research, each with a small coterie of loyal graduate students. Talking with students at all was apparently a rare phenomenon for most professors; speculative talk was bad form; and the unknown was of no interest whatsoever. Honorton was undaunted. He advertised, gave lectures, and quickly gathered about himself a collection of students with an interest in parapsychology. With them he formed the Minnesota Society for Psychical Research to promote discussion, research, and education in the field of parapsychology. This was the first of many influences Honorton would have upon the institutional structure of parapsychology. Not finding a faculty sponsor among psychologists, Honorton turned to a political scientist named Mulford Q. Sibley. Sibley was an anarchist who always

wore a red necktie as a symbol of his support for intellectual freedom and rebellion. He also had a long-standing interest in psychical
research. He became an enthusiastic defender of Honorton and an
ally in offering lectures, seminars, and debates on and off campus.
Rhine himself arrived to inaugurate the founding of the organization in January, 1965, and gave a lecture, supported by the Psi Chi
society, on the state of the field. Rhine was to make other trips as
well for public discussion with other scholars, all arranged by Honorton and some filmed. Rhine so favored the organization that its
rent off campus was paid by the Duke laboratory. Apparently Jack
Darley, then chairman of Psychology at Minnesota, was very upset
about this infestation and was about to attempt to squelch the organization, until dissuaded by Paul Meehl, another champion of
free inquiry.

Friends at the time remember Honorton as intense, bubbly, serious, with a good sense of humor, and an impressive absence of
flakiness, in spite of his preoccupation with this "fringe area." Many
lectures, debates, and symposia were sponsored by his society at the
university, in that community, and on other campuses. These were
usually conducted largely by Honorton himself. Thus began a long
career of education and debate. His professional opponents in these
contests often mistook this short, chubby, friendly boy as an easy
target. Perhaps Honorton was what clinicians term "counter-phobic"
about authority. He leapt upon it and took it on, armed with an
arsenal of facts, clear reasoning, and wit. He did very well in these
exchanges. Less adversarial discussions were also held with participants that included the philosopher Herbert Feigl, the psychologist
Gardner Murphy, Rhine, and others. The society lived up very well
to its mission to inform and educate. It also did well with scientific
discussion and research. The heart of the Society was its Research
Committee, membership on which could be secured only by passing
a difficult exam on experimental parapsychology, with at least an
80% score. This group held three official two-hour seminars each
week for mutual education and discussion, and countless hours outside planning research, carrying out pilot studies and digesting results. Honorton was very dominant in all this. He insisted that the
group keep a strictly experimental focus. Many pilot studies and
some formal research were carried out by the Society before Honorton left Minnesota. In the first year alone, over 73,000 ESP trials
were collected from over 500 subjects on topics as varied as emotional relatedness and ESP performance, the assessment of alleged
psychic training techniques, the utility of a "PK pinball" machine,

and the effects of environmental variables such as temperature, humidity, and air pressure on performance. Besides the hypnosis replication, three other studies were developed to the point that Honorton at least briefly reported them. All of them illustrate how eager he was to seize upon promising work, past and current, and develop it. His research credo came largely from Rhine, but he gave it his own emphases and charged it with his own energy.

He published a statement of this credo in an essay in the newsletter of the YG. For the first time he took on a role he was to express many times later: the parapsychologist's parapsychologist, reproaching and prodding his colleagues to move their thinking and work in directions he thought best. Titled "A Question for Researchers: How Uncontrollable is Psi?" (Honorton, 1965a), this paper argued that to consider psi innately "elusive" is lazy and unproductive. Work in the field, he said, is too often piecemeal and not followed up systematically. Making a comparison to the mainstream research literature on hypnosis (which he already knew well), he argued that an ostensibly "elusive" phenomenon can come to be seen as quite sensible and lawful when research becomes programmatic and sustained and when operations and definitions become standardized. He cited the sheep-goat research as evidence that the same can be true in parapsychology.

An illustrative bad example pertinent to these ideas was provided by a paper by a psychologist named Sprinthall that was published in a mainstream psychology journal (Sprinthall, 1964). In a review written with Morris (Honorton & Morris, 1965), the paper was dissected with succinct precision, making it clear what foolishness can be produced by someone given enough ignorance of prior literature, disregard for standard definitions, and generally poor method. In such a chancey field, only very good work could be tolerated, and it should be programmatic.

Honorton applied his beliefs to his own early research at Minnesota. Anxiety was a hot topic among researchers in Rhine's laboratory during this period (e.g., Nielsen & Freeman, 1965; Rao, 1965). The Taylor Manifest Anxiety Scale (MAS) was the main measure of anxiety used, and rather mixed results had been reported. Several of the YG took up the problem. Honorton (1965b), for his part, displayed a preference he would show with increasing conviction over the years. He wished to move away from findings that were purely empirical to ones that were empirically reliable but that also seemed to make sense. Reasoning from the theory of Spence, he predicted that the effect of anxiety upon ESP performance could be mediated by the perceived complexity of the psi task. He carried out two experiments. In the first, 88 subjects carried out 352 ESP runs, half using the BT procedure, and half the DT method, while being told that the BT procedure was the more complex of the two. More anxious subjects were expected to score well on the "simple" task and below-chance on the "complex" one, and less anxious people were expected to do the opposite. All trends were in the right directions, but only the below-chance scoring of the more anxious group on the "complex" targets was independently significant. Another study used a similar design, except that the procedural contrast was between DT clairvoyance and precognition runs. Three groups of subjects were run, with one being told that the DT condition was the more complex, another that the precognition was more complex, and the third that they were equally complex. The results were not significant.

The next study was reported informally (Honorton, 1966c). It was carried out with students at Macalester College in St. Paul and showed Honorton's commitment to the strategy of combining research leads in hopes of securing more replicable effects. Each student at the college was solicited to take part in a 40-trial ESP test, using a self-testing booklet. In 20 trials subjects were asked to try to hit the targets, and in the other 20 to try to miss. The MAS and three versions of the sheep-goat question were used as predictors of performance, and cash prizes were offered. All targets were generated on an early random-event generator (the Taylor ESP Machine). In all, 234 subjects completed the task. Results were not significant.

The last study to come out of the Minnesota days did give significant results, but it was only informally reported (Honorton, 1966a). Some of the YG had been playing with the idea of pairing some ESP targets with emotionally arousing material (unknown to the subjects) to try to make the material more salient, and also to try to arouse unconscious defenses that might affect performance. Honorton (1966a), in a typically straight-ahead approach, simply hoped that greater emotional salience could strengthen the ESP performance. In this study, two subjects carried out a long-distance ESP experiment between Chicago and Minneapolis, guessing four decks of ESP cards on each of three nights. Two of the decks in each session were laced with an erotic word on a slip of paper. Although the subjects did not know of the target difference, performance was significantly higher in the "erotic" condition, as predicted. Although small, this is the sort of study (significant results, clearly related to a growing little body of similar findings) that ordinarily would have been formally reported or at least followed up at Rhine's lab. The fact that both were discouraged by him was meaningful in itself, an ill omen.

One other little study bears mentioning here because of what it portends, even though it was never reported. I remember it only because I was involved and kept the data. During the summer of 1964, a half-dozen of the YG, under Honorton's direction, experimented with the "telepathic drawing" procedure of Carington (1940). In a pilot study, each member played the roles of sender and receiver, to see if any apparent ability emerged. One person showed very strong results as a receiver, and a small confirmatory series was carried out with her as the single subject. The results of this were also strongly positive, and statistically significant. Honorton went eagerly in to see Rhine the next morning to share the results and schedule discussion about the work at a laboratory meeting. He emerged with a grim and darkened look, a rare phenomenon for Honorton in those days. Rhine was not interested in research done with such old-fashioned methods, did not want the study discussed, and would have no further time spent on the matter in his laboratory. Honorton obeyed his orders, but in this and other similar events (such as the non-publication of results suggesting that psi has an interest in dirty words) seeds of rebellion were planted. In fact, when he returned to Minnesota, Honorton went on to continue work with the drawing technique, with encouraging results. He clearly maintained his own resolve to persist with what came to be called the "free-response" methods.

In the spring of 1966, Honorton had finished with the University of Minnesota (not graduated, but finished), and packed up, new wife in tow, to end his long seasonal commute and begin a lifetime future at the FRNM, now in its new, non-Duke location. Kennedy had been shot, but Camelot was alive and well in Durham.

He settled happily to work. The next two studies he reported were not particularly remarkable and are probably best taken as illustrating the sorts of things he elected not to pursue in his subsequent work. One problem being pondered by the FRNM staff at the time was the relation between ESP and memory. On the basis of some theoretical ideas of W. G. Roll, Honorton (1969b) carried out two studies in which subjects were required to memorize targets of one type, but not of another, and then were given an ESP test with both. Performance was expected to be better with the non-memorized targets. The results were significantly as expected in the pilot study, but not in the confirmation.

With J. Stump, Honorton (1969a) reported on a series of three studies carried out to follow up on one of Rhine's observations. In a restricted-calling situation (in which the subject is required to call exactly five each of the ESP symbols in each run), Rhine had noted the occurrence of significant psi-hitting in the last segment of the run, when the subject was having to tally prior calls and use only what was left. The new studies replicated the effect, and specified it further: it was found only in runs that were done before, and not after, a comparison free-calling condition. This work showed Honorton as a team player at FRNM, but this sort of research—driven by blind empiricism, not readily interpretable, and dependent on complex internal analyses of data—was the sort he would later eschew.

By contrast, the last study to come out of his FRNM years (Honorton, 1967a; Honorton, Carlson, & Tietze, 1968) was a good indicator of his future interests. By the mid-60s several thinkers, including Gardner Murphy (1963), had argued for the likelihood of a positive relationship between a subject's level of creativity and his/her ability in psi tests, and empirical confirmation had been found by Levine and Stowell (1963), and Schmeidler (1963, 1964). Honorton undertook a large-scale test of the hypothesis. Using state-of-the-art measures for creativity (the Ice Question Test of Burkhart and Bernheim and the Personal-Social Motivation Inventory of Torrance), he organized the testing of a total of 305 high-school and junior high-school students in five different schools. The students were tested in groups, each by a different experimenter. All subjects filled out the Torrance measure and those in two of the groups did the Ice Question Test as well. Each also carried out 4 to 10 precognition runs. The results were strongly significant and consistent across series: more creative people, in terms of both measures, did produce higher precognition scores. This was the sort of strong, intuitively cogent result that would appeal to Honorton later. Both creativity and psi ability require an "openness to experience," he reasoned. On such findings research programs can be built.

The last published piece of this period shows another side of Honorton that would blossom later: as the defender of the field to its most important critics. C. E. M. Hansel (1966) had published a book that was very critical of the field in general, including the Duke work. He started with the principle that psi effects are "a priori unlikely," hence any plausible counter-hypothesis, including that of experimenter incompetence or dishonesty, has to be preferred even when evidence for its validity cannot be had. Hansel did some arm-chair detective work, speculating on ways various reports could represent misunderstanding or fraud, and considered the matter settled. Honorton, in a review (1967b) of the book, engaged him with clarity, energy, and style. Citing the philosophers Feigl and Bridgman, he made clear that the "a priori unlikely" line of reasoning would rule out anything not currently established in science at any given moment and would bring all progress to a grinding halt if it were applied seriously. Even more pointedly, he went on to spell out instance after instance in which Hansel was highly prejudiced in his presentation, showing either gross lack of familiarity with the material he was purporting to assess, or a willful misrepresentation of it. The whole collection of selections, omissions, and distortions pointed to a man who believed that he could practice shoddy scholarship on an unpopular field with impunity. It is Hansel's own authority as a critic that was left exposed as implausible. This review shows a spirit that Honorton would display later. He wanted to press the debate between parapsychology and others in mainstream science, but also to insist that all parties be well informed and use high standards of reason and fairness.

What had Honorton learned from his professional and scientific activities by his twenty-first birthday? He had learned to favor cogent, meaningful research hypotheses and to avoid efforts to replicate uninterpretable results dependent upon internal analyses of data. He had also learned to avoid episodic new departures in research, stimulated only by "interesting ideas," and he preferred to focus upon previously successful work, often combining several of them to generate stronger predictions. He knew that the creativity of the subject was somehow an important ingredient in success. He knew that the procedure of hypnosis, and perhaps an accompanying altered state of mind, was a powerful facilitator of psi performance. He also knew, even though he had not announced it to the world, that the emotionality of targets is an important factor, and that methods of freely responding to complex targets had potential. Professionally, he had learned that he could influence many of his colleagues with his ideas and convictions, and that he could organize his own research facility. In regard to mainstream science, he had learned that persistence in pressing discussion can be productive if the work one represents is really good. He also knew that some critics are more fair and reasonable than others, and that debate should focus upon them and should be carried out with an insistence upon high standards of discourse.

Why is this the end of a chapter in Honorton's career, and not just part of a smoothly flowing stream? It is because he left FRNM abruptly in 1967, and many things changed for him. The eruption that expelled him is still an emotional matter for many of those who were connected with it. It is a vivid measure of the great esteem in which Honorton was held by those who knew him best that they rallied behind him when he was dismissed. He did not ask them to. This was the group that Rhine had groomed to carry his laboratory into the next generation. Some who had just joined FRNM left with Honorton, with nowhere to go. Others who were planning to go there when their doctorates were finished relinquished that option. It all took many years to heal, and many years before any of the YG (by then an OG) again took up employment at FRNM.

The particular event that led to the eruption was a quarrel between Honorton (together with some colleagues) and Rhine over the quality of another man's work. Whatever the facts in the situation were, I believe that in the longer view, they are incidental. The basic problem was control, and if an explosion had not ignited then, it surely would have done so not too much later. Honorton's career was already running headlong down a long, straight track with no spurs or detours, aiming straight for the repeatable ESP experiment with which to choke the words of acknowledgment out of the throat of reluctant Science. He already had strong ideas about how to do this, and his will was uncompromising. He was also young, with the kind of fierce idealizations that lead to fierce disappointments and stark alternatives. Rhine, for his part, was a dominant person who had always exercised great control over the research program of his laboratory and had no tolerance for what he construed as insubordination. He was an impeccable scientist, an inspirational figure, and an indomitable warrior for his field, but he could be a hard man to work for. Many very strong men, founders of movements, share a cluster of traits that flaw and humanize them. They can be overbearing and too stubborn, and then be vulnerable to the flattery of sycophants. They can also value too little the defiance of friends. Rhine had his share of such humanity. In any case, on one early fall day the conflict that had been simmering caught fire and burst. In a few hot minutes lines were drawn, and then Honorton, so recently come home to the center of the world, was cast out to its edges. What would he do with his devotion? Where would he take his energy, his burning questions? What next?

REFERENCES

CARINGTON, W. W. (1940). Experiments on the paranormal cognition of drawings. *Proceedings of the Society for Psychical Research*, **46**, part 162, 34–151.

CASLER, L. (1962). The improvement of clairvoyance scores by hypnotic suggestions. *Journal of Parapsychology*, **26**, 77–87.

HANSEL, C. E. M. (1966). *ESP: A scientific evaluation*. New York: Charles Scribner's Sons.

HONORTON, C. H. (1964). Separation of high- and low-scoring ESP subjects through hypnotic preparation. *Journal of Parapsychology*, **28**, 250–257.

HONORTON, C. H. (1965a). A question for researchers: How uncontrollable is psi? *Psi Worker's Newsletter*, **1**, 1–2.

HONORTON, C. H. (1965b). Relationship between ESP and manifest anxiety level. *Journal of Parapsychology*, **29**, 291–292.

HONORTON, C. H. (1966a). Emotional arousal in long-distance ESP experiments. *Psi Worker's Newsletter*, **3**, 13–14.

HONORTON, C. H. (1966b). A further separation of high- and low-scoring ESP subjects through hypnotic preparation. *Journal of Parapsychology*, **30**, 172–183.

HONORTON, C. H. (1966c). The Macalester College series. *Psi Worker's Newsletter*, **3**, 14–15.

HONORTON, C. H. (1967a). Creativity and precognition scoring level. *Journal of Parapsychology*, **31**, 29–42.

HONORTON, C. H. (1967b). Review of *ESP: A scientific evaluation*. *Journal of Parapsychology*, **31**, 76–82.

HONORTON, C. H. (1969a). Position effects in restricted calling tests. In W. G. Roll (Ed.), *Proceedings of the Parapsychological Association*, Number 4. Bruges, Belgium: St. Catherine Press.

HONORTON, C. H. (1969b). Role of associative habits in ESP preference. In W. G. Roll (Ed.), *Proceedings of the Parapsychology Association*, Number 4. Bruges, Belgium: St. Catherine Press.

HONORTON, C. H., CARLSON, T., & TIETZE, T. (1968). Combined methods in subject selection. In J. B. Rhine & R. Brier (Eds.), *Parapsychology today*. New York: The Citadel Press.

HONORTON, C. H., & MORRIS, R. (1965). A critique of Sprinthall's article "ESP: Some attitudinal factors relating to ability." *Journal of Parapsychology*, **29**, 200–203.

LEVINE, F., & STOWELL, J. (1963). The relationship between creativity and clairvoyance. *Journal of Parapsychology*, **27**, 272.

MURPHY, G. (1965). Creativity and its relation to extrasensory perception. *Journal of the American Society for Psychical Research*, **4**, 203–214.

NIELSEN, W., & FREEMAN, J. (1965). Consistency of relationship between ESP and emotional variables. *Journal of Parapsychology*, **29**, 75–88.

RAO, K. R. (1965). ESP and the Manifest Anxiety Scale. *Journal of Parapsychology*, **29**, 12–18.

SCHECHTER, E. I. (1984). Hypnotic induction vs. control conditions: Illustrating an approach to the evaluation of reliability in parapsychological data. *Journal of the American Society for Psychical Research*, **78**, 1–28.

SCHMEIDLER, G. R. (1963). Tests of creative thinking and ESP scores. *Indian Journal of Parapsychology*, **4**, 51–57.

SCHMEIDLER, G. R. (1964). An experiment of precognitive clairvoyance: IV. Precognition scores related to creativity. *Journal of Parapsychology*, **28**, 102–108.

SPRINTHALL, R. C. (1964). ESP: Some attitudinal factors relating to ability. *Journal of Psychology*, **57**, 65–69.

THE MAIMONIDES ESP-DREAM STUDIES

By Stanley Krippner

I remember September 25, 1967, as if it were yesterday. Charles Honorton telephoned me from Durham, North Carolina, telling me that he had decided to accept Montague Ullman's offer of a research position at our Dream Laboratory at Maimonides Medical Center in Brooklyn. I had joined Ullman in 1964, and several of our articles on ESP and dreams had been published (e.g., Ullman, Krippner, & Feldstein, 1966). Honorton had already gained a solid reputation in parapsychology with his studies involving the hypnotic preparation of percipients for psi tasks (e.g., Honorton, 1964) and psi and creativity test scores (e.g., Honorton, 1967).

After several years of pilot studies in the area of telepathy and dreams, Ullman had launched the Maimonides Dream Laboratory in 1962 where the monitoring of Rapid Eye Movement (REM) sleep could be incorporated into a psi-task design. These studies paired a volunteer subject with a "telepathic transmitter"; the pair interacted briefly, then separated and spent the night in distant rooms. An experimenter randomly selected an art print (from a collection or "pool") and gave the print to the transmitter in an opaque sealed envelope, to be opened only when the transmitter was in the distant room. The experimenter awakened the subject near the end of each REM period and requested a dream report. These reports were transcribed and sent to outside judges who, working independently, matched them against the pool of potential art prints from which the actual print had been randomly selected. Statistical evaluation was based on the average of these matchings, as well as by self-judgings of the percipients at the conclusion of the experiment. Precautions were taken to prevent sensory cues or fraudulent subject/transmitter collaboration from influencing the dream reports or the statistical results.

One example of a finding in an experiment that obtained statistically significant results occurred on a night when the randomly selected art print was "School of the Dance" by Degas, depicting a dance class of several young women. The subject was William Erwin, a psychoanalyst; his dream reports included such phrases as "I was in a class made up of maybe half a dozen people; it felt like a school." "There was one little girl that was trying to dance with me." An examination of the dream reports and the matched art prints indicates a similarity in this process to the way day residue, psychodynamic processes, and subliminally perceived stimuli find their way into dream content. Sometimes the material corresponding to the art prints was intrusive (for example, "There was one little girl that was trying to dance with me"), and sometimes it blended easily with the narrative (for example, "It felt like a school"). At times it was direct, at other times symbolic (Ullman & Krippner, 1970, p. 78).

Honorton joined us as we were concluding a study with a prominent psychologist and parapsychologist, Robert L. Van de Castle (1977), whose eight-night ESP dream study was accompanied by psychodynamically oriented, in-depth interviews with Ullman each morning (Krippner & Ullman, 1970). Not only did Van de Castle obtain the most robust statistical results of any of the percipients, but the interviews provided another dimension to the experience. For example, on one night the target was Rousseau's "Repast of the Lion," which depicts a lion feeding on its kill of a smaller animal. After a night filled with dreams about an attempted strangulation, karate chops, a suicide, and fighting dogs, Van de Castle surmised that the target would contain aggression, "but the aggression would have to be in some kind of disguise" (Ullman & Krippner, with Vaughan, 1989, p. 112). The psychoanalytic interview probed, not only the way aggression came into the dreams, but also why Van de Castle postulated "some kind of disguise."

Honorton (1972b) set to work completing a clairvoyance study with hypnotically induced imagery or "hypnotic dreams." He divided 60 percipients into two equal groups, one of which received a hypnotic induction and one of which received instructions to facilitate imagination. The suggestibility level of all the percipients had been ascertained by a standardized test, and there was little difference between the two groups. However, Honorton had selected the percipients so that there would be 10 persons in each of 6 groups: a high-suggestible hypnosis group, a high-suggestible imagination group, a medium-suggestible hypnosis group, a medium-suggestible imagination group, a low-suggestible hypnosis group, and a low-suggestible imagination group.

For all percipients, a sealed envelope containing an art print was placed on the arm of each subject's chair. The hypnosis percipients were told, "You are going to have a dream, a very vivid and realistic dream about the target in the envelope." The imagination percipients were told, "You are going to have a daydream, a very vivid and realistic daydream about the target in the envelope." This procedure was repeated four times as four randomly selected pictures were used per subject. Later, in interviews, the percipients described the quality of their dreams or daydreams and the degree to which they felt their consciousness had been altered.

The percipients evaluated their own material immediately after their interview was over. Only the high-suggestible hypnosis group attained statistically significant results. It was observed that the hypnosis (but not the imagination) percipients who described their dreams as "like watching a film" or "as though I was in a dream world" did significantly better at the task than those percipients who said they were "just thinking." Finally, the percipients in the hypnosis (but not the imagination) group who reported major alterations in consciousness did significantly better that those reporting little change.

One of the percipients in the hypnosis group was Felicia Parise, a hematologist working at Maimonides. One of her target pictures was Hiroshige's painting "The Kinryuszan Temple," which portrays a red and gold ceremonial lantern hanging down from a temple doorway. Parise reported:

> a room with party decorations. . . . I saw a gold chest, like a pirate's chest, but shining and new. The party decorations were colorful. No decorations on the floor, they were on the ceiling and walls. There was a table with things on it. Red balloons, red punch bowls. (p. 96)

When asked to associate to her hypnotic dream, Parise recalled her "sweet sixteen" birthday party at which her parents had strung party decorations of Japanese lanters. A few weeks later, Parise brought a photograph of that party to Honorton; it bore a striking resemblance to the Hiroshige painting.

Honorton and I (Honorton & Krippner, 1969) agreed that hypnotic induction provides one of the few available techniques for affecting the level of psi performance. But is this due to the demand characteristics of the situation, the subject's preconceived ideas about hypnosis, or some factor specific to hypnotic induction itself and the condition it evokes? Honorton (1977) was to explore these issues further in what he referred to as "internal attention states," those conditions in which "conscious awareness is maintained in the absence of patterned exteroceptive and proprioception information. These conditions include spontaneously generated states, such as hypnagogic reverie, as well as those which are deliberately induced, such as meditation and hypnosis" (p. 435). Honorton surveyed the available data and suggested an empirical generalization: "*Psi functioning is enhanced (i.e., is more easily detected and recognized) when the receiver is in a state of sensory relaxation and is minimally influenced by ordinary perception and proprioception* (p. 466; italics in original). For Honorton, the evidence lent support to a "filter theory" of the mind. As Aldous Huxley (1963) so eloquently put it: "To make biological survival possible, Mind at Large has to be funneled through the reducing valve of the brain and nervous system" (p. 23). Honorton and other parapsychologists always have been challenged to find ways to bypass this filter, obtaining information or exerting influence that transcend ordinary constraints of time, space, and energy.

During his years at Maimonides, Honorton also pursued his interest in studying the effects of immediate feedback on psi scoring. He used card-guessing tasks, alternating runs with no feedback with runs involving immediate feedback on each guess. In general, the runs involving immediate feedback obtained higher scores when compared to the previous runs with no feedback (e.g., Honorton, 1970). However, the results were not clear-cut enough to support an interpretation compatible with learning theory (Palmer, 1978, p. 185). A more clear-cut finding was Honorton's (1972a) survey of dream recall; he was the first to present convincing data that people who remember their dreams tend to obtain higher scores on ESP tests.

Honorton was also instrumental in inaugurating studies of alpha rhythm biofeedback at Maimonides. He (Honorton, 1969) was one of the first to report a fragile but intriguing relationship between alpha activity and ESP performance, and he later took this work a step further (Honorton, Davidson, & Bindler, 1971). Instead of relaxation, he and his colleagues used the biofeedback technique to generate alpha; they compared ESP scores during this period with a period in which alpha was suppressed by the same method. Self-reports were used to rate change of consciousness during the session. Percipients with the highest self-reports during the generation of alpha also produced the highest ESP scoring rate. Those who produced the greatest subjective shift in consciousness during alpha generation obtained significantly higher ESP scores than those reporting only minor shifts. Later, Honorton (1975) proposed that relatively large and rapid shifts in one's conscious state would be associated with enhanced ESP performance; this observation was to evolve and change, but it guided Honorton's development as an astute researcher and led to some of his most important contributions.

One morning in 1969, I had a telephone call from Arthur Young, inventor of the Bell helicopter and president of the Foundation for the Study of Consciousness. Young asked me if we would be interested in initiating a formal study of Malcolm Bessent, an Englishman who had reported spontaneous precognitive dreams over the years. We agreed and were assisted by Donald C. Webster, a Canadian industrialist, in bringing Bessent from England for a summer of experimental work. Initially, Honorton (Honorton, 1971b) had Bessent guess which of two colored lights would next be lighted by an electronically controlled random number generator. Both Bessent's predictions and his "hits" were automatically registered. The total number of trials was set in advance: 15,360. There were 7,859 "hits," 179 more than expected by chance, with odds against coincidence on the order of 500 to 1.

Honorton joined Ullman and me (Krippner, Ullman, & Honorton, 1971) in designing an eight-night study that would test Bessent's purported abilities in a situation closer to his spontaneous dreams that purportedly matched future events. Once Bessent's last dream had been collected for the night, an elaborate random number system was used to choose a word from Hall and Van de Castle's (1966) manual, *Content Analysis of Dreams;* this, in turn, was matched with an art print from our collection, and a multisensory experience was designed around it—all *after* Bessent had awakened. The experimenters who designed the experience had not been present during the night, and the experimenters who had monitored the electroencephalograph (EEG) were not present during the designing or execution of the multisensory event.

For example, on one night, Bessent dreamed about "a concrete building," "a patient from upstairs escaping," "a white coat..., like a doctor's coat," and "doctors and medical people." The randomly selected word on the following morning was *corridor*, and the matching art print was Van Gogh's painting "Hospital Corridor at St. Remy." When Bessent was ushered out of the sleep room, he was met by a man wearing a white doctor's coat daubed with acetone, and was greeted as "Mr. Van Gogh." He was given a pill with a glass of water, and was led through a darkened corridor to a room where he was presented with paintings by mental patients as well as the Van Gogh art print while, in the background, hysterical laughter and music from a film about a mental hospital could be heard. The outside judges were able to match Bessent's dreams with an account of the "corridor" experience at high levels, giving him a "direct hit." He obtained five other "direct hits" during the study and two "hits" with more moderate scores. If chance had produced these results, one would have to have carried out 5,000 additional experiments.

The results of his experiment were so extraordinary that critics seemed unable to grasp the protocol. For example, Zusne and Jones (1982) imply that at least one of the experimenters had a chance to know the identity of the target. The authors state: "After the subject falls asleep, an art reproduction is selected from a large collection randomly, placed in an envelope, and given to the agent" (pp. 260–261). In fact, the target was already in the envelope at the time the session began, having been placed there by a person who was not present during the night. Zusne and Jones write that "three... judges rate their confidence that the dream content matches the target picture," implying that the judges knew the identity of the target while making their evaluations. In reality, each judge was presented with a dream transcript and a pool of potential targets and was asked to evaluate the degree of similarity between the transcript and each target in the pool. These misrepresentations pale by comparison with an assertion that research participants were "primed prior to going to sleep" so that they could better incorporate the target material in their dreams. It is claimed that they were "primed" through the experimenter's

> preparing the receiver through experiences that were related to the content of the picture to be telepathically transmitted during the night. Thus, when the picture was Van Gogh's Corridor of the St. Paul Hospital [sic], which depicts a lonely figure in the hallway of a mental hospital, the receiver: (1) heard Rosza's Spellbound played on a phonograph; (2) heard the monitor laugh hysterically in the room; (3) was addressed as "Mr. Van Gogh" by the monitor; (4) was shown paintings done by mental patients; (5) was given a pill and a glass of water; and (6) was daubed with a piece of cotton dipped in acetone. The receiver was an English "sensitive," but it is obvious that no psychic sensitivity was required to figure out the general content of the picture and to produce an appropriate report, whether any dreams were actually seen or not. (pp. 260–261)

In actuality, rather than being "primed," Bessent was not shown the Van Gogh painting until after his dreams had been monitored and tape recorded. Indeed, when he was shown the Van Gogh painting, he exclaimed, "My God—that's my dream!"

Bessent returned during the summer of 1970 for another precognition study (Krippner, Ullman, & Honorton, 1972). This time, a target pool was prepared by an experimenter who planned to be in Europe while the entire study was run. He prepared 10 slide-and-sound sequences on the topics of "authoritarian signs," "beards," "birds," "crucifixion," "death," "Egyptian art," "police," "saints," and "2001." Each slide collection, made up of from 10 to 22 slides, was accompanied by 10 minutes of appropriate music or sound effects that Bessent could listen to with stereophonic head-phones. The materials were placed in boxes that were numbered, taped, and sealed.

The 16 nights of the study were arranged in pairs so that on the first night Bessent would attempt to dream precognitively about the target sequence he would experience the next night, and on that night he would attempt to dream more conventionally about the sequence he had just seen. Thus, on the odd-numbered nights he would dream about the future and on the even-numbered nights he would dream about the past. As an additional control, the EEG technicians who monitored Bessent's sleep and dreams were psy-chology students from New York University who knew little about the experimental design. The target was selected the following eve-ning, some 12 hours after the tape recording of Bessent's dreams had been mailed to the transcriber.

The results of this study were again significant, with five "direct hits" and two more moderate "hits." On the control nights, there were no "direct hits"; only when "death" was the topic, did a control night (in which Bessent dreamed about the past) obtain higher scores than an experimental night (when Bessent attempted to dream about the future). One night, Bessent dreamed about "peo-ple in motor uniforms," "conflict between students and the armed guard," "five hundred National Guardsmen," and "a police state." The slide-and-sound sequence for that night was "police." On the control night, Bessent mentioned "some sort of conflict" but had no other dreams that matched the target.

Taken together, the two Bessent dream studies have lent exper-imental credence to the precognition hypothesis. Bessent appeared to dream precognitively 14 out of 16 times in experiments that were tightly controlled against subliminal clues, sensory leakage, or fraud. And Honorton (1974b) observed: "It appears at least for this subject that extrasensory stimuli may be more easily incorporated into dreams than sensory stimuli" (p. 624).

Additional ESP Dream Studies

Honorton was a valued co-experimenter in the additional studies we conducted on dreams and ESP at Maimonides. In one of them,

Alan Vaughan was a subject partly because of a letter I received from him on June 4, 1968. Writing from Freiburg, Germany, Vaughan cited several dreams that he felt might be premonitory of Robert Kennedy's being murdered in the near future. I immediately discussed this letter with Honorton, and the next day we were saddened by Kennedy's assassination.

Vaughan and three other percipients each spent eight nights in the Dream Laboratory. A transmitter concentrated on the same target for four nights, then on a different art print for every REM period during each of the remaining four nights. The latter condition appeared to be superior, especially for Felicia Parise whose ratings of her dreams against the targets were independently significant (Honorton, Krippner, & Ullman, 1971).

For the next study, the transmitter was moved to the Foundation for Mind Research, a research center located 14 miles from Maimonides and equipped with facilities for providing the agent with a controlled audio-visual "sensory bombardment" experience. Four nights and eight percipients were involved, one of the percipants being Alan Vaughan. Such thematic sequences as "Oriental Religion" and "Space Exploration" evoked eight "hits" and no "misses," and yielded highly significant results (Krippner, Honorton, Ullman, Masters, & Houston, 1971). However, an attempted replication of this design produced only chance results (Foulkes, Belvedere, Masters, Houston, Krippner, Honorton, & Ullman, 1972).

A variation of sensory bombardment was involved for a six-night study in which the transmitters consisted of about 2,000 musical fans attending rock concerts that featured "The Grateful Dead" (Krippner, Honorton, & Ullman, 1973). While the rock band played, the audience viewed a slide sequence for 15 minutes, attempting to transmit the contents of a randomly selected art print (projected on a giant screen, along with instructions) to Malcolm Bessent located at the Dream Laboratory some 45 miles distant. Felicia Parise, sleeping at home, served as a control subject. The judges' scores for Bessent were marginally significant; those for Parise were not.

The final ESP-dream study carried out at the Maimonides Dream Laboratory before we closed our doors in 1978 involved a comparison of ESP and pre-sleep influences on dreams (Honorton, Ullman, & Krippner, 1975). Target stimuli were four films, two of them emotionally toned and two of them neutral. On each of the first two experimental nights, a transmitter was shown a different film, and the percipient tried to dream about it. On the two pre-sleep nights, the percipient viewed the films before falling asleep.

Forty percipient-transmitter pairs were involved; percipients making high scores on personality tests measuring "field independence" obtained significantly higher scores for the emotional films than for the neutral films in the ESP condition. Neither type of film was incorporated into dreams at a significant level on the ESP nights. However, the pre-sleep nights yielded significant incorporation scores.

This finding may have been a disappointment for parapsychologists, but it supported some preliminary findings in sleep psychology. Shortly before we initiated our studies at Maimonides, Witkin and Lewis (1967) showed percipients an emotionally threatening film before they went to sleep, for example, a monkey hauling her dead baby about by the limbs while nibbling at it, or an Australian aboriginal puberty rite in which an incision was made across the surface of an initiate's penis with a sharp stone. Witkin and Lewis observed that there were no direct incorporations of film content, but that their judges were able to find elements of the film in the dream reports, often in disguised, symbolic form.

Had this been a parapsychological study, the researchers would never have been taken seriously. They would have been accused of the possible cueing of the percipients' responses, of projecting their expectations while collecting the dream reports, and (because blind judging was not used) of "reading" purported symbolism into the dream content. However, Witkin and Lewis's study did not study anomalous phenomena; hence, a less than rigorous approach appears to have been permissible. In the case of parapsychology, however, it is often pointed out that claims of extraordinary phenomena require extraordinary proof; for parapsychological studies to be taken seriously, their data need to be scrupulously collected and carefully evaluated. We were pleased that our data, collected and evaluated at a more rigorous level, supported Witkin and Lewis's earlier claims.

In another influential study, dream reports were collected from patients who were about to undergo surgery; the investigators claimed that the upcoming operation was featured symbolically in the patients' dreams (Breger, Hunter, & Lane, 1971). However, the investigators who collected the dream reports were well aware of the type of surgery each patient was facing. They easily could have found specific relationships between dream content and the scheduled operation, given the vagueness and variety of dream symbols. Again, this was not a parapsychological experiment and therefore there was little criticism of this study's obvious flaws.

To evaluate whether or not our target/transcript correspondences were due to chance, we sent copies of the dream reports and post-sleep associations to three outside judges who worked blind and independently. All judges had worked previously with dream reports and/or with "free response" parapsychological material (in which the variety of potential targets is unlimited rather than circumscribed). Each judge was sent *copies* or *duplicate sets* of the targets used in the study; no judge was sent the actual target that had been used because it might have been possible that a smudge or written note on the picture would have cued the judge that someone had been concentrating upon that particular item. The averages of the judges' evaluations were used as data for statistical analysis.

In 1985, Child published a meta-analysis of the Maimonides studies. He found that the only form in which the data were available for all series of sessions was a count of "hits" and "misses." If the actual target was ranked or rated in the upper half of the target pool for similarity to the dreams and the post-sleep interview, the outcome was considered a hit. If the actual target was placed in the lower half of the pool, the outcome was considered a miss. Parapsychological experiments are often criticized on the grounds that the evidence they provide for psi phenomena is gleaned from very small effects detectable only when large bodies of data are amassed. Child pointed out that the Maimonides experiments are exempt from this criticism; significant results from some studies are attributable to just 8 data points each, that is, a total of 16 dream transcripts. All told, the Maimonides data were statistically significant to the extent that there was only one chance in 1,000 that coincidence could have accounted for the results.

Various types of criticism have been leveled against the Maimonides experiments from the time of our first publications in scientific journals. The most serious problem is that several other laboratories have not been able to replicate our effects when they followed our basic design. In one psychology text, Neher (1980) stated:

> A...series of studies of great interest are the dream-telepathy tests done at the Maimonides Medical Center in New York, in which, it is claimed, dreams are influenced telepathically. However, some other investigators have failed to obtain similar results. One unsuccessful replication used a subject who was "successful" in the Maimonides studies; another was conducted by the Maimonides investigators themselves. (p. 145)

It is certainly the case that some of our own replication attempts failed and that an independent attempt to replicate our work with Van de Castle did not support the psi hypothesis (Belvedere & Foulkes, 1971).

Nevertheless, our dream studies at Maimonides played a small but vital role in parapsychological inquiry and the search for knowledge. Perhaps our data base and our research protocols will be a continuing source of material for serious researchers who are attempting to encompass the study of anomalous phenomena within the scientific enterprise. If so, future investigators will recognize the vital role played by Charles Honorton in bringing these studies to fruition.

Psychokinesis and Sensory Deprivation

Although our laboratory was best known for its work in ESP and dreams (Krippner, 1991), Honorton initiated some provocative PK studies. Honorton and Barksdale (1972) tested their subjects with a random number generator (RNG), comparing conditions of muscular tension versus relaxation, and also active concentration versus passive attention to the target. Honorton conducted the first series in which the six subjects worked as a group to influence the RNG. Before one half of the runs, they were given suggestions to induce relaxation; before the other half, suggestions were given for sustained muscular tension. Relaxed-state scores were nonsignificant, but the tension scores were highly significant, especially in those trials that combined muscle tension with passive attention to the task.

In the second series, which Barksdale conducted, 10 subjects tried individually to influence the RNG under the same conditions; their scores were nonsignificant. Barksdale then served as experimenter for a third series in which Honorton served as the subject. The score for each condition was highly significant, that for tension being positive and that for relaxation almost equally negative. In commenting on this experiment, Rush (1977) says that "Honorton's remarkable success in the third series raises the most vexing ambiguity of all, the covert role of the experimenter" (p. 64).

Ullman and I had both visited parapsychologists in the Soviet Union, and were delighted when a friend offered to show our staff a film featuring alleged PK in that country. Felicia Parise observed the film and was inspired to undertake several weeks of persistent practice, eventually seeming to move small objects and rotate a compass needle. Ullman and I observed some of these feats under informal conditions, but Honorton (1974a) made a careful investigation of the phenomena, eventually taking Parise to the Foundation for Research on the Nature of Man, his former place of employment. According to the researchers in Durham (Watkins & Watkins, 1974), Parise deflected a compass needle, altered the signal from a metal detector, and produced anomalous effects on photographic film.

The directors of the Foundation for Mind Research had constructed a "witches' cradle" which was based on medieval sensory deprivation devices. There are historical accounts of cradle-like contraptions in which so-called witches suspended themselves from trees. Upon being covered with a sheath and after ingesting (or being coated with) belladonna, thorn apple, or some other mind-altering substance, the adept would have out-of-body experiences and other unusual adventures. The modern version of this cradle is a metal swing in which the subject stands upright, supported by broad bands of canvas. He or she wears earplugs to eliminate outside sound, and opaque goggles to eliminate visual stimuli. The swing acts as a pendulum, carrying the subject from side to side and rotating in response to involuntary movements.

Harry Hermon, a psychiatrist practicing at Maimonides, lent us his cradle for our study (Honorton, Drucker, & Hermon, 1973). Thirty percipients participated in the study; they were told that a transmitter in a distant room would view an art print during the last 10 minutes of the session. They were also taught the self-report scale that Honorton had devised to quickly evaluate alterations in consciousness. About 63% of the percipients in the study obtained "hits," a result that is not quite statistically significant. However, the subjects with high self-reports obtained a significant number of "hits." Further, the average shift in self-reports from the first 10 minutes to the last 10 minutes was higher for those making "hits" than for those making "misses."

This difference supported Gardner Murphy's (1966) hypothesis that shifts in consciousness are favorable to the emergence of psi. Murphy was pleased to hear the news. He had procured the original funding for the Dream Laboratory from the Ittleson and Scaife Foundations and had recommended me to Ullman once the laboratory needed a director. Murphy's hypothesis on shifts of consciousness was among several factors that stimulated Honorton's continued interest in partial sensory deprivation as one of many conditions that could produce a psi-conducive state characterized by a withdrawal of attention from the external world and a shift toward internal thoughts and images. After reading about a study of thought patterns and imagery during sleep onset (Vogel, Foulkes,

& Trosman, 1966) and after recalling that stilling the mind, or reducing the internal noise level, is the object of self-regulated concentration in Patanjali's system of Raja yoga, Honorton developed an innovative procedure known as the *ganzfeld*, a German term denoting a "uniform visual field."

In this procedure, research percipients were asked to relax in a soundproof room with halved pingpong balls fastened over their eyes. A colored light was placed 6 inches in front of their face, and a recording of seashore sounds was played through headphones. This method had been used earlier by Bertini, Lewis, and Witkin (1972) in an attempt to study the effect of emotional-involving films on hypnagogic imagery—in which the incorporated material was found to be more direct and less symbolic (Bertini, Lewis, & Witkin, 1972). The major procedural difference made in Honorton's study was that, rather than a presleep stimulus, a transmitter in a distant room was concentrating on randomly selected target material.

Following the session, Honorton's percipients inspected a duplicate set of four possible target materials, choosing the one they felt corresponded most closely to their thoughts and images. They ranked the other three as well, allowing all data to be categorized on a "hit" or "miss" basis. As there was a different target pool and a different percipient for each session, the problem of independence in judging was virtually eliminated. Since Honorton's (Honorton & Harper, 1974) original report, successful ganzfeld experiments have been reported from a number of different laboratories. Between 50% and 60% of these ganzfeld studies have produced significant data (Stanford, 1984)—a result that fulfills the promise of the high psi yield in the "twilight states" investigated at Maimonides.

The ganzfeld work will stand as Charles Honorton's most important contribution to parapsychological research. However, there were many other parts of the Honorton legacy, both in the laboratory, in the research literature, and in the politics of responding to critics of psi research. When Honorton arrived at Maimonides, I (Krippner, 1975) referred to him as "just about the most capable experimenter in the field" (p. 59). I have never regretted my enthusiastic evaluation; indeed, it has been reinforced over the years. I will miss him as a colleague and as a friend. And where will parapsychology find another of his stature?

REFERENCES

BELVEDERE, E., & FOULKES, D. (1971). Telepathy and dreams: A failure to replicate. *Perceptual and Motor Skills, 33,* 783–789.

BERTINI, M., LEWIS, H. B., & WITKIN, H. A. (1972). Some preliminary observations with an experimental procedure for the study of hypnagogic and related phenomena. In C. T. Tart (Ed.), *Altered states of consciousness* (2nd ed., pp. 95–114). Garden City, NY: Anchor Books.

BREGER, L., HUNTER, L., & LANE, R. (1971). Effects of stress on dreams. *Psychological Issues,* **7** (3, Monograph 27).

CHILD, I. (1985). Psychology and anomalous observations: The question of ESP in dreams. *American Psychologist,* **40,** 1,219–1,230.

FOULKES, D., BELVEDERE, E., MASTERS, R. E. L., HOUSTON, J., KRIPPNER, S., HONORTON, C., & ULLMAN, M. (1972). Long distance "sensory bombardment" ESP in dreams: A failure to replicate. *Perceptual and Motor Skills,* **35,** 731–734.

HALL, C. S., & VAN DE CASTLE, R. L. (1966). *Content analysis of dreams.* New York: Appelton-Century-Crofts.

HONORTON, C. (1964). Separation of high- and low-scoring ESP subjects through hypnotic preparation. *Journal of Parapsychology,* **28,** 251–257.

HONORTON, C. (1967). Creativity and precognition scoring level. *Journal of Parapsychology,* **31,** 29–42.

HONORTON, C. (1969). Relationship between EEG alpha activity and ESP card-guessing performance. *Journal of the American Society for Psychical Research,* **63,** 365–374.

HONORTON, C. (1970). Effects of feedback on discrimination between correct and incorrect ESP responses. *Journal of the American Society for Psychical Research,* **64,** 404–410.

HONORTON, C. (1971b). Automated forced-choice precognition tests with a "sensitive." *Journal of the American Society for Psychical Research,* **65,** 476–481.

HONORTON, C. (1972a). Reported frequency of dream recall and ESP. *Journal of the American Society for Psychical Research,* **66,** 369–374.

HONORTON, C. (1972b). Significant factors in hypnotically-induced clairvoyant dreams. *Journal of the American Society for Psychical Research,* **66,** 86–102.

HONORTON, C. (1974a). Apparent psychokinesis on static objects by a "gifted" subject. In W. G. Roll, R. L. Morris, & J. D. Morris (Eds.), *Research in parapsychology 1973* (pp. 128–132). Metuchen, NJ: Scarecrow.

HONORTON, C. (1974b). Psi-conducive state of awareness. In J. White (Ed.), *Psychic exploration: A challenge for science* (pp. 616–638). New York: G. P. Putnam's Sons.

HONORTON, C. (1975). ESP and altered states of consciousness. In J. Beloff (Ed.), *Current directions in parapsychology* (pp. 38–59). Metuchen, NJ: Scarecrow.

HONORTON, C. (1977). Psi and internal attention states. In B. B. Wolman (Ed.), *Handbook of parapsychology* (pp. 435–472). New York: Van Nostrand Reinhold.

HONORTON, C., & BARKSDALE, W. (1972). PK performance with waking suggestions for muscle tension versus relaxation. *Journal of the American Society for Psychical Research,* **66,** 208–214.

HONORTON, D., DAVIDSON, R., & BINDLER, P. (1971). Feedback-augmented EEG alpha, shifts in subjective state, and ESP card-guessing performance. *Journal of the American Society for Psychical Research,* **65,** 308–324.

HONORTON, C., DRUCKER, S. A., & HERMON, H. (1973). Shifts in subjective state and ESP under conditions of partial sensory deprivation: A preliminary study. *Journal of the American Society for Psychical Research,* **67,** 191–196.

HONORTON, C., & HARPER, S. (1974). Psi-mediated imagery and ideation in an experimental procedure for regulating perceptual input. *Journal of the American Society for Psychical Research,* **68,** 156–168.

HONORTON, C., & KRIPPNER, S. (1969). Hypnosis and ESP performance: A review of the experimental literature. *Journal of the American Society for Psychical Research,* **63,** 214–252.

HONORTON, C., KRIPPNER, S., & ULLMAN, M. (1971). Telepathic transmission of art prints under two conditions. *Proceedings of the 80th annual convention of the American Psychological Association,* pp. 319–320.

HONORTON, C., ULLMAN, M., & KRIPPNER, S. (1975). Comparison of extrasensory and presleep influences on dreams: A preliminary report. In J. D. Morris, W. G. Roll, & R. L. Morris (Eds.), *Research in parapsychology 1974* (pp. 82–84). Metuchen, NJ: Scarecrow.

HUXLEY, A. (1963). *The doors of perception* and *Heaven and hell.* New York: Harper & Row.

KRIPPNER, S. (1975). *Song of the siren: A parapsychological odyssey.* New York: Harper & Row.

KRIPPNER, S. (1991). An experimental approach to the anomalous dream. In J. Gackenbach & A. A. Sheikh (Eds.), *Dream images: A call to mental arms* (pp. 31–54). Amityville, NY: Baywood.

KRIPPNER, S., HONORTON, C., & ULLMAN, M. (1973). A long-distance ESP dream study with the "Grateful Dead." *Journal of the American Society of Psychosomatic Dentistry and Medicine,* **20,** 468–475.

KRIPPNER, S., HONORTON, C., ULLMAN, M., MASTERS, R., & HOUSTON, J. (1971). A long-distance "sensory bombardment" study of ESP in dreams. *Journal of the American Society for Psychical Research,* **65,** 468–475.

KRIPPNER, S., & ULLMAN, M. (1970). Telepathy and dreams: A controlled experiment with electroencephalogram–electro-oculogram monitoring. *Journal of Nervous and Mental Disease,* **151,** 394–403.

KRIPPNER, S., ULLMAN, M., & HONORTON, C. (1971). A precognitive dream study with a single subject. *Journal of the American Society for Psychical Research,* **65,** 192–203.

KRIPPNER, S., ULLMAN, M., & HONORTON, C. (1972). A second precognitive dream study with Malcolm Bessent. *Journal of the American Society for Psychical Research,* **66,** 269–279.

MURPHY, G. (1966). Research in creativeness: What can it tell us about extrasensory perception? *Journal of the American Society for Psychical Research,* **60,** 8–22.

NEHER, A. (1980). *The psychology of transcendence.* Englewood Cliffs, NJ: Prentice-Hall.

PALMER, J. (1978). Extrasensory perception: Research findings. In S. Krippner (Ed.). *Advances in parapsychological research* (vol. 2, pp. 59–243). New York: Plenum.

RUSH, J. H. (1977). Problems and methods in psychokinesis research. In S. Krippner (Ed.), *Advances in parapsychological research* (vol. 1, pp. 15–78). New York: Plenum.

STANFORD, R. G. (1984). Recent Ganzfeld-ESP research: A survey and critical analysis. In S. Krippner (Ed.), *Advances in parapsychological research* (vol. 4, pp. 83–111). Jefferson, NC: McFarland.

ULLMAN, M., & KRIPPNER, S. (1970). *Dream studies and telepathy; An experimental approach.* New York: Parapsychology Foundation.

ULLMAN, M., KRIPPNER, S., & FELDSTEIN, S. (1966). Experimentally induced telepathic dreams: Two studies using EEG-REM monitoring. *International Journal of Neuropsychiatry, 2,* 420–437.

ULLMAN, M., & KRIPPNER, S., with VAUGHAN, A. (1989). *Dream telepathy: Experiments in nocturnal ESP* (2nd ed.). Jefferson, NC: McFarland.

VAN DE CASTLE, R. L. (1977). Sleep and dreams. In B. B. Wolman (Ed.). *Handbook of parapsychology* (pp. 473–499). New York: Van Nostrand Reinhold.

VOGEL, G., FOULKES, D., & TROSMAN, H. (1966). Ego functions and dreaming during sleep onset. *Archives of General Psychiatry, 14,* 238–248.

WATKINS, G. K., & WATKINS, A. M. (1974). Apparent psychokinesis on static objects by a "gifted" subject: A laboratory demonstration. In W. G. Roll, R. L. Morris, & J. D. Morris (Eds.), *Research in parapsychology 1973* (pp. 132–134). Metuchen, NJ: Scarecrow.

WITKIN, H., & LEWIS, H. (1967). *Experimental studies of dreaming.* New York: Random House.

ZUSNE, L., & JONES, W. H. (1982). *Anomalistic psychology: A study of extraordinary phenomena of behavior and experience.* Hillsdale, NJ: Erlbaum.

Saybrook Institute
1550 Sutter St.
San Francisco, CA 94109

GANZFELD AND RNG RESEARCH

By Mario P. Varvoglis

I arrived at Maimonides in 1974 as a kind of tourist, prodded by a friend who was patiently trying to overcome my skepticism—and ignorance—about parapsychology. Indeed, I was converted, largely because of Honorton's work; but for several years I remained only a part-time volunteer at Maimonides, squeezing in what time I could between undergraduate studies and jobs to pay the bills. It was only toward the latter few years at Maimonides and, of course, in my years at Psychophysical Research Laboratories (PRL), from 1979 to 1985, that I can claim to have worked closely with Chuck.

The Early Ganzfeld Work

At the time I arrived at the Maimonides lab, the original Honorton and Harper (1974) study had already been completed. Several others, using identical methodologies, were in process. As in the earlier study, the sender viewed a viewmaster reel randomly selected out of a large number of possibilities and attempted to mentally convey to the receiver its visual elements and overall theme. The receiver, located in an Industrial Acoustics Corp. (IAC) sound-isolation room, was put into ganzfeld (wearing halved ping-pong balls over the eyes and headphones with "white noise" over the ears) and was asked to "think out loud," reporting all thoughts, images, or feelings that came to mind. The experimenter, who was "blind" as to the target viewmaster reel, was situated between the sender's and receiver's rooms, and monitored the latter's mentation via intercom. At the end of the sending period, the receiver would be taken out of ganzfeld and, presented with four viewmaster reels, would attempt to select the target, based on his or her earlier impressions.

When I was asked to write about Charles Honorton's later years at the Maimonides Division of Parapsychology and Psychophysics I hesitated for some time; I do not consider myself the most knowledgeable person concerning that important period of Chuck's life. I hope I can overcome my spotty recollection of the Maimonides years and do some justice to his seminal work.

Assessment of psi effects for an experimental series was thus based upon a statistical comparison of the total number of direct "hits" against the expected 25% hit rate.

Terry and Honorton (1976) report two of these follow-up ganzfeld studies. The first involved 12 undergraduate students who were following an experimental parapsychology course given by Honorton. The cumulative result, based upon 27 sessions, was significant (p = .003). The second study, involving 6 self-selected sender-receiver pairs contributing 10 sessions each, yielded highly significant results (p = .00059). Also highly successful was a shorter series (Honorton, 1976) involving rather unusual conditions: Sessions were conducted under the cameras of different TV crews. The receivers correctly selected the target in 6 out of the 7 sessions (p = .0013), suggesting that such high-pressure situations may actually be conducive for experienced subjects (Honorton, 1977b). Significant results (p = .025) were also obtained in a series with 17 visiting scientists and journalists contributing one session each (Honorton, 1977b).

As in the original Honorton and Harper study, all these experiments provided not only clear-cut statistical evidence for psi, but also a wealth of strong qualitative correspondences. While pointing to the real value of the ganzfeld procedure, these correspondences also highlighted the weakness of our quantitative evaluation method, which essentially reduced all that richness to a single psi trial with a ¼ probability of a hit. Noting the insensitivity and wastefulness of this approach, Charles Honorton (1975) proposed an alternative way for evaluating free-response psi material. The method yielded analytical data on the information content of the target, the subject's mentation, and their correspondence. By coding each target as a unique combination of 10 possible content-categories (color, activity, mythical characters, animals, human characters, artifacts, food, body parts, architecture, nature scenes) and coding the receiver's mentation using the same categorization scheme, we could immediately derive the number of matches, ranging from 0 to 10. The approach thus allowed for more precise comparisons of psi information transfer rates under different conditions, while also promising to enhance the efficiency of free-response research paradigms. As Honorton (1975) showed, given that each session would involve 10 independent guesses, with a binomial expectation of 5, a statistically meaningful result could be obtained even within a single session (i.e., with 8 or more matches out of 10).

To ensure category independence, the target pool had to consist of all possible combinations of presence or absence of the 10 content categories, ranging from 0000000000 for a target showing just a black and white geometric shape to 1111111111 for one with instances of all 10 categories present. This meant that 2^{10} or 1,024 targets had to be composed, each one showing the presence of just those content categories its code prescribed. If, for example, a target code was 1 just for body parts and food, the selected image could only show some food (without showing, say, a table, or forks and knives), and only a pair of hands, or a mouth, or nose (without showing someone's full face). Needless to say, construction of the binary target pool was a major project. When I arrived at Maimonides in 1974, Jim Terry and Sharon Harper and others were right in the middle of this, and they immediately channeled my budding curiosity about psi research into several weeks of cutting and pasting magazine images.

The first study involving the binary code target material (Terry, Tremmel, Kelly, Harper, & Barker, 1976) sought to establish the utility of this approach. Thirty volunteer sender-receiver pairs were divided into two equal groups. In one, receivers went through the ganzfeld mentation period prior to deciding which content categories were present versus absent in the target; in the other group, they simply guessed. The results were significant for the ganzfeld group ($p = .018$), and nonsignificant for the control group. This study thus pointed both to the utility of abstract coding schemes in free-response research and to the general effectiveness of the ganzfeld procedure (also suggested by an independent study by Braud, Wood, & Braud, 1975).

In parallel with this study, Smith, Tremmel, and Honorton (1976) undertook a very interesting investigation of the sender's role in the ganzfeld. Twenty sender-receiver pairs contributed two sessions each. In one, the target was presented to the sender for 10 minutes; in the other it was presented tachistoscopically for 1 millisecond. The sender was then put into ganzfeld and asked to "think out loud," just as the receiver did. At the end of the session, both sender and receiver encoded their mentation in terms of the 10 content categories. Overall psi results were significant ($p = .015$) and, interestingly enough, were comparable to results for the senders' retrieval rate ($p = .016$). Even more interesting was the finding that the overall significance for psi results was largely due to the condition in which the sender had been exposed to the target subliminally. However, a similar study conducted around the same time, and involving 17 subjects, yielded nonsignificant results in all conditions (Terry, 1976).

The binary target pool was one of Charles Honorton's many innovative efforts to enhance the replicability and efficiency of psi research. Honorton's initial hope was that this pool could become a powerful standardized tool for laboratories engaged in ganzfeld or other free-response research. But while the above studies showed its overall utility in free-response research, they did not demonstrate its superiority in terms of results (e.g., in effect size). Nor did they demonstrate that this approach really advanced our understanding of the psi process itself. Though we expected it to yield a more detailed picture of the types of information best communicated through psi, we found that the overly literal orientation of the content categories led to an insensitivity to metaphorical, synaesthetic, or global facets of the ganzfeld experience, and just ended up frustrating subjects who couldn't "squeeze" their mentation into the 10 categories.

Eventually, when we took up ganzfeld studies again at PRL, we moved back to the older, more global evaluation approaches. Chuck was singularly capable of sensing promising lines of research, but he was equally capable of "letting go" of a particular direction, even if he had invested time and effort in it, when it did not seem to be paying off. He had a strong pragmatic sense of priorities, and was well aware of his responsibilities as research director and as spokesman for the field.

It is also worth noting that, rigorous as Honorton may have been in his methodology and his attempts to quantitatively establish the reality of psi, he also was very sensitive to the experiential qualities of his research and its meaningfulness for participants. Unlike some other psi-testing procedures (e.g., forced-choice tasks using ESP cards), the ganzfeld is a novel and stimulating experience for subjects: It provides a unique opportunity for individuals to explore altered states of consciousness, mental imagery, and personal symbolism as well as psychological openness and sharing with another person. Honorton was well aware of all this, and he especially appreciated subject-intensive studies, which permit in-depth explorations of one's own mental events over a series of ganzfeld sessions. He also emphasized the need for us, the experimenters, to go through the experiments we asked our subjects to go through, and was, himself, more than willing to set the example. I think that whenever Chuck himself served as experimenter, subjects could sense that he had an "insider's feel" of the ganzfeld; this inspired confident anticipation of a positive experience and of success.

Any new research approach must pass through phases of exploration and of trial and error. Inevitably, problems will be located and will have to be ironed out. There certainly have been a number of methodological improvements in the ganzfeld over the years, which attests to the cumulative nature of scientific parapsychology; but despite some minor weaknesses the approach, from the outset, was quite sound. I think it is a tribute to Honorton that his very first ganzfeld experiment—the Honorton and Harper (1974) study—can still be referred to as "prototypical" of the research paradigm. From those early days of exploration, through the spirited defense of the paradigm's robustness (Honorton, 1983, 1985), and on to the empirical demonstration of its value in the PRL autoganzfeld studies (Honorton et al., 1990), Charles Honorton has left a permanent trace in the history of the field.

Random Number Generator Studies

Besides initiating the ganzfeld work, Honorton was also among the first to recognize the potential of Schmidt's random number generator studies and to attempt theory-driven research in this area. Beginning with his very first RNG experiment (Honorton & Barksdale, 1972, reviewed in Stanley Krippner's tribute), he came face to face with the challenge that psi-mediated experimenter effects pose to the interpretation of experimental outcomes and to model-testing. A few years later, in a seminal RNG study, he demonstrated that experimenters can also shape experimental outcomes through the manner in which they relate to subjects (Honorton, Ramsey, & Cabbibo, 1975). Thirty six participants were assigned either to an experimenter acting in a supportive or outgoing manner, or to one acting cold and aloof. Each group completed 200 RNG trials, attempting to guess which of two lamps would light up next. Subjects in the "positive interaction" group scored significantly above chance; those in the "negative interaction" group scored significantly below chance; and the difference was highly significant. The validity of the study's conclusions was reinforced by split-half reliability tests of internal consistency for each group's scores, and by subjects' responses to a post-experimental questionnaire, confirming that they had indeed perceived the two experimenters in the manner intended. To this day, this experiment constitutes some of our best evidence for the importance of interpersonal experimenter effects in parapsychology.

Perhaps because of these personal encounters with both psi-mediated and interpersonal experimenter effects, Honorton increasingly sought to develop protocols that would strongly link testing procedures to the experience, needs, traits, or physiology of participants. Having been recently introduced to the Yoga Sutras of Patanjali, Honorton became especially interested in exploring the possible roles of absorption and concentration in RNG-PK tasks. Meditation, emphasizing the disciplining of attention, seemed to be a natural starting point for such investigations, and a study by Honorton and May (1976) indirectly pointed to the potential of meditation in RNG-psi results. Ten subjects were involved, 6 of whom were regular meditators. Each subject contributed 5 high-aim and 5 low-aim 100-trial runs while receiving continuous visual feedback. Five of the 10 subjects obtained significantly more hits in the high-aim than the low-aim condition ($p = .00006$); 4 of these subjects were meditators.

In a more direct assessment of the influence of meditation on psi, Honorton (1977a) hooked up a Transcendental Meditation instructor to an EEG apparatus and examined RNG outputs in relation to different attentional and physiological conditions. Situated in a room adjacent to that of the RNG, the meditator first received event-by-event RNG feedback over 500 trials. Psi scoring during this phase was nonsignificant, though in the right direction (i.e., more hits in the high-aim than in the low-aim condition). In the second phase, the instructor simply meditated for 25 minutes, without receiving any RNG feedback. The RNG, however, continued to be sampled, its data being automatically segregated or "gated" according to whether or not the meditator's EEG was predominantly in the theta/alpha range (4–13 Hz). RNG results here were near-significant ($p = .058$) during the gated trials, in which the meditator was within the theta/alpha range. Finally, in the third phase, the subject again received trial-by-trial feedback; this time, a significant difference between high- and low-aim trials was obtained ($p = .0054$), suggesting that meditation may have helped the instructor achieve a state conducive to volitional PK. However, in a follow-up study with 10 practitioners of Ajapa yoga (Winnett & Honorton, 1977), significant results were obtained prior to meditation ($p = .005$), but not following meditation. In contrast to the TM instructor's increment in performance, the results here declined following meditation.

The above psychophysiological studies with meditators were in line with Honorton's objective of tightly "coupling" participant parameters to psi data, and thus linking experimental outcomes to the participants rather than to investigators' expectations. Two subsequent studies (Honorton & Tremmel, 1979) further explicated the possible links between RNG activity and subjects' attentional state and psychophysiology. Framed within the conceptual context of Eccles's interactionist dualism (1977), this theory-driven study focused exclusively upon unintentional PK. As in the second phase of the study with the TM instructor, the RNG here was sampled while subjects were absorbed in another task. The difference, however, was that in these studies participants were totally unaware of the import of the RNG and believed that they were simply engaged in an EEG-alpha biofeedback task. RNG data were automatically gated whenever the participant met pre-established alpha (8–13 Hz) brainwave criteria. In the first study involving 10 subjects, these gated RNG samples showed significant departures from expected levels of variance. The results suggested a relationship between RNG activity and either the subjects' physiological state (i.e., alpha brainwaves) or their volitional activity (success in the control of these brainwaves). In a second experiment, involving 7 subjects, Honorton and Tremmel focused in on a test of these alternative explanations, by taking both gated and ungated RNG samples as well as RNG samples gated during the rest period, when no attempt was made to control EEG frequencies. Once again, significant results were obtained in the alpha-gated samples during the feedback periods; however, RNG samples were at chance during both feedback-ungated periods and rest periods. Furthermore, the feedback-gated RNG results were significantly stronger than the rest-period gated results, thus suggesting a link specifically between RNG-PK and volitional success in accomplishing the EEG task.

While he recognized this was only a "feasibility study" with "many conceptual and methodological problems to be overcome" (Honorton, 1978, p. 43), Charles Honorton considered the gating work to hold major theoretical potential. He suggested that such research could add some empirical substance to the eternal debate on the mind-body problem; at the very least it could elevate the debate to a new level by demonstrating that both monistic and dualistic perspectives must come to terms with "extended psychophysical interactions," and not just personal consciousness and experience.

I was, myself, strongly intrigued by the gating work, and when the Maimonides lab closed down and Chuck invited Tremmel and me to join him in Princeton, I decided to consecrate my doctoral thesis to a replication and extension of this research. I was perplexed by the finding of "field-like" correlates of volition, and, in an effort to pinpoint their nature, designed a multifactorial experiment examining RNG-gated/ungated data under a number of different attention, intention, and awareness conditions. My own research design thus departed considerably from the studies which had inspired it, and, although the overall results were significant, for both "feedback" and "hidden" RNG conditions, the particular condition most pertinent to Honorton and Tremmel's gated findings did not yield significant results (Varvoglis, 1982; Varvoglis & McCarthy, 1986). Nevertheless, I feel that the original gating work is a conceptually intriguing and empirically productive research paradigm; it deserves far more attention than it has thus far received.

Two more RNG studies by Honorton and Tremmel deserve mention (Honorton & Tremmel, 1980; Tremmel & Honorton, 1980). Involving 93 and 40 subjects, respectively, and yielding modestly significant results, these studies were among the first to explicitly attempt to blend the rigor of automated RNG research with the motivational appeal and absorptive qualities of video games. In this context, they were forerunners to PRL's PsiLab project, which was not only a means to promote interlaboratory computer/RNG research, but also a testing ground for introducing "psi games" to the general public.

In my opinion, Honorton sensed, early on, that psi-testing software disguised as games could lead the way to a "univeralist" form of parapsychological research (Varvoglis, 1992) whereby the field moves beyond its precarious dependence upon a few good laboratories and experimenters, and flourishes in entertainment centers, in homes, even in schools. Of course, at the time all this began, at Maimonides and elsewhere, the technology simply was not adequate to create truly psi-conducive software. Furthermore, the identification of such software with psi games may have been premature. As I have argued elsewhere (Varvoglis, 1992), to encourage psi in the general public through computer-based experiments, we need to go beyond the superficially entertaining games popular in video arcades and create multimedia programs which explicitly induce mental states and mindsets congruent with psi functioning. I believe that Chuck was well aware of this, and that his efforts to provide the field with reliable and meaningful testing procedures would ultimately have centered upon software which integrates RNG tasks with meditative, hypnotic, hypnagogic, or other psi-conducive states.

Charles Honorton certainly had his shortcomings. We each have our particular palette of strengths and weaknesses, both of which serve us or disserve us in different circumstances, and Chuck was no exception. He was not very good in managing those who worked with him; he did not know how to bring out the best in us, and he frequently allowed his own preconceptions and feelings to get in the way of cooperative work. Practically all of those who directly worked with him, whether at Maimonides or at PRL, have some recollection of unfair criticisms, intimidations, or slights. But in the end, death is a harsh reminder of the larger perspective, of what has really counted in one's life. And what has counted in the case of Charles Honorton is his long, tireless, loving dedication to parapsychology, his eloquence and intelligence as spokesman of the field, his integrity as researcher, his deep commitment to the scientific method, his intuitive grasp of promise and potential, his sharp perception of patterns and trends in a plethora of z scores, and his search for the deeper meaning of it all.

He used his short time on earth well.

REFERENCES

BRAUD, W. G., WOOD, R., & BRAUD, L. W. (1975). Free response GESP performance during an experimental hypnagogic state induced by visual and acoustic ganzfeld techniques: A replication and extension. *Journal of the American Society for Psychical Research*, **69**, 105–113.

ECCLES, J. (1977). The human person in its two way relationship to the brain. In J. D. Morris, W. G. Roll, & R. L. Morris (Eds.), *Research in parapsychology 1976* (pp. 251–262). Metuchen, NJ: Scarecrow Press.

HONORTON, C. (1975). Objective determination of information rate in psi tasks with pictorial stimuli. *Journal of the American Society for Psychical Research*, **69**, 353–359.

HONORTON, C. (1976). Length of isolation and degree of arousal as probable factors influencing information retrieval in the ganzfeld. In J. D. Morris, W. G. Roll, & R. L. Morris (Eds.), *Research in parapsychology 1974* (pp. 50–53). Metuchen, NJ: Scarecrow Press.

HONORTON, C. (1977a). Effects of meditation and feedback on psychokinetic performance: A pilot study with an instructor of TM. In J. D. Morris, W. G. Roll, & R. L. Morris (Eds.), *Research in parapsychology 1976* (pp. 95–97). Metuchen, NJ: Scarecrow Press.

HONORTON, C. (1977b). Psi and internal attention states. In B. Wolman (Ed.), *Handbook of parapsychology*. New York: Van Nostrand-Reinhold.

HONORTON, C. (1978). A parapsychological test of Eccles' "neurophysiological hypothesis" of psychophysical interaction. In B. Shapin & L. Coly (Eds.), *Brain/mind and parapsychology* (pp. 35–43). New York: Parapsychology Foundation.

HONORTON, C. (1983). Response to Hyman's critique of psi ganzfeld studies. In W. G. Roll, J. Beloff, & R. A. White (Eds.), *Research in parapsychology 1982* (pp. 23–26). Metuchen, NJ: Scarecrow Press.

64

HONORTON, C. (1985). Meta-analysis of psi ganzfeld research: A response to Hyman. *Journal of Parapsychology,* **49,** 51–91.

HONORTON, C., & BARKSDALE, W. (1972). PK performance with waking suggestions for muscle tension versus relaxation. *Journal of the American Society for Psychical Research,* **66,** 208–214.

HONORTON, C., BERGER, R., VARVOGLIS, M., QUANT, M., DERR, P., SCHECHTER, E., & FERRARI, D. (1990). Psi communication in the ganzfeld: Experiments with an automated testing system and a comparison with a meta-analysis of earlier studies. *Journal of Parapsychology,* **54,** 99–140.

HONORTON, C., & HARPER, S. (1974). Psi-mediated imagery and ideation in an experimental procedure for regulating perceptual input. *Journal of the American Society for Psychical Research,* **68,** 156–168.

HONORTON, C., & MAY, E. C. (1976). Volitional control in a psychokinetic task with auditory and visual feedback. In J. D. Morris, W. G. Roll, & R. L. Morris (Eds.), *Research in parapsychology 1975* (pp. 90–91). Metuchen, NJ: Scarecrow Press.

HONORTON, C., RAMSEY, M., & CABIBBO, C. (1975). Experimenter effects in extrasensory perception. *Journal of the American Society for Psychical Research,* **69,** 135–150.

HONORTON, C., & TREMMEL, L. (1979). Psi correlates of volition: A preliminary test of Eccles' "neurophysiological hypothesis" of mind-brain interaction. In W. G. Roll (Ed.), *Research in parapsychology 1978* (pp. 36–38). Metuchen, NJ: Scarecrow Press.

HONORTON, C., & TREMMEL, L. (1980). Directional PK effects with a computer-based random number generator system: A preliminary study. In W. G. Roll (Ed.), *Research in parapsychology 1979* (pp. 69–71). Metuchen, NJ: Scarecrow Press.

SMITH, M., TREMMEL, L., & HONORTON, C. (1976). A comparison of psi and weak sensory influences on ganzfeld mentation. In J. D. Morris, W. G. Roll, & R. L. Morris (Eds.), *Research in parapsychology 1975* (pp. 191–194). Metuchen, NJ: Scarecrow Press.

TERRY, J. C. (1976). Comparison of stimulus duration in sensory and psi conditions. In J. D. Morris, W. G. Roll, & R. L. Morris (Eds.), *Research in parapsychology 1975* (pp. 194–198). Metuchen, NJ: Scarecrow Press.

TERRY, J. C., & HONORTON, C. (1976). Psi information retrieval in the ganzfeld: Two confirmatory studies. *Journal of the American Society for Psychical Research,* **70,** 207.

TERRY, J. C., TREMMEL, L., KELLY, M., HARPER, S., & BARKER, P. (1976). Psi information rate in guessing and receiver optimization. In J. D. Morris, W. G. Roll, & R. L. Morris (Eds.), *Research in parapsychology 1975* (pp. 194–198). Metuchen, NJ: Scarecrow Press.

TREMMEL, C., & HONORTON, C. (1980). Psitrek: A preliminary effort toward development of psi-conducive software. In W. G. Roll (Ed.), *Research in parapsychology 1979* (pp. 159–161). Metuchen, NJ: Scarecrow Press.

VARVOGLIS, M. (1982). Psychokinesis, intentionality, and the attentional object: Specificity and generality in mind-matter interactions. Ann Arbor, Michigan: University Microfilms International.

VARVOGLIS, M. (1992). *La rationalité de l'irrationnel*. Paris: InterEditions.

VARVOGLIS, M., & MCCARTHY, D. (1986). Conscious-purposive focus and PK: RNG activity in relation to awareness, task-orientation, and feedback. *Journal of the American Society for Psychical Research, 80,* 1–30.

WINNETT, R., & HONORTON, C. (1977). Effects of meditation and feedback on psychokinetic performance: Results with practitioners of Ajapa Yoga. In J. D. Morris, W. G. Roll, & R. L. Morris (Eds.), *Research in parapsychology 1976* (pp. 97–98). Metuchen, NJ: Scarecrow Press.

PSYCHOPHYSICAL RESEARCH LABORATORIES

By Ephraim I. Schechter

Charles (Chuck) Honorton and the late James S. McDonnell, CEO of McDonnell-Douglas Corporation, established Psychophysical Research Laboratories (PRL) in 1979. The laboratory in Princeton, NJ, opened in the fall of 1979 and closed ten years later in October, 1989. The primary research mission was "to increase the strength and reliability with which psi effects can be detected and studied under controlled conditions" (Psychophysical Research Laboratories, 1984, Sect. I, p. 1).

Other articles in this memorial series about Chuck deal with details of the various lines of research begun or continued at PRL. I will try, instead, to suggest what it was like at PRL by talking about the major projects and the formal and informal research groups that resulted from who was there, when they were there, and what their research interests and strengths were.

The list of PRL staff and contributors is long. Don McCarthy was Chuck's long-time friend and constant formal and informal collaborator before, during, and after the PRL years. The regular research staff included at one time or another Chuck himself, Pat Barker, Rick Berger, Dianne Ferraro, George Hansen, Marta Quant, Nancy Sondow, Larry Tremmel, Mario Varvoglis, and me. Visiting scientists Dick Bierman, Lendell Braud, Christine Hardy, Alianna Maren, Marilyn Schiltz, and Zoltan Vassy were part of the full-time staff for as little as a month or as long as a year. There were Rider College student Laura Csogi, and support staff Lucy Levitcher and Linda Moore, as well as colleagues who worked elsewhere but formally collaborated in or consulted on PRL research: Daryl Bem, Robert Edelberg, Ed May, Diana Robinson, and David Saunders.

I wish to thank Pat Barker, Rick Berger, George Hansen, Don McCarthy, and Nancy Sondow, who reminded me of things I'd forgotten and filled in details I didn't know. I also thank Pat and Don, and Jacquelyn Schechter, for their comments on early drafts.

This is a personal memoir. Others who were at PRL might have stressed things I've left out, or made different points. I apologize for inadvertent errors or omissions.

Mathematician Norman Herzberg and computer wizard John Bridges were informal continuing collaborators. Robert Chevako, Gene Conover, Greg Johnstone, and Tron McConnell designed or built specific pieces of equipment and software. Michael Witunski was official liaison with our funding sponsors. Colleagues, journalists, and others visited for an afternoon or a day, joined us in discussion, and became research participants. And there were many other research participants who came for a single experimental session or for many sessions.

The degree of collaboration and joint work at PRL varied over the years. The research staff planned and worked collectively on most projects at first. Later, although everyone helped run ongoing experiments, staff tended to focus on their own projects. In the final years, as the permanent research staff dwindled, projects often involved external collaborators.

To some extent, this cycle reflected Chuck's strength in research rather than management skills. He wanted bright, creative people as his co-workers and collaborators. He also insisted on substantial control of research projects—what was done, and how. Research staff chosen for enthusiasm and creativity also wanted both collaboration and control of their own projects. The resulting tension had both good and bad effects. The limits on individual projects and lines of research produced a fair amount of coherently connected work along a few major lines. Each major line benefited from everybody's input and from sub-projects reflecting individual staff members' interests. At the same time, those limits on how far individual staff could pursue their own lines and "own" their contributions aborted some projects and led to some rancorous partings.

Another pattern in PRL's work over the ten years is a rising curve of development and expansion, followed by fruition and major results from the key projects, and then a winding down that focused on summarizing already-completed work with few new projects.

Two of PRL's major lines of research had been pursued by Chuck at Maimonides Medical Center in Brooklyn. One was the ganzfeld free-response work, begun in the early 1970s. The other was the use of computerized game-like testing situations to engage participants' interest.[1] A third major line, foreshadowed in earlier

---

[1] See McCarthy (1982) for a discussion of the overall impact of microcomputers on parapsychological research.

work by Chuck and other PRL staff and formalized at PRL, was the use of statistical meta-analytic techniques to summarize and explore both the research literature and clusters of related PRL studies. All three lines drew on the work of researchers elsewhere, of course, and were pursued by others during the PRL years, but I think it is fair to say that PRL's concentration in these areas played a major role in establishing methods and approaches.

A fourth ongoing PRL project, woven through the other three, was our involvement in parapsychology's long-standing study of the relationship between research participants' characteristics and their psi-test performance.[2] PRL's contributions, later used in other laboratories as well, include an ongoing survey of participant demographics and attitudes (the "PRL Participant Information Form"), and regular use of the Myers-Briggs Type Indicator (McCaulley, 1977).

All of this was stitched together by Chuck's long-range goal of providing experimental parapsychology with more robust results to permit more effective theorizing and better understanding. The major research projects were all related to this goal, in an attempt to identify "recipes" of research procedures and participant characteristics that most consistently produced good performance on the psi tests. So also was the work to develop standard computerized protocols for experiments at PRL and other laboratories. The idea was to make it easy to keep basic procedures the same from laboratory to laboratory and, hopefully, increase the likelihood of getting similar results.

Some of the initial PRL research staff were veterans of Chuck's Maimonides projects. Larry Tremmel, who was at PRL only briefly, was a long-time Maimonides volunteer who worked on some of the early psi-testing computer games. Mario Varvoglis was also a volunteer researcher. Pat Barker, administrative assistant of the Maimonides lab between 1971 and 1975, joined PRL shortly after it opened, as both administrative assistant and researcher.

Nancy Sondow, on the other hand, had done experiments at the American Society for Psychical Research, and visiting researcher Lendell Braud had already independently established herself in psychological and parapsychological research.

Equipment also came from the Maimonides lab to PRL, such as the Cromemco System Three computer in its bookshelf-sized rack

---

[2] See, for example, Palmer's (1977, 1978) and Schmeidler's (1988) general reviews of individual-differences research in parapsychology.

(soon to be replaced by typewriter-sized but equally powerful Apple II computers), and the large, double-walled and electronically shielded sound isolation chamber used as the percipient's room in ganzfeld studies and the early computer-games research.

The first projects were continuations of Maimonides work: a ganzfeld series using the nonautomated Maimonides protocol (Sondow, Braud, & Barker, 1982), and two computer games, "PK Meter" (Honorton, Barker, & Sondow, 1983) and "Psi Trek."[3] "PK Meter," in particular, was a prototype for later PRL work. It used an RNG (random number generator) designed by Ed May for the Cromemco computer. The study's design involved both "feedback" RNG runs whose results were displayed to the participants and "silent," nondisplayed runs. The computer program that controlled participants' assignment to experimental conditions became the prototype for later experiments' "Series Manager" programs. The "Series Manager" and feedback/silent comparison were used in all subsequent PRL RNG research, including the computerized psi tasks that were part of the *PsiLab II*/℗ RNG and software package made available to other labs and still in use at some of them.

Meanwhile, Lendell completed her six-month term as visiting scientist and returned to Texas. Mario designed and ran a complex computer-controlled experiment involving both RNG and EEG feedback that would become his doctoral dissertation (Varvoglis & McCarthy, 1986); the computer program for this study was one of Don McCarthy's contributions to the early PRL research. Rick Berger and I joined the research staff late in 1981. The development and expansion stage continued through 1982 and into 1983, firming up the projects that would characterize PRL research for the next six years.

A lot of effort went into hardware and software for the computer-controlled automated ganzfeld procedure, which became more and more refined over the years as Rick focused on getting the hardware and software in place and operating properly.[4] Still pictures from the set of ganzfeld targets used in the Maimonides studies (Honorton, 1975) were videotaped; so were many short segments from movies and television programs selected to introduce sound and motion into the ganzfeld target sets. Special videotape players controlled by the Apple computers were purchased and in-

---

[3] Maimonides work on "Psi Trek" was reported by Honorton and Tremmel (1980). The PRL version of the project was never completed.

[4] See Berger & Honorton (1985) for a formal description of the fully developed version.

stalled, computer-controlled switches were constructed for the microphones and tape recorders, and initial versions of programs to coordinate it all were written. By 1982, a "debugging" series of ganzfeld trials became part of the development and fine-tuning.

Several new computer-game psi-testing tasks were designed during this early period to use Ed May's second generation of RNGs, built for the Apple II computers. Some, like "Volition" and "Psi Invaders," were developed further into long-running experimental series and were later included in the *PsiLab //*™ package developed for use at other laboratories. Others were shorter lived: "Hidden Target" never became a formal experiment, and "Psi Ball" was dropped after two test series suggested that it was not likely to produce strong results (Schechter, Barker, & Varvoglis, 1983, 1984). Another part of the RNG-research development was a series of programs that Don designed and wrote to evaluate the RNGs' randomness. Like "Volition" and "Psi Invaders," later versions of this RNG-testing software became part of *PsiLab //*™.

The methods and approach for measuring participant characteristics were also developed in the first few years. The Participant Information Form (PIF) was written, and several ways to measure participants' personality traits were considered. We selected the Myers-Briggs Type Indicator (MBTI) and, with permission from the MBTI's developers and publisher, wrote a computer program to administer and score the instrument. A variation of this program administered a special version (Stanford & Angelini, 1983) of the Tellegen Differential Personality Questionnaire's Absorption scale (Tellegen & Atkinson, 1974). Most participants in ganzfeld and RNG computer-game sessions completed all three of these instruments.

Group feeling was high during much of this first stage. There were regular meetings and a lot of collaborative design. All the research staff were at least partly involved in each project, planning, designing and producing tests, software, and gadgets, and as experimenters and participants in "debug" trials of the ganzfeld and computer-game procedures. We did have individual responsibilities and specialties—Chuck, Pat, Mario, Lendell, and Nancy were most familiar with ganzfeld procedure; Lendell worked with ganzfeld target characteristics and percipients' emotional states; Mario and Rick were the gadgeteers, and Mario, the audiovisual expert; Nancy and Pat developed the PIF; Chuck designed the "Hidden Target," "Psi Invaders," and "Volition" games; I focused on the MBTI and on

"PsiBall." We tried to stay familiar with each others' projects and progress, and gave and received lots of advice. Chuck always stated the final decisions on procedures and directions but, at first, planning was often a group process.

As the procedures that were developed in this stage became formal experiments, however, there was less and less group planning. By 1983, the group sessions stopped, and project planning and evaluation usually involved only Chuck and the staffers working on the particular task, with the key decisions clearly Chuck's. Although we all continued to be experimenters and participants in most projects, researchers gradually began to focus more and more on their own tasks.

The period between 1982 and 1985 was dominated by Chuck's debate with Ray Hyman about the interpretation and solidity of the ganzfeld data. Late in 1981 Chuck provided Ray with copies of existing ganzfeld studies for a review paper to be presented at the 1982 joint conference of the Parapsychological Association and the Society for Psychical Research. Ray's review was quite critical (Hyman, 1983), estimating that the actual "success rate" in these studies was much lower than Chuck claimed and that procedural flaws and poor statistical analysis made even the reduced estimate meaningless. A vigorous correspondence developed, as Ray and Chuck debated early drafts of Ray's paper and Chuck began to prepare a response that criticzed and offered counterarguments to Ray's review decisions, statistical analyses, and classification of procedural flaws (Honorton, 1983). By the end of the conference, Chuck and Ray had agreed to write more complete reviews, to be published together in the *Journal of Parapsychology* (Honorton, 1985; Hyman 1985). Eventually, they "agreed to disagree" and to hope that the debate had improved the quality of current and future ganzfeld research and the ways parapsychologists and critics argue (Hyman & Honorton, 1986).

The ganzfeld debate involved the entire research staff. Nancy gathered and reread the ganzfeld literature and made the preliminary classifications for the analyses of procedural flaws. We discussed Ray's letters and phone calls at length, trying to make sure we understood his arguments and clarifying our disagreements with them. Everyone contributed to or commented on drafts of responses and of Chuck's *Journal of Parapsychology* paper. And Chuck and I began exploring new methods for statistical literature review.

This was not Chuck's or my first attempt at statistical literature review,[5] but it was the first in which we used techniques of what is now called "meta-analysis" (e.g., Glass, McGaw, & Smith, 1981; Rosenthal, 1984). Karlis Osis's (1982) review led us to Glass, McGaw, and Smith's book, and meta-analytic methods quickly became a standard part of PRL research. Reports of PRL studies included meta-analytic summaries and reported effect sizes as well as the results of significance tests. Much of Chuck's later work involved meta-analytic literature reviews. Attempts to encourage this approach in parapsychology included work on meta-analytic methods (McCarthy & Schechter, 1986), a review of ESP studies involving hypnotic induction (Schechter, 1984), a roundtable at the 1984 Parapsychological Association convention,[6] and a symposium held at PRL in November 1984 with Robert Rosenthal as guest speaker.

Ganzfeld and computer-game research continued during this period, and data were presented at Parapsychological Association (PA) meetings. Comparisons of "feedback" and "silent" RNG data in "Volition," "Psi Invaders," and "PsiBall" showed interesting similarites across the three games (Berger, Schechter, & Honorton, 1986) with stronger results in the no-feedback condition. The paper included a review of RNG studies elsewhere that compared feedback and no-feedback conditions. In a related paper, Mario dealt with the theoretical implications of "silent" RNG results for the conformance-behavior and observational models of psi effects (Varvoglis, 1986). Later analyses of "Volition" and "Psi Invaders" data suggested systematic displacement relationships between the feedback and silent RNG results (Schechter, 1987a).

Ganzfeld "first timers" (i.e., initial session) results were also reported at PA meetings (Honorton et al., 1986; Honorton & Schechter, 1987) and at a conference of the Association for Psychological Type, the MBTI researchers' and users' association (Honorton & Schechter, 1985). The data suggested that ganzfeld performance was related to participant characteristics measured by the PIF and the MBTI and to interactions between these characteristics and experimental conditions, such as whether the "sender" for the session was a PRL staff member or someone brought by the percipient.

Interactions with participant characteristics also occurred in the computer games data (Berger, Schechter, & Honorton, 1986;

---

[5] See Schechter (1987b) for references to earlier statistical reviews of parapsychological research.

[6] The roundtable "Meta-Analysis: Integrating Results Across Studies" is summarized in White and Solfvin (1985), pp. 112–118. Participants included Irvin Child, Chuck Honorton, Ray Hyman, John Palmer, and Ephraim Schechter (chair).

Schechter, Honorton, Barker, & Varvoglis, 1984). In PRL Annual Reports, Pat and I regularly summarized the PIF and MBTI data for all participants, including otherwise unpublished analyses such as factors related to belief in psi (Psychophysical Research Laboratories, 1986, pp. 119–130). An early summary of PRL participant characteristics was reported at a meeting of the Southeastern Regional Parapsychological Association (Barker & Schechter, 1983, see pp. 62–63). Later, as other labs began to use both the PIF and the MBTI, a SERPA panel reported on similarities and differences between PRL and Institute for Parapsychology participants (Barker et al., 1985, see pp. 263–264).

Meanwhile, RNG and computer-game development continued. Dick Bierman, of the Research Institute for Parapsychology and Physics (RIPP) in Amsterdam spent a month at PRL as Visiting Scientist in 1983. As a result, Rick began comparing the performance of RIPP's RNG design with Ed May's RNGs that we had been using. After extensive testing, and further consultation with Robert Chevako of the electronics engineering firm NWS Associates, PRL adopted a modified version of the RIPP design.

Rick also refined the "Psi Invaders" and "Volition" programs, and began a series of studies later completed at Science Unlimited Research Foundation (SURF) in San Antonio, Texas (Berger, 1988a, 1988b). Mario began developing a sophisticated video-feedback game we called "PK Dancers," in which the strong RNG scores moved an animated image through a series of dance moves. Plans for this game, never completed at PRL, included personalizing the dance image with a computerized portrait of the participant's face. I designed the ESP game "Dowser," which reached the preliminary data-gathering stage but also never became a formal study. Chuck began work on *ESPerciser*®, a four-choice ESP test later used in experiments with high-scoring participant Malcolm Bessent (Honorton, 1987).

"Volition" and "Psi Invaders" also became part of the *PsiLab* //® package for computerized psi testing (Berger & Honorton, 1985). *PsiLab* //® included the two computer-game PK tests and their "Series Manager" and utility software, a PRL/RIPP RNG, the RNG-evaluation software that Don had developed, and a manual written by Rick, Don, and me. In 1986, *PsiLab* //® packages were in 17 different laboratories. Software for preliminary versions of *ESPerciser*® and "Dowser" were included in some later packages. Several laboratories also purchased the *PsiLab* //® MBTI module which included software for computerized administration, a user's manual, and a licensing fee to the test's publisher.

PRL research during these years attracted some national publicity beyond the parapsychological community. Material for an ABC-TV *Nightline* segment on parapsychological research was filmed early in 1984. Science writer Dan Cohen published a book about laboratory research in psi featuring PRL ganzfeld and computer-game research, for junior high school readers (Cohen, 1986).

New ganzfeld experiments were added to the "first timers" series after 1983. One compared percipients' performance with static (still pictures) and dynamic (movie and television clips) targets. Another focused on percipients who had done particularly well in their initial session. In a third series, a variation on the "first timers" protocol let percipients choose not to have a "sender" (only two selected this option). Data from these, as well as the regular "first timers" series, are summarized in Honorton et al. (1990). In addition, Rick began a series in which both the experimenter and the percipient independently judged the targets, but this series was never completed.

Other incomplete studies included a series of experiments related to William Braud's "allobiofeedback" research at Mind Science Foundation (MSF) in San Antonio (Braud & Schlitz, 1983). These studies used human psychophysiological reactions such as the galvanic skin response (GSR) as the target in a PK-testing protocol. After a visit to MSF in 1983, and working with consultant Robert Edelberg, a leading GSR researcher at Rutgers University Medical School, we began the necessary instrumentation but never brought the project far enough to collect data. In another project, David Saunders, a statistician in the Princeton area, used the Gittinger Personality Assessment System (Winne & Gittinger, 1973) to evaluate selected PRL participants. Half of these participants had scored well in PRL studies and the other half had scored poorly, and David was not to know the scoring patterns until he finished his evaluation. Some PAS data were collected, but this was never finished as a PRL project.

By the fall of 1986, most of the original research staff were gone. Nancy left early in 1983 and completed her dissertation research using American Society for Psychical Research facilities. Rick, Mario, and Pat all left in 1985. Rick became Research Associate at SURF. Mario and Christine Hardy, PRL Visiting Scientist during 1985, married and moved to France where they continued their parapsychological work. Pat and her husband moved to Colorado. My wife and I left in 1986, also for Colorado.

Meanwhile, Marta Quant and George Hansen became PRL researchers. Marta worked primarily as a ganzfeld experimenter.

George, with a background of parapsychological research and writing at the Institute for Parapsychology, participated in ganzfeld and computer-game research and programming and began a series of Monte Carlo simulations to evaluate some of the statistical methods used in the research (Hansen, 1986, 1987a, 1987b; Hansen & Utts, 1987). He continued his writing on parapsychology's association with conjuring and criticism (Hansen, 1985, 1988, 1990).

The visiting scientists during 1985 and 1986 focused mainly on their own projects. Christine took time off from her doctoral studies at the Sorbonne to concentrate on computer programs adapting some traditional prediction methods as psi tests. Zoltan Vassy, visiting from Hungary for a year, continued his previous research on the effects of sequence complexity in ESP tests with pseudorandom number sequences (Vassy, 1986). Alianna Maren applied her experience in pattern recognition research to analyzing ganzfeld percipients' mentation for complex matches to the ESP target (Maren, 1987). None of these projects became part of ongoing PRL research protocols or analyses.

In the last few years, between 1987 and 1989, PRL research became even more explicitly projects that were Chuck's, with assistance from the remaining members of the research staff. George and Marta served as experimenters, and George maintained equipment and software and worked on Monte Carlo projects. When Marta left, Dianne Ferrari, who had been a Rider College student intern at PRL for a term, joined the research staff half-time.

Meta-analytic reviews were a primary focus. In one review, Chuck reexamined all of the PRL ganzfeld studies and compared them with the earlier ganzfeld research he had reviewed for the Hyman-Honorton debate (Honorton et al., 1990). Some relationships between experimental conditions and psi-test performance were present in both the PRL and non-PRL work (Broughton, Kanthamani, & Khilji, 1990; Honorton, 1992).

Other meta-analyses covered a wider range of experimental procedures. With Dianne's help, Chuck reviewed and statistically evaluated the forced-choice precognition research since 1935 (Honorton & Ferrari, 1989); with Cornell University psychologist Daryl Bem, they examined studies of extraversion and performance in ESP tests (Honorton, Ferrari, & Bem, 1992).

The few new experiments used existing ganzfeld and computer-game procedures with special participants. One was the *ESPerciser*™ series with Malcolm Bessent, an outstanding participant and long-time friend (Honorton, 1987). Visiting scientist Marilyn Schlitz, then at Mind Science Foundation, helped to obtain participants and to design a ganzfeld series with students from the Juilliard School of Performing Arts in New York (Schlitz & Honorton, 1992). Marilyn served as experimenter for some sessions and as "sender" for others.

Encounters with parapsychology's critics continued. In 1986, Chuck participated in a workshop on the quality and potential of parapsychological research, sponsored by the Office of Technology Assessment of the United States Congress (International Security and Commerce Program, 1988). Other participants were James Alcock, Daryl Bem, Ray Hyman, Robert Jahn, John Palmer, Ted Rockwell, Marcello Truzzi, and Jessica Utts. Around the same time, Chuck, John, and Jessica wrote the Parapsychological Association's official reply to the National Research Council's highly critical report on parapsychological research (Palmer, Honorton, & Utts, 1989).

By 1989, there were no new McDonnell-based funds. Chuck ran the lab on the money that was left in the PRL account and some additional, smaller grants from the Fetzer Foundation, the ASPR, and the Parapsychology Foundation. In October the lab closed. Chuck gave the large sound isolation chamber used in the ganzfeld studies to the Fetzer Foundation; the computer-controlled audiovisual equipment went to the Institute for Parapsychology in Durham, NC. Dianne left the field. George worked as a consulting engineer, continued writing about conjuring, criticism, and parapsychology, and began some spontaneous case research (Maher & Hansen, 1992).

Chuck took the PRL archives and some of the computer equipment to his home, where he continued to analyze data and write. He reported the extraversion meta-analysis and collaborated with Marilyn on the "Juillard-student" ganzfeld report. In the fall of 1991, Chuck left New Jersey for Edinburgh, Scotland, and the PhD program at the University of Edinburgh.

PRL was a combination of people and projects. So is its legacy. Chuck's vision and forcefulness attracted people to work with him on his projects and incorporate the energy and shared information as they pursued their own. The intense focus on his own vision led some to leave so they could take that common core in their own directions, and others to prefer tapping into it by occasional collaboration. Many who were never formally involved in PRL research have responded to its quality and scope by adapting methods and approaches for their own work. It is interesting to watch the effects of contact with PRL, and with Chuck, during the PRL years as they continue to develop.

REFERENCES[7]

BARKER, P., HONORTON, C. (chair), ROBINSON, D., & ZINGRONE, N. (1985). Assessing subject characteristics [Summary]. In N. L. Zingrone, The Southeastern Regional Parapsychological Conference. *Journal of Parapsychology*, **49**, 257–264.

BARKER, P., & SCHECHTER, E. (1983). Characteristics of PRL's participant pool [Summary]. In N. Zingrone-Solomon, The Southeastern Regional Parapsychology Conference. *Journal of Parapsychology*, **47**, 49–64.

BERGER, R. E. (1988a). In search of "psychic signatures" in random data [Summary]. In D. H. Weiner & R. L. Morris (Eds.), *Research in parapsychology 1987* (pp. 81–85). Metuchen, NJ: Scarecrow Press.

BERGER, R. E. (1988b). Psi effects without real-time feedback. *Journal of Parapsychology*, **52**, 1–27.

BERGER, R. E., & HONORTON, C. (1985). *PsiLab //®*: A standardized psi-testing system [Summary]. In R. A. White & J. Solfvin (Eds.), *Research in parapsychology 1984* (pp. 68–71). Metuchen, NJ: Scarecrow Press.

BERGER, R. E., SCHECHTER, E. I., & HONORTON, C. (1986). A preliminary review of performance across three computer psi games [Summary]. In D. H. Weiner & D. I. Radin (Eds.), *Research in parapsychology 1985* (pp. 1–3). Metuchen, NJ: Scarecrow Press.

BRAUD, W., & SCHLITZ, M. (1983). Psychokinetic influence upon electrodermal activity. *Journal of Parapsychology*, **47**, 95–120.

BROUGHTON, R. S., KANTHAMANI, H., & KHILJI, A. (1990). Assessing the PRL success model on an independent ganzfeld database [Summary]. In L. A. Henkel & J. Palmer (Eds.). *Research in parapsychology 1989* (pp. 32–35). Metuchen, NJ: Scarecrow Press.

COHEN, D. (1986). *ESP: The new technology*. New York: Julian Messner, Publisher.

GLASS, G. V., McGAW, B., & SMITH, M. L. (1981). *Meta-analysis in social research*. Beverly Hills, CA: Sage Publications.

HANSEN, G. P. (1985). A brief overview of magic for parapsychologists. *Parapsychology Review*, **16**(2), 5–8.

HANSEN, G. (1986). A look at Z-scores (standardized ratings) [Summary]. In D. H. Weiner & D. I. Radin (Eds.). *Research in parapsychology 1985* (pp. 93–94). Metuchen, NJ: Scarecrow Press.

---

[7] Only the most recent or most complete version of a paper is cited.

HANSEN, G. (1987a). Monte Carlo methods in parapsychology [Summary]. In D. H. Weiner & R. D. Nelson (Eds.), *Research in parapsychology 1986* (pp. 93–97). Metuchen, NJ: Scarecrow Press.

HANSEN, G. (1987b). Examples of a need for conjuring knowledge [Summary]. In D. H. Weiner & R. D. Nelson (Eds.), *Research in parapsychology 1986* (pp. 185–186). Metuchen, NJ: Scarecrow Press.

HANSEN, G. (1988). CSICOP and skepticism: An emerging social movement [Summary]. In D. H. Weiner & R. L. Morris (Eds.), *Research in parapsychology 1987* (pp. 157–161). Metuchen, NJ: Scarecrow Press.

HANSEN, G. (1990). Some comments on the role of magicians in parapsychology [Summary]. In L. A. Henkel & J. Palmer (Eds.), *Research in parapsychology 1989* (p. 36). Metuchen, NJ: Scarecrow Press.

HANSEN, G., & UTTS, J. (1987). Use of both sum of ranks and direct hits in free-response psi experiments. *Journal of Parapsychology*, **51**, 321–335.

HONORTON, C. (1975). Objective determination of stimulus incorporation in ESP tasks with pictoral targets [Summary]. In J. D. Morris, W. G. Roll, & R. L. Morris (Eds.), *Research in parapsychology 1974* (pp. 112–115). Metuchen, NJ: Scarecrow Press.

HONORTON, C. (1983). Response to Hyman's critique of psi ganzfeld results [Summary]. In W. G. Roll, J. Beloff, & R. A. White (Eds.), *Research in parapsychology 1982* (pp. 23–26). Metuchen, NJ: Scarecrow Press.

HONORTON, C. (1985). Meta-analysis of psi ganzfeld research: A response to Hyman. *Journal of Parapsychology*, **49**, 51–91.

HONORTON, C. (1987). Precognition and real-time ESP performance in a computer task with an exceptional subject. *Journal of Parapsychology*, **51**, 291–320.

HONORTON, C. (1992, August). The ganzfeld novice: Four predictors of initial ESP performance. Paper presented at the 35th Annual Convention of the Parapsychological Association, Las Vegas, NV.

HONORTON, C., BARKER, P., & SONDOW, N. (1983). Feedback and participant-selection parameters in a computer RNG study [Summary]. In W. G. Roll, J. Beloff, & R. A. White (Eds.), *Research in parapsychology 1982* (pp. 157–159). Metuchen, NJ: Scarecrow Press.

HONORTON, C., BARKER, P., VARVOGLIS, M., BERGER, R., & SCHECHTER, E. (1986). First-timers: An exploration of factors affecting initial psi ganzfeld performance [Summary]. In D. H. Weiner & D. I. Radin (Eds.), *Research in parapsychology 1985* (pp. 28–32). Metuchen, NJ: Scarecrow Press.

HONORTON, C., BERGER, R. E., VARVOGLIS, M. P., QUANT, M., DERR, P., HANSEN, G. P., SCHECHTER, E., & FERRARI, D. (1990). Psi communication in the ganzfeld: Experiments with an automated testing system and a comparison with a meta-analysis of earlier studies. *Journal of Parapsychology*, **54**, 99–139.

HONORTON, C., & FERRARI, D. C. (1989). Meta-analysis of forced-choice precognition experiments, 1935–1987. *Journal of Parapsychology*, **53**, 281–308.

80

HONORTON, C., FERRARI, D. C., & BEM, D. J. (1992). Extraversion and ESP performance: A meta-analysis and a new confirmation [Summary]. In L. A. Henkel & G. R. Schmeidler (Eds.), *Research in parapsychology 1990* (pp. 3–38). Metuchen, NJ: Scarecrow Press.

HONORTON, C., & SCHECHTER, E. I. (1985, June). Relationship between type and ESP performance in a perceptual isolation (ganzfeld) setting. Paper presented at the Sixth Biennial Conference of the Association for Psychological Type, Evanston, IL.

HONORTON, C., & SCHECHTER, E. I. (1987). Ganzfeld target retrieval with an automated testing system: A model for initial ganzfeld success [Summary]. In D. H. Weiner & R. D. NELSON (Eds.), *Research in parapsychology 1986* (pp. 36–39). Metuchen, NJ: Scarecrow Press.

HONORTON, C., & TREMMEL, L. (1980). Psi-Trek: A preliminary effort toward development of psi-conducive computer software [Summary]. In W. G. Roll (Ed.), *Research in parapsychology 1979* (pp. 159–161). Metuchen, NJ: Scarecrow Press.

HYMAN, R. (1983). Does the ganzfeld experiment answer the critics' objections? [Summary]. In W. G. Roll, J. Beloff, & R. A. White (Eds.), *Research in parapsychology 1982* (pp. 21–23). Metuchen, NJ: Scarecrow Press.

HYMAN, R. (1985). The psi ganzfeld experiment: A critical appraisal. *Journal of Parapsychology*, **49,** 3–49.

HYMAN, R., & HONORTON, C. (1986). A joint communiqué. The psi ganzfeld controversy. *Journal of Parapsychology*, **50,** 351–364.

International Security and Commerce Program, Office of Technology Assessment, United States Congress (1988). Report of a workshop on experimental parapsychology. Reprinted in *Journal of the American Society for Psychical Research*, 1989, **83,** 317–339.

MAHER, M. C., & HANSEN, G. P. (1992). Quantitative investigation of a reported haunting using several detection techniques. *Journal of the American Society for Psychical Research*, **86,** 347–374.

MAREN, A. J. (1987). Representation and performance evaluation approaches in psi free-response tasks [Summary]. In D. H. Weiner & R. D. Nelson (Eds.). *Research in parapsychology 1986* (pp. 97–99). Metuchen, NJ: Scarecrow Press.

MCCARTHY, D. (1982). The role of microcomputers in experimental parapsychology. In B. Shapin and L. Coly (Eds.), *Parapsychology and the experimental method* (pp. 82–99). New York: Parapsychology Foundation.

MCCARTHY, D., & SCHECHTER, E. I. (1986). Estimating effect size from critical ratios [Summary]. In D. H. Weiner & D. I. Radin (Eds.). *Research in parapsychology 1985* (pp. 95–96). Metuchen, NJ: Scarecrow Press.

MCCAULEY, M. H. (1977). *Introduction to the MET for researchers:* Gainesville, FL: Center for Applications of Psychological Type.

OSIS, K. (1982). Review of *Meta-analysis in social research* by Gene V. Glass, Barry McGaw, & Mary Lee Smith. *Journal of the American Society for Psychical Research*, **76,** 191–193.

PALMER, J. A. (1977). Attitudes and personality traits in experimental ESP research. In B. B. Wolman (Ed.), *Handbook of parapsychology* (pp. 175–201). New York: Van Nostrand Reinhold.

PALMER, J. (1978). Extrasensory perception: Research findings. In Krippner, S. (Ed.). *Advances in parapsychological research, Vol. 2: Extrasensory perception* (pp. 59–243). New York: Plenum Press.

PALMER, J. A., HONORTON, C., & UTTS, J. (1989). Reply to the National Research Council study on parapsychology. *Journal of the American Society for Psychical Research,* **83,** 31–49.

Psychophysical Research Laboratories (1984). *Psychophysical Research Laboratories 1983 annual report.* Princeton, NJ: Author.

Psychophysical Research Laboratories (1986). *Psychophysical Research Laboratories 1985 annual report.* Princeton, NJ: Author.

ROSENTHAL, R. (1984). *Meta-analytic procedures for social research.* Beverly Hills, CA: Sage Publications.

SCHECHTER, E. I. (1984). Hypnotic induction vs control conditions: Illustrating an approach to the evaluation of replicability in parapsychological data. *Journal of the American Society for Psychical Research,* **78,** 1–28.

SCHECHTER, E. I. (1987a). Missing and displacement in two RNG computer games [Summary]. In D. H. Weiner & R. D. Nelson (Eds.), *Research in parapsychology 1986* (pp. 73–77). Metuchen, NJ: Scarecrow Press.

SCHECHTER, E. I. (1987b). Meta-analysis and parapsychology. *Parapsychology Review,* **18**(2), 13–15.

SCHECHTER, E. I., BARKER, P., & VARVOGLIS, M. P. (1983). A preliminary study with a PK game involving distraction from the psi task [Summary]. In W. G. Roll, J. Beloff, & R. A. White (Eds.), *Research in parapsychology 1982* (pp. 152–154). Metuchen, NJ: Scarecrow Press.

SCHECHTER, E. I., BARKER, P., & VARVOGLIS, M. P. (1984). A second study with the "Psi Ball" RNG-PK game [Summary]. In R. A. White & R. S. Broughton (Eds.), *Research in parapsychology 1983* (pp. 93–94). Metuchen, NJ: Scarecrow Press.

SCHECHTER, E. I., HONORTON, C., BARKER, P., & VARVOGLIS, M. P. (1984). Relationships between participant traits and scores on two computer-controlled RNG-PK games [Summary]. In R. A. White & R. S. Broughton (Eds.), *Research in parapsychology 1983* (pp. 32–33). Metuchen, NJ: Scarecrow Press.

SCHLITZ, M. J., & HONORTON, C. (1992). Ganzfeld psi performance within an artistically gifted population. *Journal of the American Society for Psychical Research,* **86,** 83–99.

SCHMEIDLER, G. R. (1988). *Parapsychology and psychology: Matches and mismatches.* Jefferson, NC: McFarland.

SONDOW, N., BRAUD, L., & BARKER, P. (1982). Target qualities and affect measures in an exploratory psi ganzfeld [Summary]. In W. G. Roll, R. L. Morris, & R. A. White (Eds.), *Research in parapsychology 1981* (pp. 82–85). Metuchen, NJ: Scarecrow Press.

STANFORD, R., & ANGELINI, R. (1983). The noise-silence and target-encodability variables in a ganzfeld word-association ESP task [Summary]. In W. G. Roll, J. Beloff, & R. A. White (Eds.). *Research in parapsychology 1982* (pp. 185–187). Metuchen, NJ: Scarecrow Press.

TELLEGEN, A., & ATKINSON, G. (1974). Openness to absorbing and self-altering experiences ("absorption"), a trait related to hypnotic susceptibility. *Journal of Abnormal Psychology, 83,* 268–277.

VARVOGLIS, M. P. (1986). Goal-directed and observer-dependent PK: An evaluation of the conformance-behavior model and the observational theories. *Journal of the American Society for Psychical Research, 80,* 137–162.

VARVOGLIS, M. P., & MCCARTHY, D. (1986). Conscious-purposive focus and PK: RNG activity in relation to awareness, task-orientation, and feedback. *Journal of the American Society for Psychical Research, 80,* 1–30.

VASSY, Z. (1986). Experimental study of complexity dependence in precognition. *Journal of Parapsychology, 50,* 235–270.

WHITE, R. A., & SOLFVIN, J. (Eds.). (1985). *Research in parapsychology 1984.* Metuchen, NJ: Scarecrow Press.

WINNE, J. F., & GITTINGER, J. W. (1973). *An introduction to the Personality Assessment System.* Brandon, VT: Clinical Psychology Publishing Co.

THE LAST DAYS IN EDINBURGH

BY ROBERT L. MORRIS

To understand Chuck Honorton's circumstances at Edinburgh, we should go back a few years. Chuck and I first met in 1964 at the Summer Study Program of the Parapsychology Laboratory, located then in the West Duke Building of the east Duke campus. Those were exciting days, when Rex Stanford, John Palmer, Jim Carpenter, Dave Rogers, and others would come to Durham during the summer months to train in parapsychology and conduct various research projects. At the time we met, Chuck had just finished high school, yet already had a refereed publication in the *Journal of Parapsychology*. We all became friends, and the time together in those humid Carolina summers was very important to us.

To hold us together during the rest of the year, we arranged to put out *The Psi Worker's Newsletter,* a little publication which I edited, since I was the only one who remained in Durham (I was a Duke graduate student then). We all contributed to the *Newsletter,* and it provided a way for us to keep in touch with what we were all doing and with the main activities of the Parapsychology Laboratory as it worked through its transition to becoming the Foundation for Research on the Nature of Man. For better or for worse, the contrast between the research activities in North Carolina and the slow grind of an undergraduate education at the University of Minnesota proved too much for Chuck. Half way through his sophomore year he moved south with his wife, Lori, and baby, Joey (named after Joseph Rhine), to become a full-time researcher at the FRNM. Chuck and my wife, Joanna, were already good friends, and our two families spent much happy time together. Chuck and I shared an office, which gave us many opportunities for the sort of intense discussion in which he specialized.

Some of his most productive work was done in those days, and life was good. Joanna had joined the FRNM staff as an assistant editor, and Rex Stanford came to work with us full time. Unfortunately, as often happens when things go very well, interpersonal tensions arose, and life in Durham turned sour. Chuck, Joanna, and

I left the FRNM, and Rex followed shortly after. I stayed in the area finishing my doctorate at Duke and started to work with William Roll at the Psychical Research Foundation. Thanks in part to Bill's efforts, Chuck was hired by Montague Ullman at the Maimonides Medical Center in Brooklyn. Monte, like Rhine, valued research expertise more than formal degree qualifications and recognized a gem when he saw it.

We kept in contact with Chuck in the following years, and the three of us remained strong friends. We were most saddened by the Honortons' divorce but very pleased when his son returned as a young teenager to live with him. When we were together, Joanna and I would encourage Chuck to go back to school to finish his education. It was obvious that he was occasionally the victim of a kind of artificial snobbery because of his lack of formal academic qualifications. He was proud of what he had accomplished on his own merits, however, and each little snub made him more resolved not to play the academic game. Eventually, he was funded by James McDonnell, of the McDonnell-Douglas Corporation, who also valued competence over credentials, and was invited to head his own laboratory, the Psychophysical Research Laboratories. It was clear by then that Chuck had made his point, and we did not again bring up the issue of his education.

Chuck's Days at Edinburgh

As has been chronicled elsewhere, funding for the PRL did dry up as an eventual consequence of the unexpected death of Mr. McDonnell. This left Chuck without a full-time job, although he was able to piece together support from various sources to continue his involvement with the field. In the summer of 1990 we invited Chuck to spend a month with us in Edinburgh, to stay in the "granny flat" that adjoined our house. He was happy to accept, much to the delight of all concerned, and he fit right in with our own small research group, some of whom he already knew. Carl Sargent even made a special trip up to see him, and they had a great time comparing notes on their various earlier studies, many of which had overlapped considerably in theme and method. Ed May, another old friend, also visited at that time with his family.

When I said goodbye to Chuck at the airport, I commented that both Joanna and I had been impressed that he had blended in so well, both with our group and with us as a family. Shortly afterward, we began exploring the possibility of his joining us full time, to do research and acquire his PhD degree. The University of Edinburgh had no insistence upon undergraduate credentials as a prerequisite for the doctorate and, although he had to be considered as a special case, our Faculty Postgraduate Committee agreed that his research credentials were impressive and he was offered a place without difficulty. Chuck was able to acquire funding from the Parapsychology Foundation and the American Society for Psychical Research; our unit paid for his tuition, and we found additional funds to help us redo our research space so that automated ganzfeld research could be done. He joined us in mid-1991 to begin a new phase in his life, living with us and working in the Psychology Department full time on parapsychology, without the intrusion of administrative obligations and hassles.

The entire process of redoing our facility to meet the requirements of good auto-ganzfeld work proceeded slowly, unbearably so at times. Chuck busied himself doing meta-analyses (e.g., the role of the sender in ganzfeld studies), writing other papers such as one for the Italian *CICAP Journal*, and giving public talks on his research. He presented his work to our Psychology Department, and it was very well received. Colleagues were impressed with the rigor of his research and the care with which he treated his data. He made many friends among students, the teaching and research staff, technicians, and secretarial and administrative staff at all levels throughout the Department. They treated him naturally, without implying that his work or his presence in the Department was in any way strange or inappropriate.

In the months spent with us, Chuck's health and appearance steadily improved. He lost weight and became more active, reaching the point where his cane was needed only for long walks or special circumstances.

Perhaps his crowning moments came when he gave a set of talks, one for the Society for Psychical Research in London and another for the Cavendish Laboratory at Cambridge, the latter at the invitation of Nobel Laureate Brian Josephson. At these talks his work was placed under close scrutiny and survived intact, with only minor issues remaining to be resolved.

And then, one terrible morning in November of 1992, his heart gave out and he died.

Chuck's Hopes for the Future

In the few days before his death, the future was already well upon Chuck. So much of his effort was oriented toward gaining acceptance of the ganzfeld research in particular and parapsychology in general; and he could see that happening, tangibly, in Edinburgh and elsewhere, in no small part thanks to his own efforts.

Chuck always disliked the sort of unfair and sloppy criticism to which the field is so often subjected. He was delighted, therefore, when he, along with Sue Blackmore, was asked by the Italian skeptical society, CICAP, to prepare an article offering critical commentary on papers submitted to their journal for an issue devoted to parapsychology and its prospects for the future. It gave him the opportunity to point out how criticism of serious parapsychology was starting to flounder, unable or at least unwilling to deal effectively with his own work or with the recent meta-analyses. One of his strongest hopes for the future was gradually being realized—that we be able to distinguish both for ourselves and for the public as a whole the difference between legitimate criticism of specific methodologies and the superficial, rhetoric-ridden pronouncements that so often prevailed. He valued the former and despised the latter, as befits a former champion debater.

A companion hope, also increasingly being realized, was that parapsychological researchers would focus their efforts on procedures that are both psi-conducive and theoretically relevant. Only then can we do the business of science, of replicating and extending each others' work, and developing a rich understanding of the nature of psi.

I think Chuck could see the future becoming the present, in the professional and public responses to his work and those of other major researchers. He knew that several research centers were taking up the ganzfeld work, that meta-analyses were becoming a routine aspect of parapsychological evaluation, and that the self-declared "skeptical" community was gradually being compelled to clean up its own act when referring to serious parapsychology.

This is not to say, of course, that he or anyone else regarded his work as perfect. The auto-ganzfeld procedure still needs to be sharpened—for instance by the use of duplicate tapes for sending and judging and by isolation of the VCR units from the experimenter, as we are doing now in Edinburgh. Meta-analysis is still a relatively new technique, and many questions remain regarding its usage and interpretation. Work in both areas will continue to evolve conceptually and methodologically. Both represent extremely valuable tools, helping us pass on to more systematic investigation of the real issues of the processes of psi, of the nature of experience, and the sense of self that drove the original psychical researchers, drove Charles Honorton, and will continue to fuel our efforts in the future.

Chuck knew he was living on borrowed time. He lived longer than he expected to. It is up to us now to ensure that he lived long enough to pass on a true legacy.

HONORTON THE META-ANALYST

By Jessica Utts

For anyone who has followed the history of parapsychology, there can be no doubt that the use of meta-analysis is an important part of that history. One of the principal arguments of the critics concerned the apparent lack of repeatable experiments. Meta-analytic techniques, along with attention to power and sample sizes, have revealed that the problem did not lie with the data; the problem was that *repeatable* was absurdly defined to mean that every experiment, or at least a large percentage of them, must reach "statistical significance."

Even the early meta-analyses used in parapsychology relied on this "vote-counting" method of determining whether replication was evident. As more sophisticated uses of meta-analysis were introduced, however, it became clear that these techniques provided for a different definition of the term *repeatable*, namely, that effect sizes remain homogeneous from one similar experiment to another.

Meta-analytic techniques brought other welcome additions to investigating parapsychological data. First, they allowed for quantitative testing of the alleged problem that the more flawed experiments were the ones most likely to produce statistical significance. Second, they permitted the comparison of conditions both within and across experiments. Third, they provided a means by which power calculations could become an important part of designing a new experiment.

Certainly there were quantitative reviews of broad areas of parapsychology before the introduction of meta-analysis (see Schechter, 1987, for some references); but the widespread acceptance of meta-analysis as a way to consider controversial claims in medicine and the social sciences has made it ideal for examining claims in parapsychology as well.

Charles Honorton was one of the first to recognize the potential value of meta-analysis for parapsychologists. He continued to advocate the reporting of effect sizes and other information that would simplify the work of future meta-analysts. He was the first to publish a nominal meta-analysis in parapsychology (Honorton,

1985a), and he went on to publish several more. His sophistication in the use of meta-analytic techniques grew steadily over the years, and the way he wove them together with his other work provides valuable lessons for future researchers. We now turn to the history and magnitude of Chuck's contributions to the interface of parapsychology and meta-analysis.

History

In the second half of 1982, ten years before his death, two series of events converged in a way that would change the rest of Chuck's research career and the history of parapsychology itself. The first of these was that he and psychologist Ray Hyman had exchanged the first round of their now-famous debate (resulting in: Honorton, 1985a; Hyman, 1985a; and Hyman & Honorton, 1986) at the annual meeting of the Parapsychological Association, held in Cambridge, England, in August. Much of the debate centered around the question of whether any conclusions could be drawn from the existing body of ganzfeld studies. Hyman's approach to the database centered on identifying methodological flaws that he believed negated any statistically significant findings.

The second series of events started when Chuck and colleague Ephraim Schechter read a review by Karlis Osis (1982) describing a newly published book on meta-analysis by Glass, McGaw, and Smith (1981). Upon reading the book; they immediately realized that this new field of meta-analysis had relevance to parapsychology. In light of the status of the debate with Hyman, you can imagine Chuck's reaction when he read the following passage, which alone is marked in the margin of his copy of the book:

> Respect for parsimony and good sense demands an acceptance of the notion that imperfect studies can converge on a true conclusion. An important part of every meta-analysis with which we have been associated has been the recording of methodological weaknesses in the original studies and the examination of their covariance on study findings. Thus, the influence of "study quality" on findings has been regarded as an empirical a posteriori question, not an a priori matter of opinion or judgment used in excluding large numbers of studies from consideration. (p. 222)

The emerging importance of meta-analysis in Chuck's research and thinking is evident from the progression of space devoted to its description in the annual reports of the Psychophysical Research Laboratories (PRL). By the time the 1982 report was written, crude steps had already been taken toward the meta-analysis that Honorton eventually published (1985a). The 1982 annual report spent one paragraph explaining what meta-analysis does and included descriptions of that meta-analysis, as well as the one eventually published by Schechter (1984) on hypnosis. The focus of both of these analyses was "vote-counting," that is, comparing significant with nonsignificant studies.

In contrast, the 1983 annual report of PRL devoted 10 pages to a general description of meta-analysis. These were followed by an additional 15 pages presenting more comprehensive results for the two areas of studies discussed in the 1982 report (ganzfeld and hypnosis). It is in this report that one begins to see Chuck's commitment to this emerging field, as we read: "Our feeling that the parapsychological research enterprise can benefit from meta-analysis is sufficiently strong that we are actively promoting the research" (p. 97).

Indeed, he did promote the research. On November 17, 1984, PRL hosted a one-day conference on meta-analysis, featuring Harvard psychologist Robert Rosenthal, one of the early proponents of meta-analysis, as the guest speaker. The conference was attended by five members of the PRL staff, as well as 12 other researchers, and is briefly summarized in the 1984 PRL annual report (section 5.0, pp. 96–97). In addition, PRL staff member Ephraim Schechter (1985b) organized a roundtable discussion at the 1984 Annual Convention of the Parapsychological Association, entitled "Meta-Analysis: Integrating Results Across Studies." Joining Schechter (1985b) and Honorton (1985b) as participants were Ray Hyman (1985b), John Palmer (1985), and Irvin Child (1985). The roundtable discussion was prefaced by the participants' prepared remarks, some of which will be examined in the next section of this paper.

During the next eight years, Chuck's sophistication with the use of meta-analytic techniques grew steadily. He collaborated with others to produce a few meta-analytic reviews (Honorton & Ferrari, 1989; Honorton et al., 1990; Honorton, Ferrari, & Bem, 1992), and his research reports all included effect sizes as well as sufficient details to be useful to future meta-analysts. He encouraged others to do the same. Let us now turn to a more in-depth study of this growing sophistication.

From Vote-Counter to Statistical Sophisticate

Chuck's use of meta-analysis in his research progressed through four stages, each identified by the use to which he put the analysis methods. He started with simple vote-counting, then progressed to the idea that meta-analysis could be used to identify flaws and correlate them with study outcome, thus helping to design better experiments for the future. The next stage was the realization that effect sizes could be estimated and used to plan future experiments by calculating power. In the final stage (e.g., Honorton et al., 1990), Chuck was performing a multifaceted analysis in which effect sizes were measured, tested for homogeneity, and compared across conditions to suggest more completely how to design future experiments for optimal results.

Chuck was actually performing meta-analysis in the form of vote-counting before the term had even been introduced (Honorton, 1977), and his first round of analysis of the ganzfeld data used this same technique. Vote-counting is the simple procedure of counting how many of a given group of studies achieve statistical significance at some prespecified level, usually .05. It has been shown that this procedure is actually more and more likely to lead one to the wrong conclusion as the number of studies increases (Hedges & Olkin, 1985). As late as 1989, in the meta-analysis with Ferrari (Honorton & Ferrari, 1989) vote-counting was still included as one of several measures examined, but the credence given to the procedure was so reduced over the years that it does not appear at all in the 1990 paper by Honorton et al.

The next stage incorporated the idea that meta-analysis could be used to identify and summarize flaws in previous studies so that information could be gained for designing better studies. As mentioned above, Chuck was first made aware of meta-analysis when he was in the middle of the debate with Hyman over the ganzfeld database. Because the focus of the debate was study quality and its relation to study outcome, it is not surprising that both Chuck and Ray Hyman picked up on that aspect of meta-analysis as being relevant to parapsychology. The degree to which their thinking was similar, and to which it presaged their joint communiqué (Hyman & Honorton, 1986) can be seen from their separate remarks at the 1984 roundtable on meta-analysis (Schechter, 1985b). They were both arguing that meta-analysis could be used to design better studies, which could then be used to confirm or reject the existence of the phenomena:

> As applied to the search for psi, for example, no amount of meta-analysis, no matter how well-conceived, can serve as proof for the existence or nonexistence of psi or for patterns of correlation with psi. Like any

other output of exploratory search, the findings, at best, can serve to guide the design and conduct of experiments that will carry confirmatory weight. (Hyman, 1985b, p. 115)

By coding study procedures, meta-analysis helps define and clarify important methodological issues.... Once these initial steps have been taken, researchers and critics may be able to agree upon *explicit criteria* for the design and evaluation of new sets of studies which will enable sound conclusions to be drawn. The development of such criteria is, I believe, a necessary prerequisite for resolution of the controversy over the occurrence of psi phenomena. (Honorton, 1985b, p. 116)

The major change that occurred in the quantitative assessment of groups of studies as a result of the formal introduction of meta-analysis into parapsychology was the change in focus from vote-counting to measuring effect sizes. Unlike a significance level, the magnitude of an effect size does not depend on the sample size. Consequently, it is far better to define replication in terms of similar effect sizes than in terms of the number of "statistically significant" experiments.

The shift in Chuck's thinking along these lines can be seen by comparing the ganzfeld meta-analyses presented in the 1982 and 1983 PRL annual reports. In the 1982 report we read: "Meta-analysis techniques were used to compare statistically significant and non-significant studies to assess the effects of potential artifacts" (section III, p. 2). By 1983, however, the PRL annual report addressed the problems with vote-counting:

Last year, we presented a meta-analytic review of psi ganzfeld research using the "vote counting" method.... The vote counting method has low statistical power since it is based on dichotomized rather than continuous scores. For this reason, we present here analysis using a more powerful measure, the binomial z-score for direct hits. (section 4, p. 83)

The use of z scores for direct hits still carries the problem of being affected by the number of trials in each experiment, but the shift away from significance levels was a step in the right direction. The final step, that of using effect sizes like Cohen's h, was undoubtedly a result of Chuck's interactions with Robert Rosenthal. Rosenthal's (1986) commentary on the ganzfeld debate was based almost exclusively on analyzing these effect sizes. In any case, all of Chuck's meta-analyses subsequent to the ganzfeld debate relied on effect sizes as the primary measures of interest.

The final maturation in Chuck's use and understanding of meta-analysis can be seen in his treatment of the autoganzfeld database.

The paper by Honorton et al. (1990) is technically not a standard meta-analysis because all of the experiments were performed in the same laboratory and no literature search was necessary. Nevertheless, the treatment of the data is a good example of how meta-analysis can be used to evaluate a group of experiments, and it illustrates the level of statistical sophistication Chuck had attained by that time.

In keeping with Chuck's spirit of educating the parapsychological community on meta-analysis, I will briefly review the attractive highlights of the work presented in that paper. The first good feature is that all procedures used in the laboratory and in the experiments are described in painstaking detail. This does not contribute to the meta-analysis of the data, but is necessary in all scientific reports if they are to be used for future meta-analyses. We cannot guess what aspect of an experiment might be important to some future analyst, so it is critical to include all possible details when reporting experimental work.

Turning to the numerical analyses, the main advancement over previous reviews is that this one does not focus at all on significance levels for individual studies. Instead, effect sizes are reported, along with confidence intervals for them. When z scores are reported, the focus is not on "significance," but rather on whether they were consistently in the predicted direction.

A further level of sophistication is an examination of the homogeneity of effect sizes. This is done with a chi-squared test, and the results should be used as a guideline for whether different experimenters and/or studies are getting similar results in terms of effect sizes.

Finally, this paper shows how the autoganzfeld work provided a reasonable replication of the effect sizes estimated in the earlier ganzfeld meta-analysis. It is this completion of the exploratory/confirmatory progression that illustrates one of the most useful applications of meta-analysis to parapsychology, and I suspect Chuck recognized that potential long before it became clear to most of us.

Scientific Progress

Although Chuck ventured into other psi regimes to perform meta-analyses, I believe the intertwining of the ganzfeld work with meta-analysis is an exemplary illustration of how science should proceed, and one of which he was most proud. Perhaps it is too early to know the ultimate impact of Chuck's contributions, but I believe he could rest easier knowing that the story was soon to be told in the *Psychological Bulletin* (Bem & Honorton, in press) and would thus reach a wide audience.

The general progression for which that story is such a superb illustration begins when someone, Chuck in this case, forms a theory, on the basis of previous related work, that a certain kind of experiment might succeed. In this case, Chuck noticed that attention to internal states was important in gaining information through psi and was thus led to the ganzfeld procedure (see Honorton, 1977). The next step in our ideal progression is that the initial experiment is successful enough that others might try to replicate, or more likely, improve it.

Ideally, and as happened with the ganzfeld, this initial phase of investigation includes experiments by people in different laboratories but using similar enough procedures so that the results can be used in a comprehensive review. The introduction of meta-analysis in the late 1970s and early 1980s provided the quantitative machinery necessary for a review that could most constructively lead to the next step.

It should be noted that Hyman was correct in stating that a meta-analysis of the type initially conducted on the ganzfeld data base is "Exploratory Data Analysis...[and] we should not confuse the outcomes of such explorations with Confirmatory Data Analysis (1985b, p. 115)." However, the results of such analyses are exactly what are needed to plan the confirmatory studies, and that is precisely what happened in this case.

The debate and subsequent papers connected with the initial ganzfeld meta-analysis were useful in two ways. First, the analyses of flaws led Hyman and Honorton (1986) to provide explicit rules that a proper confirmatory study should follow—rules that were followed in the autoganzfeld work. Second, they provided effect-size measures that, if matched in a confirmation, would indicate the presence of a repeatable effect. The most useful of the papers in this regard was the contribution by Rosenthal (1986) in which he analyzed the database for its effect size by Cohen's h, and made an adjustment for the flaws that had been identified.

Continuing with our ideal progression, once flaws and effect sizes have been identified, new studies can be planned to avoid those flaws and to try to confirm the size of the effects. The autoganzfeld studies were designed to meet those goals, and seem to have successfully done so. Certainly they have yet to be found flawed in any way, and the overall effect sizes are just what were predicted from the earlier exploratory meta-analysis.

Sender / No Sender Meta-Analysis
Study Coding Form

REFERENCE ID

BIBLIOGRAPHICAL

AUTHORS

TITLE

PUBLICATION

JASPR	JP	JSPR	EJP	RIP	PF MONO	YEAR 19	VOL	PAGES	ABSTRACT or JOURNAL

OTHER

SERIES ID

PSI MODE

SENDER	NO SENDER	MIXED

STATISTICS (DIRECT HITS)

N SUBJECTS	N TRIALS	PROB. OF HIT	HITS	Z	p(Z)	PROP. HITS	EFFECT SIZE

STATISTICS (SUM OF RANKS)

N SUBJECTS	N TRIALS	PROB. OF HIT	SUM OF RANKS	Z	p(Z)	EFFECT SIZE

STATISTICS (RATINGS Z)

N SUBJECTS	MEAN Z	SD	t	p(t)	Z(p)	EFFECT SIZE

STATISTICS (OTHER THAN ABOVE)

PROCEDURAL FEATURES

TASK	JUDGE :		
	FREE-RESPONSE	FORCED-CHOICE	PHYSIOLOGICAL

SET		
	INTENTIONAL	UNINTENTIONAL

SETTING			
	INDIVIDUAL	GROUP	POST

TARGETS

DISTANCE BETWEEN SUBJECT & TARGET

FIGURE 1. Example of a meta-analysis coding form.

SUBJECTS

RECRUITMENT		HISTORY		POPULATION	
VOLUNTEER		UNSELECTED		CHILDREN	
STUDENT		SELECTED		ADOLESCENT	
FRIEND		EXPERIMENTER		ADULT	
EXPERIMENTER		MIXED		STUDENT	
ADVERTS		UNKNOWN		SPECIAL GROUP	
WORD OF MOUTH				UNKNOWN	
COURSE/LECTURE					
MEDIA					
OTHER:					
UNKNOWN					

S/R RELATIONSHIP	
LAB	
FRIEND	

STUDY QUALITY CRITERIA

SENSORY CUES: STUDIES WITH NO SENDER

TARGETS IN OPAQUE CONTAINERS OR COMPUTER MEMORY	
TARGETS SCREENED & UNKNOWN TO EXPTR	
TARGETS PHYSICALLY REMOTE	
(FREE RESPONSE) SEPARATE JUDGING PACKS OR EQUIV.	

SENSORY CUES: STUDIES WITH SENDER

SENDER/RECEIVER IN DIFFERENT ROOMS	
ROOM SHIELDING DOCUMENTED	
1-WAY COMMUNICATION PATH FROM RECEIVER DOCUMENTED	
SENDER/RECEIVER MONITORING	
(FREE RESPONSE:) SEPARATE JUDGING PACKS OR EQUIV	

RANDOMISATION

TARGET SELECTION NOT DESCRIBED	
HAND SHUFFLING OR DICE	
MECHANICAL SHUFFLING	
RANDOM NUMBER TABLE OR RNG	
RANDOMNESS CHECKS REPORTED	

DATA RECORDING

NOT DESCRIBED	
MANUAL RECORDING	
DUPLICATE RECORDING	
AUTOMATED RECORDING	

DATA CHECKING

NOT DESCRIBED	
MANUAL CHECKING	
DUPLICATE CHECKING	
AUTOMATED CHECKING	

SENDER ACTIVITIES

N SENDING PERIODS		NOT DESCRIBED	
		PRESENT/NO CONTACT WITH TARGET	
SENDING DURATION:		TARGET/UNSPECIFIED SENDING METHOD	
		TARGET/FOCUS ON CONTENT	
		TARGET/FOCUS ON MEANING	
		TARGET/FOCUS ON EMOTIONAL TONE	
OTHER:			

FEEDBACK

NOT DESCRIBED	
TRIAL-BY-TRIAL	
RUN-SCORE	
SESSION STATISTICAL SUMMARY (1 = IMMEDIATE, 0 = DELAYED)	
NO FEEDBACK	
OTHER:	

98

There remains one more step in our ideal scenario, one that was identified by Hyman (1991) in his reply to my earlier description of this work (Utts, 1991):

> Honorton's experiments have produced intriguing results. If, as Utts suggests, independent laboratories can produce similar results with the same relationships and with the same attention to rigorous methodology, then parapsychology may indeed have finally captured its elusive quarry. (Hyman, 1991, p. 392)

Work In Progress

When Chuck died he was working on two projects related to meta-analysis, which he unfortunately did not see to their conclusion. The first was a new meta-analysis on the impact of sender versus no sender in the ganzfeld. To illustrate the care required to properly perform a meta-analysis, Figure 1 shows the coding sheet used to record the results of each study. Preliminary results from this meta-analysis indicated slightly higher effect sizes in studies for which senders were used, but the results were not conclusive (Honorton, 1992).

The second project Chuck had planned was one he had discussed with me and with others. It was a book summarizing the role and use of meta-analysis in parapsychology, and he referred to it as his "ESP-60." At the time of his death, he had prepared an outline with the working title "Parapsychology: A Meta-Analytic Perspective." He had planned five sections, consisting mainly of previously published work. Of the 18 chapters, only two were to be newly written, both by him. One was to be titled "Meta-Analysis and Traditional Objections to Parapsychological Evidence," and the other, to be the final chapter, was titled "Future Directions." This last was to be the only chapter of Section V, "Summing Up."

Sadly, we will never have the wisdom of Chuck's version of "Future Directions"; but it is up to the rest of us to ensure that the paths he showed by example are used to lead the science he loved into a brilliant future.

REFERENCES

BEM, D. J., & HONORTON, C. (in press). Does psi exist? Replicable evidence for an anomalous process of information transfer. *Psychological Bulletin.*
CHILD, I. (1985). Meta-analysis: Remarks suggested by a review of ESP dream research (part of a roundtable on "Meta-analysis: Integrating Results

Across Studies"). In R. A. White & J. Solfvin (Eds.), *Research in parapsychology 1984* (pp. 116–118). Metuchen, NJ: Scarecrow Press.

GLASS, G. V., McGAW, B., & SMITH, M. L. (1981). *Meta-analysis in social research.* Beverly Hills, CA: Sage Publications.

HEDGES, L. V., & OLKIN, I. (1985). *Statistical methods for meta-analysis.* Orlando, FL: Academic Press.

HONORTON, C. (1977). Psi and internal attention states. In B. B. Wolman (Ed.), *Handbook of parapsychology* (pp. 435–472). New York: Van Nostrand Reinhold.

HONORTON, C. (1985a). Meta-analysis of psi ganzfeld research: A response to Hyman. *Journal of Parapsychology,* **49,** 51–92.

HONORTON, C. (1985b). Programmatic research assessment (part of a roundtable on "Meta-Analysis: Integrating Results Across Studies"). In R. A. White & J. Solfvin (Eds.), *Research in parapsychology 1984* (pp. 115–116). Metuchen, NJ: Scarecrow Press.

HONORTON, C. (1992). Impact of sender in ganzfeld communication: Meta-analysis and power estimates. Unpublished manuscript.

HONORTON, C., BERGER, R. E., VARVOGLIS, M. P., QUANT, M., DERR, P., SCHECHTER, E. I., & FERRARI, D. C. (1990). Psi communication in the ganzfeld: Experiments with an automated testing system and a comparison with a meta-analysis of earlier studies. *Journal of Parapsychology,* **54,** 99–139.

HONORTON, C., & FERRARI, D. C. (1989). Meta-analysis of forced-choice precognition experiments, 1935–1987. *Journal of Parapsychology,* **53,** 281–308.

HONORTON, C., FERRARI, D. C., & BEM, D. J. (1992). Extraversion and ESP performance: A meta-analysis and a new confirmation. In L. Henkel & G. Schmeidler (Eds.), *Research in parapsychology 1990* (pp. 35–38). Metuchen, NJ: Scarecrow Press.

HYMAN, R. (1985a). The psi ganzfeld experiment: A critical appraisal. *Journal of Parapsychology,* **49,** 3–49.

HYMAN, R. (1985b). Searching for patterns: Meta-analysis and parapsychology (part of a roundtable on "Meta-analysis: Integrating Results Across Studies"). In R. A. White & J. Solfvin (Eds.), *Research in parapsychology 1984* (pp. 114–115). Metuchen, NJ: Scarecrow Press.

HYMAN, R. (1991). Comment. *Statistical Science,* **6,** 389–392.

HYMAN, R., & HONORTON, C. (1986). A joint communiqué: The psi ganzfeld controversy. *Journal of Parapsychology,* **50,** 351–364.

OSIS, K. (1982). Review of *Meta-analysis in social research* by Gene V. Glass, Barry McGaw, & Mary Lee Smith. *Journal of the American Society for Psychical Research,* **76,** 191–193.

PALMER, J. (1985). Meta-analysis in process-oriented psi research (part of a roundtable on "Meta-analysis: Integrating Results Across Studies"). In R. A. White & J. Solfvin (Eds.), *Research in parapsychology 1984* (pp. 117–118). Metuchen, NJ: Scarecrow Press.

100

Psychophysical Research Laboratories (1982). Annual report. Unpublished manuscript.

Psychophysical Research Laboratories (1983). Annual report. Unpublished manuscript.

Psychophysical Research Laboratories (1984). Annual report. Unpublished manuscript.

ROSENTHAL, R. (1986). Meta-analytic procedures and the nature of replication: The ganzfeld debate. *Journal of Parapsychology*, **50**, 315–336.

SCHECHTER, E. I. (1984). Hypnotic induction vs. control conditions: Illustrating an approach to the evaluation of replicability in parapsychological data. *Journal of the American Society for Psychical Research*, **78**, 1–28.

SCHECHTER, E. I. (1985a). Experimental procedures as variables in meta-analysis (part of a roundtable on "Meta-analysis: Integrating Results Across Studies"). In R. A. White & J. Solfvin (Eds.), *Research in parapsychology 1984* (pp. 117–118). Metuchen, NJ: Scarecrow Press.

SCHECHTER, E. I. (1985b). Meta-analysis: Integrating results across studies. In R. A. White & J. Solfvin (Eds.), *Research in parapsychology 1984* (pp. 112–118). Metuchen, NJ: Scarecrow Press.

SCHECHTER, E. I. (1987). Meta-analysis and parapsychology. *Parapsychology Review*, **18** (2), 13–15.

UTTS, J. (1991). Replication and meta-analysis in parapsychology. *Statistical Science*, **6**, 363–403.

THE GANZFELD EXPERIMENT

BY DARYL J. BEM

Charles Honorton had three overriding scientific goals: understanding psi, providing parapsychology with a "recipe for replication," and winning mainstream acceptance for parapsychology. His chosen vehicle was the ganzfeld experiment. It is the jewel in the crown of Chuck Honorton's work and, arguably, the jewel in the crown of contemporary parapsychology itself.

In this article, I summarize the history of Chuck's ganzfeld work and then describe in more personal terms our collaborative efforts to bring it to the attention of mainstream psychology.

The Ganzfeld Procedure

Chuck left college in 1966 to work with J. B. Rhine at the Institute for Parapsychology in Durham. By that time, a number of parapsychologists were already searching for alternative laboratory procedures that would more faithfully reflect the circumstances that seemed to characterize reported instances of psi in everyday life.

Historically, psi has often been associated with meditation, hypnosis, dreaming, and other naturally occurring or deliberately induced altered states of consciousness. For example, the view that psi phenomena can occur during meditation is expressed in most classical texts on meditative techniques; the belief that hypnosis is a psi-conducive state dates all the way back to the days of early mesmerism (Dingwall, 1968); and cross-cultural surveys indicate that most reported "real-life" psi experiences are mediated through dreams (Green, 1960; Prasad & Stevenson, 1968; Rhine, 1962; Sannwald, 1959).

There is now experimental evidence consistent with these anecdotal observations: Several studies show that meditation facilitates psi performance (Honorton, 1977); a meta-analysis of experiments on hypnosis and psi suggests that hypnotic induction might also facilitate psi performance (Schechter, 1984); and the experiments conducted during the 1960s at Maimonides Medical Center in New York provided evidence for dream-mediated psi (Child, 1985; Ullman, Krippner, & Vaughan, 1973). (Honorton played an important role in these studies and subsequently served as Director of Research for the Maimonides laboratory from 1974 to 1979.)

These several lines of evidence converged to suggest a working model of psi in which psi-mediated information is conceptualized as a weak signal that is normally masked by internal somatic and external sensory "noise." By reducing ordinary sensory input, these diverse psi-conducive states are presumed to raise the signal-to-noise ratio, thereby enhancing a person's ability to detect the psi-mediated information (Honorton, 1969, 1977). To test the hypothesis that a reduction of sensory input itself facilitates psi performance, Chuck and others turned to the ganzfeld procedure (Braud, Wood, & Braud, 1975; Honorton & Harper, 1974; Parker, 1975), a procedure originally introduced into experimental psychology during the 1930s to test propositions derived from Gestalt theory (Avant, 1965; Metzger, 1930).

Like the Maimonides dream studies, the psi ganzfeld procedure has most often been used to test for telepathic communication between a sender and a receiver. The receiver is placed in a reclining chair in an acoustically isolated room. Translucent ping-pong ball halves are taped over the eyes, and headphones are placed over the ears; a red floodlight directed toward the eyes produces an undifferentiated visual field, and white noise played through the headphones produces an analogous auditory field. It is this homogeneous perceptual environment that is called the *Ganzfeld* ("total field"). To reduce internal somatic "noise," the receiver typically also undergoes a series of progressive relaxation exercises at the beginning of the ganzfeld period.

The sender is sequestered in a separate acoustically isolated room, and a visual stimulus (art print, photograph, or brief videotaped sequence) is randomly selected from a large pool of such stimuli to serve as the target for the session. While the sender concentrates on the target, the receiver provides a continuous verbal report of his or her ongoing imagery and mentation, usually for about 30 minutes. At the completion of the ganzfeld period, the receiver is presented with several stimuli (usually four) and, without knowing which stimulus was the target, is asked to rate the degree to which each matches the imagery and mentation experienced during the ganzfeld period. If the receiver assigns the highest rating to the target stimulus, it is scored as a "hit." Thus, if the experiment employs judging pools containing four stimuli (the target and three "decoys" or control stimuli), then the hit rate expected by chance is .25. The ratings can also be analyzed in other ways; for example, they can be converted to ranks or standardized scores within each set and analyzed parametrically across sessions. The similarity ratings can also be made by outside judges using transcripts of the receiver's mentation report.

The Debate Over the Ganzfeld Database

In 1985 and 1986, the *Journal of Parapsychology* devoted two entire issues to a critical examination of the ganzfeld database, which at the time contained 42 studies, including five of Chuck's. The 1985 issue comprised a meta-analysis and critique of the studies by Ray Hyman (1985)—a cognitive psychologist and skeptical critic of parapsychological research—and a competing meta-analysis and rejoinder by Chuck (Honorton, 1985). The 1986 issue contained four commentaries on the Hyman-Honorton exchange, a joint communiqué by Hyman and Honorton (1986), and six additional commentaries on the joint communiqué itself.

Although I was already familiar with the ganzfeld procedure, it was Chuck's detailed, data-based response to Hyman's critique that persuaded me to relinquish a large measure of my previous skepticism and to seriously entertain the possibility that the psi ganzfeld effect was genuine. Chuck's rhetorical skills were considerable, but it was his ability to get the data to speak for themselves that carried the argument so forcibly.

For example, Hyman had agonized for several pages over the fact that many investigators had performed multiple statistical analyses on their data without adjusting the significance levels to account for multiple tests. In a simple but elegant response, Chuck ignored the investigators' original analyses and applied a uniform test on the proportion of direct hits across each of the 28 studies from which the hit rate could be extracted. He then added in 10 additional studies that had used the relevant judging procedure but had not reported their hit rates; conservatively, he set the hit rates on these 10 studies to chance ($z = 0$). The combined z across all 38 studies was 5.67 ($p = 7.3 \times 10^{-9}$), thereby ending in a single stroke the debate over multiple analyses.

I also felt that Chuck argued successfully against the charge that the nonindependence of studies from the same laboratory, selective reporting problems, or methodological flaws vitiated the substantive findings or fatally compromised the integrity of the ganzfeld database. Moreover, I was impressed by the sheer size of the effect: Depending on just how the studies are combined, the direct hit rate is approximately 35% (where 25% is expected by chance). This is equivalent to seeing a coin turn up heads 62% of the time, an effect size that is almost visible to the naked eye (Bem & Honorton, in press).

Apparently Hyman was not as impressed as I was. Nevertheless, he agreed with Chuck in their joint communiqué of 1986 that

> there is an overall significant effect in this data base that cannot reasonably be explained by selective reporting or multiple analysis. We continue to differ over the degree to which the effect constitutes evidence for psi, but we agree that the final verdict awaits the outcome of future experiments conducted by a broader range of investigators and according to more stringent standards. (Hyman & Honorton, 1986, p. 351)

They then spelled out in detail the "more stringent standards" they believed should govern future experiments. These included strict security precautions against sensory leakage, testing and documentation of randomization methods for selecting targets and sequencing the judging pool, statistical correction for multiple analyses, advance specification of the status of the experiment (e.g., pilot study, confirmatory experiment), and full documentation in the published report of the experimental procedures and the status of statistical tests (e.g., planned or post hoc).

The Autoganzfeld Studies

In 1983, Chuck and his colleagues at his Psychophysical Research Laboratories in New Jersey initiated a new series of ganzfeld studies designed to avoid the methodological problems he and others had identified in earlier studies (Honorton, 1979; Kennedy, 1979). These studies complied with all the detailed guidelines that he and Hyman were to publish later in their joint communiqué. The program continued until September of 1989, when a loss of funding forced the laboratory to close.

The major innovations of the new studies were the computer control of the experimental protocol—hence the name "autoganzfeld"—and the introduction of videotaped film clips as target stimuli. The automated ganzfeld protocol has been examined over the years by several dozen parapsychologists and behavioral researchers from other fields, including well-known critics of parapsychology, and "mentalists," magicians who specialize in the simulation of psi.

All have expressed satisfaction with the handling of security issues and controls.

The experimental program included three pilot and eight formal studies. Five of the formal studies employed novice (first-time) participants who served as the receiver in one session each. The remaining three formal studies employed experienced participants. Altogether 100 men and 140 women participated as receivers in 354 sessions during the research program. Eight separate experimenters, including Chuck, conducted the studies.

The overall hit rate obtained across the autoganzfeld studies was approximately 34%, which is nearly identical to the effect size found in the meta-analysis of the earlier database and is highly significant ($p = .0009$). The complete results were published in the *Journal of Parapsychology* in 1990 (Honorton et al., 1990) and are summarized in Bem and Honorton (in press).

Among the autoganzfeld participants were 10 male and 10 female undergraduates from the Juilliard School in New York City who had been recruited specifically to examine within the ganzfeld setting the frequently reported relationship between creativity or artistic ability and psi performance (Schmeidler, 1988). Eight of these students were music majors, 10 were drama majors, and 2 were dance majors. Each served as the receiver in a single session. These students achieved a hit rate of 50% ($p = .014$), one of the five highest hit rates ever reported for a single sample in a ganzfeld study. The musicians were particularly successful: Six of the eight (75%) successfully identified their targets ($p = .004$). Further details about this sample and their ganzfeld performance are reported in Schlitz and Honorton (1992).

In our summary of these studies, Chuck and I stated that

> we believe that the "stringent standards" requirement has been met by the autoganzfeld studies. The results are statistically significant and consistent with those in the earlier database. The mean effect size is quite respectable when compared with other controversial research areas of human performance (Harris & Rosenthal, 1988). And, there are reliable relationships between successful psi performance and conceptually relevant experimental and subject variables—relationships that also replicate previous findings. (Bem & Honorton, in press)

Hyman has also commented on the autoganzfeld studies:

> Honorton's experiments have produced intriguing results. If... independent laboratories can produce similar results with the same relationships and with the same attention to rigorous methodology, then para-

psychology may indeed have finally captured its elusive quarry. (1991, p. 392)

Into the Mainstream

My collaboration with Chuck had its roots in a visit I paid in 1983 to his New Jersey laboratories, where he had invited me to examine the autoganzfeld procedures from the perspective of a research psychologist, a subject, and a magician.[1] Although I was impressed with the methodology, it was not until I read the published debate three years later that I concluded that there was a body of data with sufficient probative value to warrant the attention of the wider psychological community.

Accordingly, in 1988 I prepared a section on psi for the forthcoming edition of the introductory psychology textbook that I co-author (Atkinson, Atkinson, Smith, & Bem, 1990, 1993), using the Hyman-Honorton debate as the vehicle for discussing both the ganzfeld experiments and related issues of replication, meta-analysis, and skepticism.[2] Chuck enthusiastically provided comments on the draft and photographs to accompany the textbook discussion.

During this same period, Chuck began a meta-analysis of studies reporting correlations between psi performance and the personality trait of extraversion, a correlation that had been replicated in the autoganzfeld data. Because I am a personality psychologist, he asked me if I would advise him on the interpretation of the correlation. I agreed, and this became our first joint venture (Honorton, Ferrari, & Bem, 1992). These two projects also initiated a regular E-mail correspondence between us, a fortuitous turn of events that has left me with a detailed written record of our collaboration.

When Chuck's laboratory lost its funding in 1989, we began to discuss ways in which the ganzfeld work might achieve wider recognition. He said that he wanted to write a book on psi and internal attention states using a meta-analytic framework. He also suggested that we could submit the meta-analysis of the psi-extraversion correlation to the *Psychological Bulletin*. I disagreed, believing it to be

---

[1] I have performed as a mentalist for many years and am a member of the mentalist's professional organization, the Psychic Entertainers Association. Interestingly, so is Hyman. Apparently, knowing how to fake psi is not predictive of one's beliefs concerning the real thing.

[2] A recent survey of 64 introductory psychology textbooks found that very few of them discuss contemporary psi research; our text is the only one that even mentions the ganzfeld experiments (Roig, Icochea, & Cuzzucoli, 1991).

too narrow a topic. I suggested that we aim instead for a *Psychological Bulletin* article that would provide a grander synthesis of the ganzfeld work.

This possibility appeared even more promising when Robert Sternberg was appointed editor of the *Psychological Bulletin* beginning in January of 1991. Sternberg has himself published in a diverse set of areas, including intelligence testing and romantic love. Thus, I was not surprised when in his maiden editorial, he urged prospective authors to

> take risks in choosing topics.... Many of us have had the disappointment of feeling...that the hardest articles to get accepted by mainline journals are our worst ones and our best ones—our worst because they are, well, bad, and our best because they represent too much of a departure from current conventions, whether in conceptualization or methodology. I would like to encourage authors to take risks—to submit their best and most creative work to the *Bulletin*, in exchange for which I will make every effort to ensure that top-quality work is rewarded rather than punished. (1991, p. 3)

Although we needed no further encouragement, several events intervened to postpone the actual writing of our grand opus, including Chuck's relocation to Edinburgh. Finally, in the summer of 1992, I crafted a first draft and took it with me to the August convention of the Parapsychological Association in Las Vegas, where we could work on it face to face.

It was an exhilarating experience. Even though we were both strong-minded individuals with compulsive writing preferences, our shared, slightly acid senses of humor made it unadultered fun. We debated commas and semicolons as vigorously as we did the substantive and stylistic matters.[3]

I also learned many things about the ganzfeld work that Chuck had never written down. For example, I had always assumed that he had adopted a procedure using both a sender and receiver because he believed that the operative phenomenon was more likely to be telepathy than clairvoyance or precognition. But his decision was more pragmatic. First, he believed that the *subjects* would find the telepathy procedure more plausible and hence would enter the session with more optimistic expectations. Second, he believed that by having two participants, it would make the session a team effort and remove the exclusive focus and performance pressure on the

---

[3] We also debated the order of authorship. It was only at Chuck's insistence that I became first author.

108

receiver. And finally, he had his eye on the ultimate goal of achieving mainstream acceptance of psi, believing that the scientific community would find it easier to accept evidence for telepathy than for clairvoyance or precognition.

The Las Vegas convention was to be the last time I saw Chuck. On September 9, 1992, I mailed a revised draft to him at Edinburgh, incorporating the changes we had agreed on. On September 23, we submitted the article to the *Psychological Bulletin*. As I had from the outset, I told Chuck that, as a former editor of an APA journal myself, and knowing Sternberg's own wide-ranging interests, I was almost certain that the article would be accepted.

Chuck died on November 4, 1992. Nine days later our article was accepted for publication, with all four external referees—including Hyman—recommending publication. One of the referees added, "I think this paper may well become a *Psych. Bull.* classic." In his covering letter, Sternberg wrote: "This is a blockbuster article, and one that should generate great interest from the field.... You should look at this rapid acceptance as an indication of how important I think the article is!"

I have rarely been happier. Or sadder.

REFERENCES

ATKINSON, R., ATKINSON, R. C., SMITH, E. E., & BEM, D. J. (1990). *Introduction to psychology* (10th ed.). San Diego: Harcourt Brace Jovanovich.

ATKINSON, R., ATKINSON, R. C., SMITH, E. E., & BEM, D. J. (1993). *Introduction to psychology* (11th ed.). San Diego: Harcourt Brace Jovanovich.

AVANT, L. L. (1965). Vision in the ganzfeld. *Psychological Bulletin,* **64,** 246–258.

BEM, D. J., & HONORTON, C. (in press). Does psi exist? Replicable evidence for an anomalous process of information transfer. *Psychological Bulletin.*

BRAUD, W. G., WOOD, R., & BRAUD, L. W. (1975). Free-response GESP performance during an experimental hypnagogic state induced by visual and acoustic ganzfeld techniques. A replication and extension. *Journal of the American Society for Psychical Research,* **69,** 105–113.

CHILD, I. L. (1985). Psychology and anomalous observations: The question of ESP in dreams. *American Psychologist,* **40,** 1219–1230.

DINGWALL, E. J. (Ed.). (1986). *Abnormal hypnotic phenomena* (4 vols.). London: Chuchill.

GREEN, C. E. (1960). Analysis of spontaneous cases. *Proceedings of the Society for Psychical Research,* **53,** 97–161.

HARRIS, M. J., & ROSENTHAL, R. (1988). Human performance research: An overview. Background paper commissioned by the National Research Council. Washington, DC: National Academy Press.

HONORTON, C. (1969). Relationship between EEG alpha activity and ESP card-guessing performance. *Journal of the American Society for Psychical Research*, **63**, 365–374.

HONORTON, C. (1977). Psi and internal attention states. In B. B. Wolman (Ed.), *Handbook of parapsychology* (pp. 435–472). New York: Van Nostrand Reinhold.

HONORTON, C. (1979). Methodological issues in free-response experiments. *Journal of the American Society for Psychical Research*, **73**, 381–394.

HONORTON, C. (1985). Meta-analysis of psi ganzfeld research: A response to Hyman. *Journal of Parapsychology*, **49**, 51–91.

HONORTON, C., BERGER, R. E., VARVOGLIS, M. P., QUANT, M., DERR, P., SCHECHTER, E. I., & FERRARI, D. C. (1990). Psi communication in the ganzfeld: Experiments with an automated testing system and a comparison with a meta-analysis of earlier studies. *Journal of Parapsychology*, **54**, 99–139.

HONORTON, C., FERRARI, D. C., & BEM, D. J. (1992). Extraversion and ESP performance: Meta-analysis and a new confirmation. In L. A. Henkel & G. R. Schmeidler (Eds.), *Research in parapsychology 1990* (pp. 35–38). Metuchen, NJ: Scarecrow Press.

HONORTON, C., & HARPER, S. (1974). Psi-mediated imagery and ideation in an experimental procedure for regulating perceptual input. *Journal of the American Society for Psychical Research*, **68**, 156–168.

HYMAN, R. (1985). The ganzfeld psi experiment: A critical appraisal. *Journal of Parapsychology*, **49**, 3–49.

HYMAN, R. (1991). Comment. *Statistical Science*, **6**, 389–392.

HYMAN, R., & HONORTON, C. (1986). A joint communiqué: The psi ganzfeld controversy. *Journal of Parapsychology*, **50**, 351–364.

KENNEDY, J. E. (1979). Methodological problems in free-response ESP experiments. *Journal of the American Society for Psychical Research*, **73**, 1–15.

METZGER, W. (1930). Optische Untersuchungen am Ganzfeld: II. Zur phänomenologie des homogenen Ganzfelds. *Psychologische Forschung*, **13**, 6–29.

PARKER, A. (1975). Some findings relevant to the change in state hypothesis. In J. D. Morris, W. G. Roll, & R. L. Morris (Eds.), *Research in parapsychology 1974* (pp. 40–42). Metuchen, NJ: Scarecrow Press.

PRASAD, J., & STEVENSON, I. (1968). A survey of spontaneous psychical experiences in school children of Uttar Pradesh, India. *International Journal of Parapsychology*, **10**, 241–261.

RHINE, L. E. (1962). Psychological processes in ESP experiences: I. Waking experiences. *Journal of Parapsychology*, **26**, 88–111.

ROIG, M., ICOCHEA, H., & CUZZUCOLI, A. (1991). Coverage of parapsychology in introductory psychology textbooks. *Teaching of Psychology*, **18**, 157–160.

SANNWALD, G. (1959). Statistische untersuchungen an Spontanphänomene. *Zeitschrift für Parapsychologie and Grenzgebiete der Psychologie*, **3**, 59–71.

SCHECHTER, E. I. (1984). Hypnotic induction vs. control conditions: Illustrating an approach to the evaluation of replicability in parapsychology. *Journal of the American Society for Psychical Research*, **78**, 1–27.

SCHLITZ, M. J., & HONORTON, C. (1992). Ganzfeld psi performance within an artistically gifted population. *Journal of the American Society for Psychical Research*, **86**, 83–98.

SCHMEIDLER, G. R. (1988). *Parapsychology and psychology: Matches and mismatches.* Jefferson, NC: McFarland.

STERNBERG, R. J. (1991). Editorial. *Psychological Bulletin*, **109**, 3–4.

ULLMAN, M., KRIPPNER, S., & VAUGHAN, A. (1973). *Dream telepathy.* New York: Macmillan.

A CRAFTSMAN AND HIS TOOLS: THE NEW TECHNOLOGY

By Richard S. Broughton

In the late 1970s I visited Chuck Honorton at the Maimonides Medical Center Dream Laboratory. At the time I was completing my PhD at the University of Edinburgh, and, in a separate project, I had just finished work on a computerized PK test in the form of a game that was loosely based on trading futures contracts on an imaginary commodity market. My principal reason for visiting Chuck was to pay homage to the laboratory and the remaining researchers involved in the ESP-dream work, and to learn more about Chuck's ganzfeld research.

When Chuck learned of my interest in psi testing via computer games he took me into another room and sat me in front of a television screen. He explained that I should imagine myself on the starship *Enterprise* being attacked by Klingons. The Klingons' ships would be cloaked and would not appear on the screen, so I must use my intuition or ESP to locate and destroy them. I no longer recall much else about that session apart from scenes of nifty little spaceships exploding, and the feeling that now we could really make psi testing fun.

That was my first visit with Chuck Honorton. I had my last visit with him not long before he left to do his PhD at the University of Edinburgh. I saw him at his apartment because his lab had closed, but he was busy on his new computer. We talked about old times and reviewed some new observations on his ganzfeld data base. He demonstrated some new software tools that he was planning to use when he recreated the autoganzfeld in Edinburgh. Then, with a twinkle in his eye, he said, "Wait 'til you see this. . . ."

In a few moments Chuck had me sitting in front of his computer screen, now transformed into the cockpit of some starfleet's space fighter, while sound effects—indeed, what seemed like an entire film score—blared from his stereo. Chuck had dropped me into a major intergalactic war while he sat on the sidelines alternately

I am greatly indebted to Donald McCarthy and Edwin May for broadening my perspective on Chuck Honorton's relationship with technology.

barking commands and commenting on my ineptitude as a starfight-er. Eventually, at my pleading, he took the controls and, with a se-ries of quick movements, destroyed the attacking alien spacecraft and won a commendation from whatever organization he was de-fending. No, this was not a psi test—it was a popular commercial game—but when he finished, he turned to me and expressed just what I was thinking; "Now, if we could build a psi test into this..."

Chuck Honorton and Technology

If it seems strange to focus on such a banal topic as technology in this commemorative context, let me assure the reader that those who knew Chuck concur that technology was very much part of his life. He enjoyed it, both in his home and in the lab. His love of technology was not merely gadget-collecting, however. In the labo-ratory he viewed technology in the same way that he viewed any new research technique, new statistical approach, or any new idea from any quarter: Can it improve psi research? It is no accident that the same person who brought the ganzfeld technique and meta-analysis to parapsychology should also be the one responsible for some of the most productive applications of technology for psi re-search.

Nor was Chuck a mere dilettante when it came to the technology that he chose to use. He was quick to master the hardware and soft-ware of any system that became part of his research program. My own working relationship with computers in research predated Chuck's by about five years, but it was not long before I was seeking his advice in everything from programming languages to statistical packages.

At one level or another, technology has always been part of psi research, and I must confess a certain arbitrariness in deciding to focus on the technology of digital electronics and its ability to au-tomate research as the "new technology" of this paper. Yet, there is no doubt that, during the years Chuck's research has flourished, it is this technology that has grown explosively to the point where it is a pervasive part of everyone's lives.

The Early Days

Helmut Schmidt had no sooner published his pioneering pre-cognition experiments using an electronic random number generator (Schmidt, 1970) than Chuck persuaded Schmidt to lend one of his machines to the Maimonides lab. The device Chuck obtained was a simple binary RNG with a red light, a green light, and a response button corresponding to each. The subject's task was ostensibly that of precognition—guessing whether the red or the green lamp would be illuminated following the next button-press. For Chuck, steeped in the traditions of card-guessing and well aware of its weaknesses (especially its tediousness), Schmidt's automated testing device had an immediate appeal. The device effectively precluded subject fraud, eliminated sensory leakage problems, and largely automated the data-recording chores. In addition to all that, thousands of trials could be done relatively quickly with little wear and tear on either the subject or the experimenter.

Chuck's first foray into automated ESP testing was productive. In the first Schmidt-RNG paper published, other than Schmidt's own, Chuck reported a successful series of precognition experiments with the English sensitive Malcolm Bessent (Honorton, 1971). Over 15,000 individual trials were carried out, with very significant hitting by Bessent. At the time, Chuck admitted that the study added little to our understanding of psi processes, but it did confirm the existence of the "high-scoring subject," a species thought extinct by critics and even many parapsychologists.

One of the clearest advantages of automated psi research is that it permits the researchers to spend more time investigating the psi process by relieving them of the need to attend to the time-consuming details like target preparation and data collection (see Broughton, 1982, for a discussion; see also McCarthy, 1982, for a perspective on how Honorton's lab was using computers at the time). It was precisely this advantage that Chuck exploited for the next experiment. With co-experimenters Margaret Ramsey and Carol Cabibbo, he designed an experiment to test whether the attitude of the investigator could affect the subject's results. Using Schmidt's binary RNG, this time with a chart recorder attached for a paper record of every trial, Honorton and his colleagues gave 200 trials to each of 36 subjects. One half of the subjects enjoyed a friendly and supportive interaction with the experimenter; the other half were faced with an abrupt and unfriendly experimenter. The results neatly confirmed the expected high scores for the positively treated subjects and low scores for the negatively treated ones.

Honorton was sufficiently confident of his results and methods that he submitted the resulting paper to *Science* in August 1972. It was rejected, revised, and resubmitted, and finally rejected again even though five of the eight referees had recommended publication. Eventually the paper was published in the *Journal of the American Society for Psychical Research*, along with an appendix that detailed *Science*'s treatment of the paper (Honorton, Ramsey, & Cabibbo, 1975). Honorton's use of Schmidt's new technology in a well-designed experiment thus yielded important data for both the experimenter and the sociologist of science.

In 1975, Ed May joined Honorton at the Maimonides lab and introduced him to a new generation of psi-test technology. In his presidential address of 1975, Honorton relates his encounter with an advanced RNG test device that May had lugged around India testing gurus and yoga adepts (Honorton, 1976). May's approach to RNG testing was to create an RNG with easily set parameters that permitted researchers to investigate different "physics type" questions on the fly, but with good control.

May constructed a multifunction RNG for the Maimonides lab that was unlike any RNG seen before in parapsychology (May, 1976). The device, dubbed PSIFI, combined the output of an RNG with physiological signals (EMG, EEG) from the subject. Feedback from all three sources could be presented to the subject in various combinations ranging from simple RNG feedback in a straightforward PK task to integrated PK, EMG, and EEG feedback that amounted to a complex psi-bio-feedback tesk. Another feature permitted "gating" RNG trials so that PK data would be collected only during periods when specific physiological criteria were met. In this way researchers could easily compare PK trials done in different physiological states. PSIFI was used in several experiments in the mid-1970s (Honorton, 1977; Honorton & May, 1976; Winnette & Honorton, 1977).

The microcomputer revolution reached the Maimonides lab early, and by 1978 Honorton and his colleague Lawrence Tremmel had traded conventional ESP tests for space battles. Honorton and Tremmel had developed a simple computer game that involved fantasy situations using names and terminology from the popular television series *Star Trek*. It was this game to which I was introduced during my visit. To win the game, the subject had to use psi (either ESP or PK). The story line associated with the game was that the subject was defending his or her own starship from the attacking Klingons, whose ships were equipped with a cloaking device that rendered them invisible to the observation screens. You, the subject, had to rely on ESP or intuition to determine in which quadrant to fire your photon torpedoes.

The reason for embedding psi tests in a computer game was to see if the motivational aspects of the game would enhance the subject's demonstration of psi. Instead of relying on the often highly variable abilities of the experimenter to motivate the subject to perform, this approach attempted to capitalize on the inherent motivation to do well in what was perceived as playful challenge. Behind the playful facade, however, lay a sophisticated experiment, controlled by a Cromemco Z80-based microcomputer that, in addition to displaying the various components of the game, collected the data, changed conditions, and analyzed the results. Two physically different RNGs, designed and constructed by Ed May, were used in the experiment and could be systematically compared. There were ESP and PK versions of the test to provide variety (as well as contrasting conditions), and the ESP version could switch between clairvoyance and precognition.

PSITREK, as the game/test was called, appears to have been used in only one major project before Honorton moved his research from the Maimonides lab to the Psychophysical Research Laboratories. That project ran for about one year and employed 93 participants, who played 443 games. The overall results were significant, but equally interesting were some secondary findings. In the ESP condition, precognition seemed better than clairvoyance, and virtually all the ESP effect was found in the sessions using the RNG based on quantum mechanical tunneling effects, in contrast to the pure avalanche-based RNG (Honorton & Tremmel, 1980).

The PRL Period

The establishment of the Psychophysical Research Laboratories, with the generous support of the McDonnell Foundation, enabled Honorton to pursue his research goals on a broad scale. It is beyond the scope of this paper to review the goals of the PRL, but there were at least two major objectives that relied heavily on technology. The basic approach of the lab was to collect a broad spectrum of psychological and behavioral data on participants and then see how individual differences related to performance in psi tasks. The latter consisted of the ganzfeld ESP experiments and a variety of microcomputer-based ESP and PK tests. The goal was to "optimize" psi performance by identifying the subject-based components associated with good psi in the various contexts offered. Of course Honorton and his team were well aware that the constellation of factors pointing to success in one psi-testing context may not be the same as in another.

Underlying Honorton's basic research program was the recognition that to mount an effective attack on the problem of identifying characteristics of good psi subjects required highly standardized tests both in his own lab and in other parapsychology laboratories. Microcomputer automated research was precisely the tool he needed, and by now it was within the budget of many parapsychology laboratories. Thus, from the start, PRL's experimental research effort focussed on two principal areas: (a) a highly automated, standardized ganzfeld research program for long-term data collection at PRL, and (b) a completely automated "psi laboratory in a box" that would offer several ESP and PK tests plus all the statistical and quality control tools necessary for methodologically unassailable psi research.

It was the latter consideration—methodological quality—that informed the entire development effort for both the automated ganzfeld project and the portable psi laboratory. Honorton's experience dealing with both valid and invalid criticisms of psi research had grown considerably since his first encounter with C.E.M. Hansel's work (Honorton, 1967) and his first experiences with a Schmidt machine. Technology now enabled the researcher to do far more than automate target generation and data collection. It could guide, even force, the experimenter to follow all the appropriate steps at the right times, from the initial design stage through the data collection and control testing to final analysis.

In the early days of PRL, the Cromemco computer was still used in several projects (e.g., Honorton, Barker, & Sondow, 1983; Schechter, Barker, & Varvoglis, 1983). A particularly ambitious example of computer usage in the lab was a project by Varvoglis and McCarthy (1986) that involved several studies in which subjects attempted to influence either their own EEG, an RNG, or a hidden RNG under different conditions. By the time Honorton was ready for his principal program of research, however, automation technology had evolved further. The Apple II microcomputer was rapidly eclipsing the competition as the popular standard, and it was making rapid inroads into educational and research establishments. Dick Bierman of the University of Amsterdam and the Research Institute for Psi and Physics (RIPP) had started producing a Schmidt-type RNG that plugged directly into the Apple II bus (the computer's primary internal communication channel), and a few parapsychology labs were already using Apple II computers. Last, but by no means least, if Honorton was serious about creating a network of collaborating laboratories, was the fact that Apple Computer Corporation was rapidly establishing a wide base of dealers and service facilities.

The PRL projects represent exemplars of technology in the service of psi research, and we shall examine these in some detail so that they can be fully appreciated. Before that, however, we must note that what we shall be reviewing were the products of a hard-working and dedicated team of individuals who had worked under Honorton for many years. On the technological side, they included Rick Berger, who led the technical efforts for many years, along with George Hansen, Donald McCarthy, Ephraim Schechter, and Mario Varvoglis; Patricia Barker and Nancy Sondow developed the personal information assessments and the target pools for the ganzfeld. Everyone contributed important input to the design and analysis of the various experiments.

PSILAB II

The transportable parapsychology lab took shape in the form of PSILAB II, a combination of hardware and software that, when installed on an Apple II computer, created a comprehensive psi-testing facility. Honorton planned to produce a quantity of these testing packages and distribute them to qualified researchers at a nominal cost.

The hardware component of PSILAB was an extensively tested true random number generator. After evaluating several options, Honorton decided on Bierman's design and ordered a batch of them. When they arrived, Honorton's team subjected each board to thorough tests of individual components and of general randomness. This led to certain modifications by Robert Chevako, and, after further testing, final acceptance.

The RNG consisted of twin independent Zener noise diodes. The output from each diode was digitalized separately, combined (in several steps), and placed in a register that was read directly through the Apple's data bus. The RNG could produce random bits at the rate of 10,000 per second. The circuitry was mounted on a 3-inch by 6-inch printed circuit board that included special shielding for the Zener diode section.

The software part of PSILAB consisted of a selection of ESP and PK tests. Only two game-tests—*Psi Invaders* (a PK test) and *ESPerciser*™ (an ESP test with training aspects)—were released officially, but at least one other, *Volition* (a PK test), was used at PRL and other labs.

Each test module consisted of a number of components representing all the principal stages of a good experiment. It is notable that today computer users are still clamoring for "consistent user interfaces" among the various types of software that they must use so that they do not have to learn completely different ways of doing the same tasks for different programs. Over a decade ago that was one of the features that Honorton's team designed into the PSILAB system—all PSILAB experiments use the same user interface for the experimenter in order to make mastering the system easier and to reduce the possibility of errors.

The experiment was controlled by a supervisory program called the "Series Manager." Access to this program required a password, followed by the date, which was used in record keeping. Before embarking on any research, the Series Manager required the experimenter to declare his or her intentions by designing an experimental series that typically included the type of study (screening, pilot, or formal), the number of participants, the number of runs for each participant, and the number of trials per run. Also, certain specifications for the RNG sampling rate and various criteria for rewards and feedback were set at this time. On completion of this phase, the Series Manager created a data file corresponding to the specified parameters.

Once the experimental series had been designed, participants could be registered as they became available. Again, the Series Manager took care of this, registering the necessary information and storing it in the data base. Because the PSILAB tests were commonly used in situations in which participants came more than once to take the test, each session was handled separately. The experimenter would log in the participant; the Series Manager would check to see that the participant was registered and would report how many tests he or she had carried out so far. Then the participant was free to play the game or take the test.

The Series Manager program "supervised" the experiment by ensuring that the various steps were performed in the correct order. It kept track of the data and politely informed each participant when he or she had completed the preset quota of runs. It also informed the experimenter when the number of participants had been reached (and declined to add any others). If for any reason a participant failed to complete a run, the experimenter received notification the next time the program was run, and the program checked to see that a PRL random generator board was installed before any session started. Each test module contained various security features that were capable of detecting "unauthorized" behavior by a subject.

Of course, the Series Manager contained a module that analyzed the accumulated data by individual runs and by concatenating them in various ways. Data analysis was confined to basic statistics, often supplemented with graphic displays of the results, but the raw data could be transferred to other programs for detailed analysis.

Finally, there was a facility for running control tests of the experiment in the form of simulated experiments that exactly mimicked the real experiment that was underway.

In addition to the simulated experiments, the PSILAB package came with a separate suite of programs for testing the RNG. These programs enabled the investigator to perform extensive randomness checks with detailed analyses and reports at any time before, after, and during the experiments.

Psi Invaders was the first test released with PSILAB, and the only one that was in the form of a game. It was based on *Space Invaders*, a popular arcade type of game in which the player positioned and fired a gun at invading aliens who conveniently lined up in rows as they marched down the screen. In *Psi Invaders*, the participant was told that the laser gun was old and prone to misfiring, but that the participant should use "the force" to make it fire more reliably. Whether the gun fired or misfired each time depended on the outcome of 100 binary trials (which were accumulated almost instantly). Points were scored for hitting aliens and for "strong use of the force," which happened when various preset scoring criteria were exceeded. *Psi Invaders* was cast as a micro-PK test though there was no mention of PK in the standard presentation. The scores (in points) that the participant viewed during the game were indirectly related to the PK results, but the actual PK data were reported only to the experimenter. If the player failed to win, however, an invading alien would end the game by stomping on the player's gun. At the design stage of the experiment, the investigator could set parameters that controlled the score necessary for a "win" on each successive game and the sampling frequency for the RNG.

More conventional ESP testing was available through a test called *ESPerciser*℠. This test produced a colorful screen with four blank windows. While the blank windows were on the screen, the participant could use the time (the length of which was up to the participant) to receive impressions of the target. When the response button was pressed, the windows filled with four images. Then the participant used the hand controller to select one image as the response. The computer asked if the participant had made his or her choice on the basis of a guess, a feeling, or an impression (these terms had been defined beforehand). When the type of response was registered, the computer indicated which image was the target; and if the trial was a hit, the word *HIT* flashed several times accompanied by electronic beeps. *ESPerciser*™ was billed as an "ESP feedback trainer" in the hope that the instant feedback coupled with the bit of self-examination about how the selection was arrived at might help participants get better at the task. The principal parameters the experimenter could set were the number of trials in a run and the number of runs per subject. The images offered on each trial were taken from a large pool of pictures and designs that provided some variety over the run.

Volition was a test module that offered a straightforward binary psi test (ostensibly PK) but with a wide range of options available to the participant to add novelty and challenge. The experimenter determined the number of trials in a run and the number of runs in a game, but the participant was free to choose the target direction (up or down), whether to play trial-by-trial or continuously, and what sort of feedback and display was to be used. Feedback was provided in the form of an accumulating graph plotting the test results against a graph of mean change expectation and standard deviation lines. When the appropriate feedback options were selected by the subject, varying high and low beeps signalled good and poor trials; good cumulative performance met with visual displays and brief musical selections.

Because the study of individual differences was an important component of the PRL program, Honorton also distributed the Participant Information Form that PRL was using, and he encouraged the use of the Myers-Briggs Type Indicator personality assessment for comparability with their data base.

Although I have described all these tests in the past tense, they are still being used, but it must be admitted that even though numbers of PSILAB packages were distributed, the network of collaborating researchers never took shape. In part, this was because not long after PRL began distributing the test kits, PRL's chief source of funds, the McDonnell Foundation, began reducing its support and Honorton chose to concentrate his resources on the ganzfeld research.

In the end, it was Honorton himself who illustrated some of the advantages of having an "instant lab" available. In 1987, he was contacted by Malcolm Bessent, the star of his first automated psi test. Honorton asked Bessent why he had not been active in research since the original Maimonides tests, and Bessent replied that no one had asked him to. Honorton invited him over for more testing and Bessent accepted on the spot. Thanks to PSILAB, Honorton could put together a top-notch psi experiment in little more than a few minutes, and over the next couple of days Bessent again confirmed that high-scoring subjects are still around (Honorton, 1987).

The Autoganzfeld

The history of science will undoubtedly view Honorton's ganz-feld research program as one of the major landmarks on the road to scientific acceptance of psi phenomena, and his accomplishments in this regard are well covered in this journal and elsewhere. Here, too, Honorton's fondness for technology and his ability to envision research applications of new technology helped propel ganzfeld research from the status of just another technique purported to improve psi results to a consistent, progressive, research program that is both yielding predictive hypotheses and winning the admiration of critics at the same time.

As ganzfeld research at the Maimonides laboratory and elsewhere began to attract the attention of parapsychologists and skeptics, it became clear that there were particular aspects of ganzfeld research that could be regarded as flaws if not handled properly in each experiment. While this is true of any experiment, the relative complexity of the ganzfeld experiment compared with other ESP research gave the critics many potential trouble spots to focus upon. This was highlighted for Honorton as he prepared for a 1982 debate with skeptic Ray Hyman on the validity of ganzfeld results (Honorton, 1983; Hyman, 1983). As a rule, the ganzfeld research by Honorton and his team had always been among the best studies; but having a friendly automaton looking after the details and reminding the humans to perform their various tasks at the correct times could make things easier and even more fool-proof.

The autoganzfeld has been described formally in print already (Berger & Honorton, 1986; Honorton, Berger, Varvoglis, Quant, Derr, Schechter, & Ferrari, 1990). I should like to review the highlights of the system here from the perspective of the user/experimenter because we have recreated the system at the Institute for Parapsychology and are about to start using it.[1]

---

[1] In 1990, after the PRL had shut down, Honorton donated the autoganzfeld

122

The basic outlines of a ganzfeld experiment are well known. The subject, designated as the "receiver," outfitted in the customary accoutrements of the ganzfeld, engages in about 15 minutes of relaxation exercises and then spends about 30 minutes describing whatever images, thoughts, or memories come to mind. During the latter 30 minutes, a "sender" tries to communicate a visual image to the receiver by ESP. At the end of the 30 minutes, the receiver views the possible target images and ranks the four options in order of similarity to his or her mentation. Implicit in this brief outline is the fact that there is a good deal of work that must be done, and done properly. The autoganzfeld was developed to ensure that all the tasks were carried out properly, yet efficiently, with a minimum of personnel.

From a user's perspective, the key design principles behind the autoganzfeld are automation and quality control. The automation, of course, is a given in this context, but the quality control had to be designed into the system by a team thoroughly familiar with the demands placed on psi research. Rick Berger was primarily responsible for the technical implementation of the autoganzfeld, but many members of the PRL team made contributions along the way.

The heart of the system is an Apple II computer with a special interface that permits it to control a video cassette recorder and switch its output to several television monitors. The VCR enables the researchers to use excerpts from films, cartoons, and so forth, as the targets in the ganzfeld. Indeed, prior research with *Viewmaster*™ slide reels had suggested that dynamic targets may have an advantage over simple still photos.[2]

As with the PSILAB system, a ganzfeld experiment is managed by a Series Manager program. Although similar in appearance to the PSILAB equivalent, the Series Manager for the autoganzfeld incorporates more automatic system checking and record keeping specific to the needs of ganzfeld research. Before starting a series, the experimenter has to specify its design, including the type of study, the number of trials in the series and the number of trials for each receiver, duration of the ganzfeld, and so forth. The program ensures that the design parameters are adhered to. It is possible to modify some parameters later, for example to add additional trials;

---

equipment to the Institute for Parapsychology. During fall and winter, 1992–1993, Kathy Dalton, with assistance from Douglas Day, rebuilt the autoganzfeld and installed it.

[2] Although *Viewmaster* slides are stills, the group of images on the reel conveyed a developing theme, often with implied action.

but the program demands an explanation that is entered in the official log of the series.

Once the series is designed, participants can be registered and entered in the data base through the Series Manager.

The experimenter sets up the session by logging in the receiver and entering several items of information related to the session, for example, name and relationship of the sender (friend, lab staff, etc.), the light intensity, and the sound level for the white noise. (The receiver would already have been prepared in the ganzfeld room, with the lights and sound adjusted.) The Series Manager confirms that the receiver is registered and that the preset number of trials has not been met.

Target selection, which can be done before or after the previous step, is the only phase of the experiment that requires a second experimenter. With the main experimenter out of the room, the target selector goes to the computer and executes the randomize-target procedure from the Series Manager. In this operation the computer uses a true RNG to select one of the 160 possible targets and its associated judging pool of three "decoys." The program then directs the target selector to insert one of the four video cassettes into the VCR (but it gives no other information about the target). The target selector inserts the cassette and covers the VCR (to hide the meters and counters) and leaves, taking the remaining three video cassettes. The program records all the pertinent data concerning target selection. The VCR automatically winds the video cassette to its center position to further reduce the possibility that the experimenter could glean any clues to the target identity by the length of time the VCR takes to locate a target.

Once the session has been set up and the target is prepared, the session is ready to begin. The computer starts issuing instructions to the experimenter to insert the relaxation/white noise tape in the tape deck, set various switches and level controls, and start the tape (synchronizing it with the computer). The relaxation tape is played to both the receiver and the sender.

As the relaxation period draws to a close, the experimenter is notified and given further instructions to start the tape that records the mentation and to initiate the target-sending sequence on the computer. The computer begins operating the video controller, first turning off the experimenter's console and then displaying some instructions to the sender. After a few minutes the computer displays the name of the target on the sender's screen, followed by the 73-second video segment showing the target. During the half hour, the display is repeated for a total of six viewings, after which the VCR returns the tape to the center position.

As the mentation period ends, the experimenter is signaled by a tone, and the computer turns off the sender's video and turns on the experimenter's video. Again, the experimenter is given detailed instructions for bringing the subject out of the ganzfeld and for starting the judging period. Before the judging begins, however, the experimenter is prompted by the computer to answer a number of questions about the quality and quantity of the mentation. For the judging, the experimenter's TV and the TV in the receiver's room are turned on. The computer begins the judging by first showing brief excerpts (4–5 seconds) of each of the four video segments (to minimize "first impression" effects); and then, on command from the experimenter, the computer presents each of the video segments in its entirety. The receiver is given the opportunity to review any of the video segments.

Up to this point, the receiver has only viewed the possible targets. Next the computer displays a "rating form" on the screen asking the receiver to rate the degree of correspondence between his or her ganzfeld experience and each of the segments (in turn, by name). The receiver turns the knob on the hand controller to move a pointer on a scale of 0 to 100 that is displayed on the screen. The procedure is repeated for each possible target. If the receiver produces tied ratings the computer asks the receiver to re-rate the targets and to take the opportunity to change any ratings before the judging is completed.

When the judging is completed, the computer informs the experimenter that it is ready to show the target. At this point the experimenter gets the sender, and both join the receiver in the receiver's room. The sender reveals the correct target, and the computer displays it on the receiver's TV.

The final phase of the experiment requests the experimenter to enter any comments, and the program stores all the data on a floppy disk (and a back-up as well, just to be safe). The experimenter then causes the computer to produce a printed report of the session that is placed in the subject's file.

If I have burdened the reader with too much detail about the autoganzfeld, I apologize; I am myself a "hands-on" experimenter and I cannot help but share my appreciation of what I regard as a particularly well-crafted research tool. Unfortunately, apart from the staff of a couple of laboratories, few people will have the opportunity to appreciate this craftsmanship.

The point of good craftsmanship is to produce a fine product, and that is precisely what the autoganzfeld has done in a way that all scientists can appreciate. When the "ganzfeld debate" finally settled down and Honorton and critic Ray Hyman agreed on the standards of research that should be acceptable to parapsychology's critics, the autoganzfeld research already met those standards. The eleven ganzfeld studies done with the autoganzfeld system are among the strongest experimental evidence for psi phenomena to date and have been accorded a rarely achieved measure of recognition outside the field (Atkinson, Atkinson, & Bem, 1990; Bem & Honorton, in press).

When Chuck died, he had just completed re-creating the autoganzfeld at the University of Edinburgh. The new autoganzfeld used the latest computer and programming tools, as well as a new generation of video equipment. Fortunately, that project will continue, and undoubtedly there will be new versions of the autoganzfeld that will use technology which Chuck could only dream about. The highest tribute that Chuck Honorton's successors in this endeavor can pay to this pioneer will be to ensure that their efforts achieve the high level of craftsmanship that he and his laboratory colleagues brought to psi research.

REFERENCES

ATKINSON, R. L., ATKINSON, R. C., & BEM, D. J. (1990). *Introduction to psychology* (10th ed.). San Diego: Harcourt Brace Jovanovich.

BEM, D. J., & HONORTON, C. (in press). Does psi exist? Replicable evidence for an anomalous process of information transfer. *Psychological Bulletin*.

BERGER, R. E., & HONORTON, C. (1986). An automated psi ganzfeld testing system. In D. H. Weiner & D. I. Radin (Eds.), *Research in parapsychology 1985* (pp. 85–88). Metuchen, NJ: Scarecrow Press.

BROUGHTON, R. S. (1982). Computer methodology: Total control with a human face. In B. Shapin & L. Coly (Eds.), *Parapsychology and the experimental method* (pp. 24–42). New York: Parapsychology Foundation.

HONORTON, C. (1967). Review of *ESP: A scientific evaluation* by C. E. M. Hansel. *Journal of Parapsychology, 31,* 76–82.

HONORTON, C. (1971). Automated forced-choice precognition tests with a "sensitive." *Journal of the American Society for Psychical Research, 61,* 476–481.

HONORTON, C. (1976). Has science developed the competence to confront claims of the paranormal? In J. D. Morris, W. G. Roll, & R. L. Morris (Eds.), *Research in parapsychology 1975* (pp. 199–223). Metuchen, NJ: Scarecrow Press.

126

HONORTON, C. (1977). Effects of meditation and feedback on psychokinetic performance: A pilot study with an instructor of Transcendental Meditation. In J. D. Morris, W. G. Roll, & R. L. Morris (Eds.), *Research in parapsychology 1976* (pp. 95–97). Metuchen, NJ: Scarecrow Press.

HONORTON, C. (1983). Response to Hyman's critique of psi ganzfeld studies. In W. G. Roll, J. Beloff, & R. A. White (Eds.), *Research in parapsychology 1982* (pp. 23–26). Metuchen, NJ: Scarecrow Press.

HONORTON, C. (1987). Precognition and real-time ESP performance in a computer task with an exceptional subject. *Journal of Parapsychology,* **51,** 291–321.

HONORTON, C., BARKER, P., & SONDOW, N. (1983). Feedback and participant selection parameters in a computer RNG study. In W. G. Roll, J. Beloff, & R. A. White (Eds.), *Research in parapsychology 1982* (pp. 157–159). Metuchen, NJ: Scarecrow Press.

HONORTON, C., BERGER, R. E., VARVOGLIS, M. P., QUANT, M., DEER, P., SCHECHTER, E. I., & FERRARI, D. C. (1990). Psi communication in the ganzfeld: Experiments with an automated testing system and a comparison with a meta-analysis of earlier studies. *Journal of Parapsychology,* **54,** 99–139.

HONORTON, C., & MAY, E. C. (1976). Volitional control in a psychokinetic task with auditory and visual feedback. In J. D. Morris, W. G. Roll, & R. L. Morris (Eds.), *Research in parapsychology 1975* (pp. 90–91). Metuchen, NJ: Scarecrow Press.

HONORTON, C., RAMSEY, M., & CABBIBO, C. (1975). Experimenter effects in extransensory perception. *Journal of the American Society for Psychical Research,* **69,** 135–149.

HONORTON, C., & TREMMEL, L. (1980). PSITREK: A preliminary effort toward development of psi-conducive software. In W. G. Roll (Ed.), *Research in parapsychology 1979* (pp. 159–161). Metuchen, NJ: Scarecrow Press.

HYMAN, R. (1983). Does the ganzfeld experiment answer the critic's objections? In W. G. Roll, J. Beloff, & R. A. White (Eds.), *Research in parapsychology 1982* (pp. 21–23). Metuchen, NJ: Scarecrow Press.

MAY, E. C. (1976). PSIFI: A physiology-coupled, noise-driven random number generator to extend PK studies. In J. D. Morris, W. G. Roll, & R. L. Morris (Eds.), *Research in parapsychology 1975* (pp. 20–22). Metuchen, NJ: Scarecrow Press.

McCARTHY, D. J. (1982). The role of microcomputers in experimental parapsychology. In B. Shapin & L. Coly (Eds.), *Parapsychology and the experimental method* (pp. 82–99). New York: Parapsychology Foundation.

SCHECHTER, E. I., BARKER, P., & VARVOGLIS, M. (1983). A preliminary study with a PK game involving distraction from the psi task. In W. G. Roll, J. Beloff, & R. A. White (Eds.), *Research in parapsychology 1982* (pp. 152–154). Metuchen, NJ: Scarecrow Press.

SCHMIDT, H. (1970). A quantum mechanical random number generator for psi tests. *Journal of Parapsychology,* **34,** 219–224.

VARVOGLIS, M. P., & MCCARTHY, D. (1986). Conscious-purposive focus and PK: RNG activity in relation to awareness, task-orientation, and feedback. *Journal of the American Society for Psychical Research,* **80,** 1–29.

WINNETTE, R. ., & HONORTON, C. (1977). Effects of meditation and feedback on psychokinetic performance: Results with practitioners of Ajapa yoga. In J. D. Morris, W. G. Roll, & R. L. Morris (Eds.), *Research in parapsychology 1976* (pp. 97–98). Metuchen, NJ: Scarecrow Press.

LEARNING TO LURE THE RABBIT: CHARLES HONORTON'S PROCESS-RELEVANT ESP RESEARCH

By Rex G. Stanford

None of the students who, in the early to mid-60's, eagerly imbibed the words of their hoary mentor and psi meister, J. B. Rhine, could easily forget his pithy advice to all who would study psi in the laboratory: "If you want to have rabbit stew, first catch the rabbit." It meant, "If you want to study psi in the laboratory, you must provide the circumstances that will insure the presence of psi in your study." Deliberate planning was needed to insure that there was "rabbit" in your larder from the beginning. These words came from the man who had regularly managed to elicit psi in the laboratory and had helped to put parapsychology on the scientific map. They had to be taken seriously by anyone planning a career as a laboratory parapsychologist, as all of us were. Failing to heed them would be the scientific equivalent of giving a party and no one turning up!

Perhaps no student of Rhine ever learned this lesson better or applied it more successfully than Charles Honorton. He always seemed to be having rabbit stew, while others were spending most of their time chasing the rabbit. There were probably several reasons for this, and this essay will touch on some of them. In essence, though, Honorton knew that if you wanted the rabbit, you had to lure it, not go chasing after it! You had to know something about rabbit psychology, even if learning about rabbit psychology was not your main objective.

A driving force—perhaps *the* driving force—in Honorton's professional life was to effectively put before the broader scientific community a reliable demonstration of ESP, a dependable recipe for rabbit stew, if you will. Honorton might well have cared less about rabbit psychology than about putting rabbit stew on his and on other scientists' intellectual menus. Studying rabbit psychology

I am grateful to St. John's University for granting a reduction in teaching load (Research Reduction) that substantially aided the preparation of this paper. I also gratefully acknowledge the assistance of John Palmer, whose vast knowledge of the ESP literature was helpful more than once.

was a necessary step toward his ultimate goal, and he learned much about luring the rabbit. He learned it from his research and from diverse other sources, and he worked hard to pass this knowledge on to other researchers. (For this extended Rhineian metaphor I offer apologies to my fellow vegetarians and to animal rights advocates.)

If Honorton's interest in the psychology of psi function was in considerable degree a means to an end, this does not mean that he lacked interest in basic theoretical and even philosophical issues related to psi reality. My review of Honorton's research and writings persuades me that in these larger matters of the intrinsic nature of psi and its implications for a broader understanding of reality, he had keen interests. His tough-minded pragmatism probably shaped his important theoretical, methodological, and empirical contributions to process-oriented work, but that pragmatism itself seemed driven by his conception of psi reality as perhaps the single most important topic confronting science. In the contemporary world-view, rabbits just should not exist.

For Honorton, mind was a reality that could be demonstrated through psi research. This philosophical bent showed up, for example, in his concept (1977, pp. 466–467) of "Mind at Large." Following writers such as Henri Bergson and Aldous Huxley, he considered the brain and nervous system as filters that help to make manageable the potential influx of information from Mind at Large. The concept of mind as real also emerged in his naming his laboratory in Princeton, New Jersey, the Psychophysical Research Laboratories. He adopted the term *psychophysical* because it was his objective, in working at the laboratory, to research interactions between the mental and the physical (personal communication at the time he was selecting that name).

Learning to Recognize a Rabbit: The Pursuit of Individual Differences Predictive of ESP-Task Performance

Who Responds Positively to Hypnotic Suggestions for ESP Success?

To make rabbit stew, you must do more than catch any old animal. It must be a rabbit of some kind. One way of looking at the metaphor is that "rabbit" means "psi." Another way is to consider "rabbit" to be an individual who can produce psi in your laboratory.

In his earliest published parapsychological work, during his junior year in high school in West St. Paul, Minnesota, Honorton tried to identify the kind of person for whom hypnosis would facilitate ESP (Honorton, 1964). Identifying people who respond favorably to a psi-conducive setting was a theme he would repeat with variations throughout his career. The unique ideas behind his first such study show his creative genius. That this hypnosis work would and could have been carried out at a high school by a high-school student shows the boldness of Honorton and the respect he engendered in those who were privileged to know him.

He reasoned that hypnosis, especially hypnosis combined with confidence-building suggestions, might enhance the natural tendencies of individuals to score above or below mean chance expectation (MCE) on ESP tests. His idea was that hypnotically induced attitudes toward personal psi ability and toward the capacity to demonstrate it would enhance the subject's usual tendency, predicted from scores on an interest inventory (validated as an ESP predictor by Stuart and Humphrey; see Honorton, 1964), to perform either above or below MCE. To know whether this had happened, one also had to test without hypnosis.

Honorton's first such study was based on a small number of participants recruited in his high school. The experimenter remained blind to the interest-scale results while ESP testing was still underway. The results supported the major expectations, especially regarding the low-scoring group under hypnosis. In a replication study (Honorton, 1966), he obtained very similar, generally confirmatory, outcomes using a substantially improved methodology. His hypothesis assumed that the predicted extrasensory outcomes are mediated by changes in expectancies about ESP-task performance induced by the suggestions given under hypnosis. Accordingly, he also demonstrated in his 1966 study that his hypnotic manipulation increased expectations of success. This had not been measured in the first study, and this was a major step toward supporting his hypothesis.

Here was a high-school student who developed and experimentally supported a sophisticated hypothesis about a Person × Situation interaction—and who did so at a time when research on "Person × Situation interactions" was rare in psychology. Even today, the studies in parapsychology that examine this type of interaction are few. This circumstance clearly identified Honorton, from his earliest research, as a conceptually sophisticated process-oriented researcher.

His hypothesis in this work and in its subsequent replication (Honorton, 1964, 1966) was built around the important suggestion that different factors may determine the *direction* and the *magnitude* of the deviation from MCE. (In the present case, a person variable was seen as determining the former and a situational one, hypnosis, as determining the latter.) Palmer's later reviews of the ESP literature found support for the generalization that altered states affect the magnitude, rather than the direction (relative to MCE), of ESP-task performance (1978, p. 205; 1982, p. 56).

In a later paper on this topic (Honorton, 1969a), in which he summarized his earlier results, Honorton reported additional, supplementary, studies that examined whether comparable results could be produced simply by giving the expectancy-manipulating suggestions in the waking state. If they could not, Honorton reasoned, variables other than simply the suggestions themselves—perhaps degree of relaxation or cognitive factors—would be implicated. If they could be produced by suggestion without hypnosis, the suggestions themselves could be presumed to be the locus of the effect. The extrasensory effect did not appear with waking suggestions, but there was a complicating outcome. Although waking suggestions were associated with statistically enhanced reported expectancy, the consequences of the waking suggestions for expectancy were not so great as when the suggestions were given with hypnosis. We therefore have to ask what it is about the hypnotic situation that makes the suggestions more effective in elevating expectations. This work (Honorton, 1969a) also indicated that direct suggestions (during the waking state) about success were more effective in boosting stated expectancies than were indirect or implicit suggestions.

Here, again, Honorton showed himself to be a thoughtful process-oriented researcher by measuring the hypothesized mediating factor, attitude enhancement, and by asking whether hypnosis was necessary for his ESP results or whether suggestions alone might be sufficient. As Honorton himself acknowledged, methodological refinements in subsequent work would be needed to pin down the loci of his effects.

Manifest Anxiety and Perceived Complexity: Turning Anxiety Into an Asset and Assessing Its Role in ESP-Task Performance

A little-known episode in Honorton's research (1965, Honorton's first paper presented at the Parapsychological Association) clearly showed him to be a conceptually oriented thinker. Although the results from these two studies were not significant by normative standards, this work deserves mention because of its extrapolation to ESP testing of an idea borrowed right out of behaviorist psychology! (Honorton always liked the idea of blending parapsychological and psychological concepts.) In Kenneth Spence's behaviorist theorization (e.g., Spence, Farber, & McFann, 1956) manifest anxiety was conceived as a drive. As such, it tends to energize responses in a multiplicative fashion. Each response is energized by anxiety, and this drive factor should multiply extant response strength. If there is a dominant response, it should therefore be particularly energized. In complex tasks, the proper response is not dominant, and heightened anxiety (drive) should deter performance. On the other hand, those with lower anxiety (drive) might be able better to succeed at the demands of complex tasks. On simple tasks, the dominant response is correct. Therefore, high-anxious (high-drive) persons should do well, but low-anxious (low-drive) persons, less adequately. (Honorton's 1965 work seemingly assumed that the demands of learning tasks—the original domain in which this hypothesis was developed—bear some similarities to what we find in ESP testing and that expectancies about complexity are equivalent to the real thing.) Honorton extended this reasoning to ESP tasks by experimentally manipulating whether the subject perceived the task as simple or complex and by measuring anxiety level. (In his first study this was done by a home-made test; in the second, by the Taylor Manifest Anxiety Scale.) He hypothesized above-chance performance for high-anxious (HA) subjects on simple tasks, but performance at or below chance for HAs on complex tasks. He also predicted that low-anxious (LA) subjects would score at or below chance on simple tasks, but above chance on complex tasks. (I am not certain of the rationale for this latter prediction.) In line with this kind of thinking, high-anxious subjects performed objectively better on an ESP task that they had been led to think of as simple than on one they had been led to believe was complex. Also as expected, low-anxious subjects showed the opposite pattern.

Here, as always, Honorton showed a readiness to recognize the limitations of an earlier study and subsequently to improve his work. In his first study he had presented BT and DT ESP tests to the participants as "simple" and "complex," respectively. Recognizing that he had confounded what might be objective and subjective complexity and desiring to know about the role of subjective complexity, in his second study he crossed objective and perceived complexity. He did this by telling one group of subjects that the DT test was simple but that a precognition test was complex. He told another group the opposite. He also had a third, control, group who were told that the tasks were equally difficult. The nonsignificant results were in line with the predictions from his hypothesis.

This work showed Honorton's incisive critical acumen and his readiness to persevere toward better research designs. It also showed his readiness to borrow from nonparapsychological domains. Later, with ganzfeld, he would borrow from perceptual-cognitive psychology.

Creativity

Honorton (1967) ventured briefly into "creativity" and ESP-task performance. He again showed himself a careful process-oriented methodologist. In his five series in the work on this theme, he always administered the ESP task before the creativity tests, and subjects never learned their ESP scores during the testing session because these were precognition tests. These circumstances precluded the possibility that performance on the creativity test (which might have been obvious to subjects, even if feedback was not given) could have affected ESP-task performance by inducing expectancies or affecting mood. It is not plausible that the reverse would have happened. Feedback about ESP results was given weeks after the test session. Honorton's concerns about test order reappeared in his recent meta-analysis of the correlation between extraversion and forced-choice ESP-task performance (Honorton, Ferrari, & Bem, 1992).

By pooling across his series of studies and using chi-square for consistency of direction of deviation above or below MCE, Honorton showed that the results contrasting dichotomized high- and low-creative subjects were significantly different. He also reported statistics for the individual series, based on a CR_d contrast of high- and low-creative subjects.

This was a bit early in his career for him to have done meta-analysis, so I have helped him, retrospectively, by combining the z scores for the creativity-group contrasts for the several series, using the method recommended by Rosenthal (1991). For the Ice Question Test (IQT, a performance measure), $z = 4.06$, $p < .00006$. For the creative motivation scale of the Personal-Social Motivation Inventory (PSMI), $z = 3.19$, $p < .002$. If the z scores for the given series are weighted according to the total number of subjects (pooled across high- and low-creative persons) in each series, for the IQT, $z = 3.62$, $p < .00035$; and for the PSMI, $z = 2.78$, $p < .006$.

Although Honorton succeeded in making a case that high-creative, as contrasted with low-creative, subjects turned in higher scores on the precognition task, he neglected in his Discussion to point out that essentially all the statistical evidence of ESP in this work came from the low-creative subjects (albeit as psi-missing). My compilation of the ESP-task performance data for the two series involving the IQT shows that the low-creative individuals scored significantly below MCE ($z = -3.44$, $p \approx .0006$, two-tailed), whereas the high-creative ones did not differ reliably from MCE ($z = +0.92$), $p \approx .358$, two-tailed). The comparable data for the PSMI five series show (by my computation) that the low-creative individuals collectively turned in sigificant below-chance performance ($z = -3.47$, $p \approx .0005$, two-tailed), whereas the high-creative ones again showed a net result not different from chance ($z = +0.26$, $p \approx .795$, two-tailed). These facts must be considered in interpreting this work. They might mean that in Honorton's work the low-creative individuals, rather than lacking ESP ability, had such ability but tended to reject the correct impression. (For broader discussion of the work on creativity and ESP-task performance, see Palmer, 1978).

Honorton's interest in a possible relationship between creativity and ESP-task performance reappeared recently (Schlitz & Honorton, 1992) in a ganzfeld-ESP study with students from the Juilliard School in New York. I will ignore that work here because the relevance of its findings to the other creativity work is unclear and because it concerned a small, highly specialized sample of talented individuals who, oddly, scored relatively poorly on a standardized test related to creativity.

Hypnotic Susceptibility, "Depth," and Suggestibility

Early in his work with hypnosis and suggestibility, Honorton took an interest in whether hypnotic susceptibility, "depth," or suggestibility correlated with performance on the ESP task. In his second study (1966) on whether the interest inventory interacted with hypnotic induction in affecting ESP-task scores, he found no significant relationship between depth of hypnosis and ESP performance, but he did not report the magnitude of the observed correlation. (This was normative at the time. Investigators rarely reported the values for inferential or descriptive statistics if the former was nonsignificant.) Honorton, however, did report the correlation of suggestibility (measured by objective scores on the Barber Suggestibility Scale, BSS) and ESP-task performance in his work with waking suggestions and the interest inventory (Honorton, 1969a). The reported correlation ($+$ .31) comes close to statistical significance ($p <$ .09, two-tailed, my computation).

One searches the considerable ESP-hypnosis literature in vain for correlational data for standardized hypnotic-susceptibility tests and ESP-task performance under hypnosis. Honorton has to be credited here again with being out ahead of most investigators, although his reported correlation with the BSS is for waking imagination, not for a hypnosis condition. It is possible, though, that his reported correlation might have been contaminated by his having administered the BSS before the ESP test and in the same context. Expectancies based on BSS success or failure might have influenced ESP performance, given that suggestions were made, albeit in the waking state. The possibility that the above correlation was not spurious is supported by the following observation. Stanford (1972) reported a significant tendency for higher-suggestible (above median) subjects to score better on a precognition task than lower-suggestible ones (below median), with BSS as the suggestibility measure. The significant t value (Stanford, 1972, p. 57) associated with this effect is equivalent to $r = +$ .25, $N = 65$, $p <$ .05, two-tailed (based on a conversion formula in Rosenthal, 1991, p. 66). This correlation is reasonably close to the $+$ .31 value found by Honorton (1969a, p. 80), with a waking imagination condition and clairvoyance testing. The Stanford finding is not subject to the interpretation that ESP performance was biased by subjects' knowledge of their BSS scores; the BSS was given after the ESP task. Also, BSS performance could not have been affected by sensory knowledge of ESP scores in this precognition task. Here, then, is evidence supporting Honorton's finding (1969a) of a low positive correlation of ESP-task performance and suggestibility even when there was no hypnotic induction.

Honorton and Krippner (1969), in their review of the hypnosis-ESP literature, made many excellent suggestions for future research. One was that reseachers should use standardized measures of hypnotic susceptibility (or suggestibility) to describe the population studied—a potentially important element in replicability in the hypnosis-ESP domain. In a related vein, these authors also suggested that investigators study susceptibility (using standardized instruments) as an independent (or predictor) variable in potential interaction with manipulated variables in affecting ESP-task performance (or other measures of interest). Among other things, this arrangement allows determination of whether the consequences of an experimental manipulation (e.g., hypnotic induction versus control) depend on the susceptibility of participants. Exploration of this possible interaction of the hypnosis and susceptibility variables is important both to efforts at replication and to interpreting the findings.

Honorton followed this sage advice in his 1972b study of hypnotically induced ESP dreams. He used a 2 × 3 factorial design with hypnotic induction and waking-imagination as the levels of the first variable and high, medium, and low susceptibility (measured by the BSS) as the levels of the second.

This study was intended to examine the potential interaction of susceptibility and the hypnosis manipulation. Honorton went further and had participants make state reports, using a rating scale, in the hope of relating extrasensory success to the actual state of the subject and, particularly, to shifts in state. (He also used these to check the consequences of his experimental manipulation.) He was concerned also with how dreamlike subjects' dreams were—the dreams that were supposed to supply mediating vehicles for the occurrence of ESP—and how this related to ESP-task performance. This was an ambitious and, in many ways, brilliant study.

Regrettably, it suffered from methodological problems that make its results difficult to interpret. Such is often the fate of first efforts in a given area. The problems in this study included: (a) no direct analysis of the expected interaction; (b) problematic statistical analysis related to assuming independence of trials when this was doubtful (Kennedy, 1979); (c) violation of random assignment to hypnosis and waking conditions; (d) administration of the BSS before ESP testing in the same setting and apparently by the same experimenter; (e) subject judging of the same target materials that were presented during the ESP task; and (f) state report measures that were potentially reactive.

The state-report-related results of this study are tantalizing. Change in state was the best predictor of ESP-task performance. Honorton seemed to interpret such findings as indicating that change in state per se facilitates ESP-task performance. However, there is an alternative interpretation. To make a state report, the subject must make an attribution concerning (i.e., an interpretation about) why he or she is experiencing what is being experienced. This attributional effort might not occur spontaneously, but only because the experimenter requested it. (In other words, this is a potentially reactive methodology.) This attribution, which is made in response to an experimenter request, might then influence subject expectations of success (e.g., "Good, I just entered an altered state and that should mean I'll do well on the ESP task"). If these kinds of attribution-induced expectations influence ESP-task performance, they might be the cause of (or contaminate) any correlation between state report (or state-report shift) and ESP-task performance, rather than there simply being a causal role related to state (Stanford, 1988, October).

The problem of nonduplicate target materials was also present in the earlier work on hypnotically induced dreams (Honorton & Stump, 1969). Psi researchers, Honorton included, had typically been trained in forced-choice methodology. Time was needed (and some published criticism, e.g., Kennedy, 1979) for all the potential problems with this new method to become obvious and for satisfactory solutions to be deployed.

Honorton's second study of hypnotically induced clairvoyant dreams (1972b) provided a research paradigm that, with improved methodology, could help unravel one of the puzzles of parapsychology, the facilitation of ESP-task performance with hypnosis. The methodological problems in the original study are understandable, considering the difficulties of doing complex, groundbreaking work. The study again showed Honorton's recognition of and interest in studying the interaction between person characteristics (i.e., susceptibility/suggestibility) and situations provided by the experimenter (i.e., hypnotic induction or waking imagination). It inspired considerable additional research on hypnotically induced dreams, work that provided some independent replication (see Palmer, 1978).

Honorton's (1972b) study of hypnotically induced dreams was unusual in work on altered states and ESP in that it contrasted a hypnotic-induction condition with something resembling a proper control condition (i.e., waking-imagination circumstances that were parallel in many ways to the hypnotic condition). Honorton specified operationally, but not conceptually (i.e., not for the relevant psychological variables), what it was about the hypnosis condition that he wished not to be included in the waking-imagination control condition. Such conceptual specification seems necessary to test the validity of the control condition and to assure the interpretation of outcomes.

Perhaps the critical psychological difference between Honorton's hypnosis and waking-imagination control conditions was whether the subject would come to believe that she was undergoing hypnosis (and whatever added expectations that might entail). Perhaps, though, Honorton thought that the difference might be a special state produced by the induction. He examined some possible psychological consequences of his manipulation, namely, dream quality and state (i.e., degree of internalized attention), but he did not examine expectancies.

Unfortunately, Honorton (1972b) did not report the correlations between susceptibility (or suggestibility) and ESP-task performance for the hypnosis and waking-imagination groups. The data in his Table 1 for the hypnosis condition suggest the possibility of a positive correlation; for the waking-imagination condition, there would seem to be no correlation (based on subject-classification breakdowns in Table 1).

Reported Frequency of Dream Recall and ESP-Task Performance

Honorton was deeply interested in individual differences in what he termed *internal sensitivity* (1972a) or what psychologists term *introception*. In his view, sensitivity to internal cues was needed for successful performance on an ESP task. Persons who could not discriminate their own thoughts from those that appeared in their minds through extrasensory means could never succeed on an ESP task. Also, those not inclined to or perhaps afraid of looking inward could obviously not make such discriminations. Honorton was interested both in individual differences in this regard and in special environments that might enhance persons' readiness to focus on inward impressions undisturbed by distracting sensory noise and thoughts. His interest in these topics was based on his model of psychophysical noise reduction (e.g., Honorton, 1977). He thought that self-reported recall of dreams might predict ESP-task performance because it could index sensitivity to (or perhaps interest in) internal processes. He found significant evidence of a positive relationship of reported frequency of dream recall and performance on a precognition task. This confirmed an earlier such finding by Johnson (1968).

Mental Imagery and ESP-Task Performance

Honorton's growing concern with internal sensitivity led him to an interest in what Tyrrell (1946) had termed the *mediating vehicles* for extrasensory information. Honorton, Tierney, and Torres

(1974) specifically noted that in spontaneous cases of ostensible ESP the relevant information often seems mediated into consciousness through mental imagery and that seemingly gifted percipients often emphasize the role of mental images in their impressions. They suggested that psi communication should be enhanced under conditions that favor imagery or in persons inclined toward imagery.

In the first study of this kind, Honorton et al. (1974) found that "strong imagers" (median split) scored significantly above chance and that "weak imagers" scored significantly below. The difference of performance of these two groups was, as expected, significant as measured by a subject-based statistic. He also reported that strong imagers did significantly better on their confidence calls than weak imagers, and, in his Discussion section, he seems to take this difference as meaning that in making psi responses the high imagers have available and use cues that weak imagers do not. It is presumably those cues on which they base their confidence calls.

This is an appealing interpretation, especially given that Honorton here links it with the finding of McCallam and Honorton (1973) that subjects using multiple cues as the basis of their confidence calls in initial testing showed greater post-feedback-training enhancement of confidence-call accuracy than did those who did not report internal cues on which their confidence calls were based. Regrettfully, there was a serious statistical error in Honorton's assessment (Honorton et al., 1974) of the difference of confidence-call accuracy for strong and weak imagers (and in the McCallam & Honorton, 1973, work).

The problem is this: Honorton contrasted confidence-call accuracy for these strong and weak imagers but neglected to consider that the former group had a significantly higher rate of hitting than the latter. Consequently, simply by chance alone, their percentage of correct confidence calls should be higher (see R. Schechter, Solfvin, & McCollum, 1975). Interestingly, the difference in proportions of confidence-call accuracy for strong, as contrasted with weak, imagers (+ 5.4%) is very similar to the difference of the proportions of hitting for the two groups (+ 3.2%). My analysis (based on data in the Honorton et al. 1974 report) shows that (a) the strong imagers did not perform significantly above MCE on confidence calls, given their actual hit rate in the ESP task ($z = + 0.52$), (b) the weak imagers did not perform significantly below MCE in confidence-call accuracy, considering their hit rate ($z = - 0.80$), and (c) in view of these figures, the two levels of confidence calling do not differ significantly.

Honorton's theoretical reasoning in this work on mental imagery and ESP-task performance may not go far enough. I suggest that he did not sufficiently integrate his interest in psi-relevant internal cues and his concerns about psychophysical noise reduction. It is clear, as he suggested, that ESP-test participants need to have available mediating vehicles (e.g., visual imagery) that can encode and communicate to consciousness target-relevant information. This potential asset, however, can become a liability if the imagery is so abundant and free-flowing that it serves as a serious source of cognitive noise when the subject is trying to identify and report information about the ESP target. (This might be especially the case in free-response work, but I also do not understand why an abundance of highly vivid imagery should be needed for forced-choice work.) For this reason, I think it is specious to predict a monotonic relationship between imagery ability and ESP-task performance. Any relationship between individual differences in imagery and ESP-task performance might depend on the nature of the ESP task (free-response versus forced-choice) and factors in the test environment that influence the disposition to produce imagery.

Honorton frequently quoted the important paper by White (1964) that, in part, concerned how outstanding percipients prepared themselves to receive information. It is true, as Honorton et al. (1974) pointed out, that many of the sensitives White discussed found that their psi-mediated information came through the mediating vehicle of visual imagery. It is also true that an important part of White's paper concerned how these experienced percipients tried to insure that they would wait and watch for the psi-mediated information at a time when their minds had been cleared of extraneous material, including imagery. They engaged in precisely what Honorton might have called "a deliberate act of psychophysical noise reduction." Regrettably, Honorton et al. (1974) seemed to ignore this consideration, although Honorton later made use of White's paper when discussing psychophysical noise reduction (Honorton, 1977, p. 451). He even quoted the section concerned with stilling the body and mind.

The conclusion that a lack of abundant, vivid imagery need not deter ESP is reinforced by the work of R. Schechter, Solfvin, and McCollum (1975), who attempted replication of the Honorton et al. (1974) study but found: (a) a nonsignificant tendency toward psi-missing among strong imagers and (b) significant psi-hitting among weak imagers. R. Schechter et al. (1975) found in their work that it was the weak imagers who did better on the confidence calls, but they noted that, in both their study and that of Honorton et al. (1974), accuracy on confidence calls closely followed the hit rate on the ESP task. Differences in confidence-call accuracy for the two groups of imagers therefore reflected nothing more than chance success at identifying hits.

This consideration undermines a fundamental tenet of Honorton's argument. Under these circumstances, it cannot be assumed that high imagers had special awareness of the accuracy of their psi processes. Thus, level of imagery per se cannot, on the basis of this work, be regarded as an index of internal sensitivity. Merely having much imagery may neither facilitate psi nor be an indicator of internal sensitivity.

Honorton (1975b), like R. Schechter et al. (1975), subsequently questioned the construct validity of the Betts QMI Vividness of Mental Imagery Scale (Sheehan's shortened version), the instrument used in the series of studies on imagery ability and ESP-task performance. Honorton's own review of this area (1975b) showed a total of three forced-choice studies using this instrument, two of which showed significantly better ESP-task performance for weak than for strong imagers, a consensus opposite to the significant findings of the original study (Honorton et al., 1974). Honorton (1975b) also noted, in the case of three studies with free-responses ESP tasks, no evidence of an artifact-free relationship of imagery-test performance and ESP outcomes. He correctly suggests that there may be serious construct-validity problems with the imagery instrument used in this work. The test is based on self-report, instead of performance, and scores might easily be influenced by such factors as demand characteristics.

Nonetheless, the literature in this area (reviewed by George, 1981) shows a striking incidence of statistical significance in research with the Betts QMI, with results often in conflicting directions. It may not be enough to say that there is likely a problem in the validity of the imagery test. That would not explain the odd pattern of contradictory, but often significant, results. Honorton (1975b) suggested using several measures related to imagery, including subjective, behavioral, and psychophysiological measures—an excellent suggestion. Nonetheless, it is possible that this wealth of contradictory, but significant, results says something besides commenting on conceivable vicissitudes of the Betts QMI. After all, the test does seem to be tapping into something relevant to ESP-task performance. There is need for refinement of theoretical ideas about imagery and ESP-task performance and for the development of a model that makes precise predictions for particular kinds of ESP tasks. As noted above, there are reasons to think that a curvilinear relationship might exist between imagery abundance and performance on certain types of ESP tasks, including free-response ones. The point of the break in the curve might depend on the requirements of the ESP task. Significant results with conflicting directions can sometimes derive from separate studies that tap into different parts of a nonmonotonic function. Significant contradictory results perhaps more clearly suggest the need for rethinking the problem area than for blaming the instrument used in the work. Having said that, the points made by Honorton (1975b), R. Schechter et al. (1975), and George (1981) about the need for better instruments are well taken. Perhaps combining other instruments with the Betts QMI might help to untangle the empirical puzzle that has emerged. Nonetheless, changing instruments alone will not do the job. It cannot replace the need for more refined, careful thinking about how imagery may relate to ESP-task performance.

Extraversion

One personality variable that has been widely researched as a predictor of ESP-task performance is extraversion (reviewed by Palmer, 1978). Meta-analysis is the tool best suited to assess whether and in what degree extraversion scores have correlated with ESP-task performance across the available studies. Honorton, Ferrari, and Bem (1992) reported such an analysis.

For forced-choice studies, a significant average (positive) correlation of extraversion and ESP-task performance existed only for work in which ESP testing preceded the measurement of extraversion. The correlation differed significantly for the two testing orders, and this finding was deemed independent of test setting (individual or group), nature of extraversion measure, and ESP mode (e.g., telepathy versus clairvoyance).

Honorton et al. (1992) suggested that for forced-choice ESP studies in which ESP testing came first, the observed (significant) correlation of extraversion and ESP might have been artifactual because the subjects' knowledge of their ESP scores could have affected their extraversion scores. Here is another indication of Honorton's sensitivity to the possibility that the results of one test can affect another. The conclusion Honorton et al. (1992) reached may be regarded by some as premature, but their significant pattern of findings needs to be explained. Honorton and colleagues provided an excellent example of how meta-analysis can aid in developing potential explanations for sets of findings and can encourage new work intended to investigate such explanations.

Work has already begun to test the order-artifact hypothesis proposed by Honorton and colleagues (Krishna & Rao, 1991). The findings of Krishna and Rao provided no support for predictions they derived from the order-artifact hypothesis of Honorton et al. (1990), but, for several reasons, Krishna and Rao are probably correct in their conclusion that the order-artifact hypothesis cannot be dismissed solely on grounds of their results. Considerable additional work is needed to evaluate the order-artifact hypothesis. Failure to do this work would leave in limbo whether an extraversion-ESP correlation exists in the forced-choice domain. Also, parapsychologists would make a substantial contribution to psychometrics if they could show that this kind of artifact exists.

The finding of a possible order artifact in the forced-choice extraversion-ESP correlation might provoke theoretical advances—a happy thought. Has anyone proposed a cogent theoretical framework that would predict an ESP-extraversion correlation in *both* free-response and forced-choice tasks? That the correlation should hold up in both situations seems peculiar (or at least needs explanation), given the differences in the two types of tests.

In the free-response work, Honorton et al. (1990) found evidence of a small, but significant, average correlation of extraversion and ESP-task performance. They also concluded that this correlation was not artifactual. The correlation held up across various measures of extraversion. As confirmation of their meta-analytic finding, they reported a small but significant large-sample-based, positive, extraversion-ESP correlation in the ganzfeld work at Psychophysical Research Laboratories in Princeton, NJ. It was remarkably similar in magnitude to the mean effect size derived from their meta-analysis of free-response results.

Rabbits Will Be Rabbits

Honorton used meta-analysis in many ways to advance parapsychology. Another of his meta-analytic findings (Honorton & Ferrari, 1989) is relevant to the present topic of individual differences and ESP-task performance.

Within the vagaries of testing error, if ESP tests have some validity, superior performance on an ESP test at one time should be associated with greater chances of outstanding performance at another time. In their meta-analysis of forced-choice precognition studies, Honorton and Ferrari (1989) identified eight subject populations, among which were "selected subjects." Studies that used individuals selected because of their previous performance in experiments or pilot tests showed significantly larger effect sizes than those that used unselected subjects. Honorton and Ferrari also found that a substantially higher percentage of the studies with selected subjects produced significance than did those with unselected subjects. Studies with selected subjects also tended (albeit not significantly) to be more rigorous than those with unselected subjects.

These data suggest that if you want to find out whether what you have is a rabbit, see if it behaves like one. If it does so in a compelling way, it will likely continue to do so in the future. By identifying and studying individuals with bona fide ability, it may be easier to reach scientific conclusions about psi function.

This meta-analytic finding suggests that psi performance may be *relatively* reliable among those who are particularly talented and that this reliability probably extends in some degree across types of ESP tests. If it does, the personal characteristics of these talented individuals might contribute to their successful laboratory performance on varied tasks. Perhaps parapsychologists should, then, attempt to study the personal characteristics that such talented persons might hold in common that distinguish them from less successful, less reliable, participants. This approach could be useful for understanding process, but it has historically been lacking, for the most part, in parapsychology. Personality-ESP research has typically focused on groups of relatively unselected participants tested on a single psi task.

The Honorton-Ferrari meta-analysis points toward a new approach to studying individual differences and psi-task success. It suggests the importance of identifying and studying the characteristics of those who show reasonably reliable ESP-task performance, both over time and over different tasks.

Predicting the Success of Ganzfeld First-Timers

At the Psychophysical Research Laboratories (PRL), Princeton, NJ, Honorton and colleagues tried to discover the characteristics of individuals who did and who did not succeed in the ganzfeld-ESP task the first time they participated. This effort was built around the use of several tests. One that was regularly administered to participants was a lengthy questionnaire called the Participant Information Form (PIF). It elicited data on demographics, attitudes toward parapsychological claims, presence or absence of personal experiences seeming to be of one or more psi types, information on prior participation in nonganzfeld psi experiments, and other information. A standard personality test that was administered to most participants was the Myers-Briggs Type Indicator (MBTI). These two instruments were the basis of the efforts to predict first-time ganzfeld ESP-task performance. Workers at the Institute for Parapsychology (IP), Durham, NC, later joined the effort to predict the success of first-timers in ganzfeld (Broughton, Kanthamani, & Khilji, 1990). Four major empirical papers have appeared on predicting who are successful ganzfeld first-timers (Broughton, Kanthamani, & Khilji, 1990; Honorton, 1992; Honorton, Barker, Varvoglis, Berger, & Schechter, 1986; Honorton & Schechter, 1987).

It is appropriate that Honorton, the originator of this line of individual-differences work and the man whose life and work we honor in this issue of the *Journal*, should have the last word on this matter. His paper "The Ganzfeld Novice: Four Predictors of Initial ESP Performance," at the 1992 Parapsychological Association Annual Convention, was his final presentation before this organization whose work he had so much enriched. This paper was an updating of the status of work predicting the success of ganzfeld first-timers, and I will touch here on some of its major findings and conclusions.

Honorton (1992) examined the original PRL first-timers series (from Honorton & Schechter, 1987), first-timers from the automated ganzfeld series (Honorton, Berger, Varvoglis, Quant, Derr, Schechter, & Ferrari, 1990), and the IP data (Broughton, Kanthamani, & Khilji, 1990), singly and in combination. On the basis of Honorton (1992), let us look at these data collectively.

Participants who were predicted to do well the first time in ganzfeld were those (a) who had had prior psi testing in a nonganzfeld setting, (b) who reported at least one type of psi experience, (c) who were the Feeling-Perceiving [FP] type as measured by the MBTI, or (d) who had practiced mental discipline. The net outcomes across all these series can be summarized as follows: For all four individual predictors of first-time ganzfeld ESP-task performance and for the combined-predictor model (i.e., subjects meeting the criteria for all of these), those predicted to do well scored significantly above MCE. In no case did those predicted to do less well score significantly above MCE. Nevertheless, only in the case of prior testing and FP did the difference for these two groups reach statistical significance.

These summarized ganzfeld first-time results involved hundreds of subjects in multiple series in two laboratories. Although the effect sizes are modest in this work, the consistency of outcomes across a massive database at two laboratories is impressive. To extend the metaphor, Honorton really had learned the field marks distinguishing the rabbits from the hares.

What he did not do was to show that a combination of field marks provided better rabbit-hare discrimination than any single field mark taken alone. Less metaphorically, his combined model did not provide—and he did not claim it provided (Honorton, 1992)—better discrimination than certain of his specific predictor variables. Nevertheless, his advice to ganzfeld investigators to recruit persons meeting as many of his criteria as possible was prudent because presumably there is some degree of unrealiability in measuring individual predictors.

Some Reflections on Honorton's Individual-Differences Findings

1. Free-response procedures in which the subject is the judge (of correspondences) provide correlations of individual differences and ESP-test scores that are affected by extrasensory responsiveness, ability to judge, and motivation for judging. The individual-difference measure might be predicting extrasensory proficiency, judging skill, motivation for judging, or some combination of these. This should be kept in mind in interpreting these correlations and in attempting to replicate them (e.g., consider the consequences of using external judges instead of subjects as judges). Honorton was well aware of the multiple determinants of success with participants as judges, and this awareness was reflected in various of his publications, including his last paper at the Parapsychological Association (1992, final paragraph under "Reported Personal Psi Experiences," p. 54).

2. Individual-difference-based correlations are not always self-explanatory. Process-oriented experimentation and, sometimes, supplementary analysis can aid in understanding their meaning. Honorton was keenly aware of these considerations. For example, in his first paper on a model for initial ganzfeld success (Honorton & Schechter, 1987), he successfully tested a deduction from the premise that FP correlates with ganzfeld success because ganzfeld is a novel situation and novelty motivates FPs. Another possible deduction from the same premise is that the outstanding performance of FPs should regress under repeated testing because novelty wears off. I do not know whether Honorton empirically evaluated this particular deduction. In this case, a control group of initially successful non-FPs would be

needed (if such exist). They should not exhibit such a strong decline in performance with recurrent testing as FPs do.

3. Honorton's labors in the individual-differences domain, like those of most all such investigators, concerned prediction of performance during a first testing episode. From personal discussions with him, I know him to have been well aware that the predictors of sustained performance might be different from those for initial success. To effectively pursue the agenda he has placed before us, we need to investigate the predictors of long-term, sustained performance. (That individuals can sustain performance across time and tasks was suggested by the Honorton-Ferrari precognition meta-analysis, discussed earlier under "Rabbits Will Be Rabbits!".)

4. On the basis of Honorton's individual-difference findings, it might be easy to suppose that making rabbit stew is as easy as being sure one locates rabbits instead of hares—that one must simply get the right persons into one's laboratory.

It is almost certainly not that simple. The "right person" can come into a laboratory, but if circumstances there are not suitable, his or her behavior might not be as expected. He or she might not produce successful ESP-task performance.

Honorton did not investigate in a formal way, over a sustained period, what a psi-conducive laboratory might be like but he certainly investigated this informally. Honorton et al. (1990) make it clear that humanistic considerations are of primary importance in conducting a successful ganzfeld-ESP study. The section on "Participant Orientation" provides glimpses of a social setting that should help each person to do his or her best. It makes clear that the things that are said and done by the experimenter depend in considerable part on the reactions of the individual subject to the information being supplied (e.g., whether or not the subject becomes anxious about performance). Parapsychologists have known these things at least since the days of J. B. Rhine, but Honorton may have known them better than any of us.

Social psychologists have discussed similar concerns in their research. Elliot Aronson, a leading social psychologist, has for years taught—as I learned in coursework with him in the late '60s—and stated in his writings that trying to bring individuals to a common desired understanding of the research situation, far from being unscientific, is part of what is essential to a successful study (see, e.g., Aronson, Ellsworth, Carlsmith, & Gonzales, 1990, chap. 7). This means, in part, that there is a genuine effort to communicate with and to one's participants, not a rigid set of words that are uttered when they enter the laboratory. In a similar spirit, Honorton (1991) emphasized that we must not confuse rigor and rigidity in our laboratory work. The former is possible without the latter, but with too much of the latter, all the rigor in the world may count little.

Honorton (1991) appreciated the vulnerability of participants in a study such as ganzfeld and urged investigators to make them individually feel safe and comfortable and to motivate them toward the desired goal. Without these, he said, "...there is really no reason why you should expect success" (p. 74).

Stated differently, Honorton's successful participants (e.g., FPs and those with prior experience) were successful in a given kind of situation, the excellent social environment that participants experienced in his laboratory. It is gratuitous to assume that that type of person necessarily would be successful in a different situation.

Honorton et al. (1990) also convey the impression that the job of the successful ganzfeld researcher is, in major part, one of persuasive communication, communication that convinces the participants of the likelihood of success, that motivates them, and that reassures those with anxieties. If my experience as a percipient and as an agent at Honorton's laboratory is typical, the participant gained the impression that he or she was the focus of interest for the moment, instead of that focus being a long-range research objective or a study per se. It was a bit like a friend inviting you to go on a little adventure with him or her, one that promised both excitement and fun.

Enhancement Paradigms

The previous discussion might leave the impression that the driving force behind Honorton's parapsychological research was individual differences. That would be misleading. Most of his individual-differences work was done in the context of a test environment intended to foster ESP-task performance. Examples already discussed include: hypnosis, hypnotic dreaming, and ganzfeld. The additional enhancement paradigms explored by Honorton in his ESP work included: training sensitivity to extrasensory cues, training alpha rhythms to enhance ESP, and partial sensory deprivation.

Attempted Insight Training

Given Honorton's intense interest in what he termed "internal sensitivity," a logical step was to explore whether research participants could, through feedback training, learn to discriminate correct and incorrect ESP-test responses. This he did in a total of four series of studies reported in three publications (Honorton, 1970, 1971; Mc-Callam & Honorton, 1973). This potentially very important research also inspired work by others (Jackson, Franzoi, & Schmeidler, 1977; Kreiman & Ivnisky, 1973).

Conceptually, Honorton's is perhaps the most important work done in efforts to train ESP performance through immediate trial-by-trial feedback about ESP-task success. It was intended to get at the heart of what was supposed to be trained through such procedures: insight about discriminating psi from nonpsi cues.

The ideal evidence for the supposition that such feedback leads to insight would seemingly be a combination of (a) enhanced ESP-task performance because of feedback and (b) evidence that this enhanced performance truly derives from increased insight into the correctness of response (i.e., increased discriminability of hits from misses). The latter was the special concern of Honorton's series of studies, but the guiding hypothesis seems to suggest that both kinds of evidence should be forthcoming.

Honorton's motivation for such work was enhanced by the following considerations: (a) ESP-test subjects can have insight into their success or lack of it on given trials, as reflected in confidence-call accuracy (see Honorton, 1970, p. 405); (b) confidence calls have usefulness with sensory stimuli so weak that they appear to be beyond the recognition threshold (see relevant citation and Discussion, Honorton, 1971, p. 160); (c) unconscious physiological processes can be trained through biofeedback (Discussion in Honorton, 1970); and (d) given the above, the accuracy of confidence calls in ESP tests might represent discrimination of psi-mediated and non-psi-mediated internal cues, rather than simply a second act of ESP. If it did, ESP might be trainable because subjects might be taught to discriminate extrasensory from nonextrasensory cues, despite skepticism by some parapsychologists of the Rhineian school who felt that ESP should be untrainable because of its being unconscious.

In typical work of this kind by Honorton (and by those who tried to replicate), unselected subjects did three runs with confidence calls (no trial-by-trial feedback), then three runs with trial-by-trial feedback about success, and finally three runs with confidence calls (no trial-by-trial feedback). The objective was to learn whether the accuracy of confidence calls (i.e., of trials for which the subject indicated confidence of success by making a check mark on the record) was enhanced following this set of feedback runs. (On confidence-call runs, the experimenter requested between 3 and 7 confidence "checks," indications of greater confidence for particular trials, per 25-trial run. An average of 5 such checks per run was specifically requested.) A control group had the same pattern of testing, but the feedback during the middle set of 3 runs was bogus. For those runs, the experimenter indicated success for each trial that immediately followed a successful trial.

Of the five studies (Honorton, 1970, 1971; Jackson, Franzoi, & Schmeidler, 1977; Kreiman & Ivnisky, 1973; McCallam & Honorton, 1973) using this or a very similar paradigm, three allegedly showed a significant increase in the proportion of correct confidence calls (Honorton, 1970, 1971; McCallam & Honorton, 1973). ("Allegedly" is appropriate because of a problematic statistical computation having been used to support this central claim.) Of these five studies, three showed a significant increase in ESP-task performance from the pre- to post-feedback periods (Honorton, 1970; Kreiman & Ivnisky, 1973; McCallam & Honorton, 1973). There will be no further comment here on the Kreiman-Ivnisky (1973) work because only an abstract is available to me.

Jackson, Franzoi, and Schmeidler (1977) had done a "systematic" (nonexact) replication of this work—one with two pre-feedback confidence-call runs, two feedback runs, and two post-feedback confidence-call runs (as contrasted with Honorton's three in each case)—and found what they believed was evidence of significantly negative performance on the pre-feedback confidence calls. They checked to see if Honorton had found that, too, but in none of his reports had he published the proportion of success with confidence calls for the pre- and post-feedback periods. At their request, Honorton supplied the relevant data for his published work, namely, means, t-test outcomes, and related p values for pre- and post-feedback, confidence-call means relative to (what Honorton had erroneously treated as being) MCE. Jackson et al. (1977) reported the means supplied by Honorton, as well as whether each such mean differed reliably from (what they, too, erroneously treated as being) MCE. They concluded that two of the three studies by Honorton confirmed their own finding of significantly poor performance on pre-feedback confidence calls. They also noted that they had found only one case of significant accuracy in post-feedback confidence calls; it was in Honorton's work. This suggested to them that the real effect tended to be one of reliably inaccurate confidence calls before feedback, but no clear evidence of accuracy in confidence calls after feedback. Jackson et al. (1977) seemed to interpret this as due to demand characteristics (or, perhaps, an experimenter effect). If it is obvious to the participant that a pre- and post-feedback difference in confidence-call accuracy is to be expected, then it makes sense to do poorly on the pretest.

Unfortunately, some of the analyses of Jackson et al. (1977) on their own data and on those supplied by Honorton are problematic. True MCE for accuracy of confidence calls is equivalent to the hit rate (on the ESP test) for the experimental condition being studied, but this was not considered in these analyses. Instead, MCE for accuracy of confidence calls was taken to be the hit probability if ESP were not operating. (Schechter et al., 1975, noted this problem in criticizing Honorton's later work on imagery.)

It is not possible to do a full, proper analysis of Honorton's data (for pre- and post-feedback conditions) because we lack information on (a) the number of confidence calls in a given phase of the study, (b) the number of correct such calls for that phase, and (c) performance of individual participants. Also, Honorton does not report in his 1971 paper the ESP-test hit rate by phase of study. This makes it impossible to estimate MCE for confidence calls for that study. For the other studies (except the pilot study of Honorton, 1970, which also must be ignored because of lack of any useful data for this purpose), MCE for confidence calls can be computed because we can compute the hit rate on the ESP task, and we have available the average confidence-call hit rates per study phase (supplied by Honorton to Jackson et al., 1977, reported therein). If we then assume that subjects made five confidence calls per run as suggested by the experimenter, we can use this with the above information to compute a critical ratio (z score) for the observed difference of empirical and theoretical confidence-call success. This is an approximation because of having to estimate the number of confidence calls made in a given phase, but the estimated number should not be far from the mark.

Table 1 provides the z scores thus computed for the three studies for which adequate information was available.

The tabled figures make it clear that, just as suggested by Jackson et al. (1977), the statistically meaningful effects in this work appear to be erroneous confidence calling in the pre-feedback period. This effect is significant when outcomes are pooled across the studies for which the analysis was possible. Unlike the analyses reported by Jackson et al. (1977), these have considered the empirical hit rate in computing mean chance expectation for confidence calls. The tabled data should discourage any claim that the feedback has resulted in statistically meaningful insights about judgments of accuracy. Jackson et al. (1977) maintain that (on the basis of data supplied to them by

TABLE 1
ACTUAL OR ESTIMATED z SCORES FOR CONFIDENCE-CALL ACCURACY,
COMPARED WITH CHANCE ACCURACY, FOR PRE- AND POST-FEEDBACK
CONDITIONS

	Accuracy		No. of confidence calls	z score
	Actual	Chance		
Honorton 1970)				
Pre-feedback cond.	.097	.157	(150)	(− 2.03)
Post-feedback cond.	.236	.211	(135)	(+ 0.72)
Jackson et al. (1977)				
Pre-feedback cond.	.150	.198	150	− 1.48
Post-feedback cond.	.177	.191	158	− 0.44
McCallam et al. (1973)				
Pre-feedback cond.	.127	.177	(210)	(− 1.91)
Post-feedback cond.	.196	.236	(210)	(− 1.36)
Meta-analysis (Stouffer) method				
Pre-feedback cond.				− 3.13[a]
Post-feedback cond.				− 0.62[b]

Note: The data in parentheses are the estimated values. The chance accuracy for confidence calls is the proportion of ESP-task hits under the condition in question.
[a] $p < .002$, two-tailed (Stouffer method, Rosenthal, 1991).
[b] $p \approx .54$, two-tailed (Stouffer method, Rosenthal, 1991).

Honorton) Honorton's 1971 study, and it alone, did find pre-feedback confidence calling that was not significantly inaccurate and post-confidence-call accuracy that was significantly above mean chance expectation. This statement was (apparently) based on a computation that did not consider the empirical ESP-test hit rate for the given test phases in question. Apparently, .20 was assumed as the hit rate, and this might again have led to erroneous statistical inference.

Also, Honorton's own contrasts of pre- and post-feedback confidence-call accuracy failed to consider that mean chance expectation for confidence calls is the proportion of hits in the runs being called. Honorton's statistical analyses in this domain therefore contain an error that brings into question his conclusions from this entire line of research.

The following finding (my computation, based on data reported in McCallam & Honorton, 1973) illustrates the fallacy of inferring learned insight from pre- to post-feedback changes in confidence-call accuracy without considering the changes in MCE for confidence-call accuracy that occur when the ESP hit rate changes. Across the four experimental groups in the McCallam-Honorton (1973) study, the objective shift in pre- to post-feedback percentage of confidence-call success is strongly correlated with the shift in ESP-test hit rates from pre- to post-feedback; $r = +.96, p < .04$, two-tailed (my computation). This correlation occurs despite a lack of evidence from the study (noted by McCallam & Honorton, 1973, p. 85) in support of the discriminative learning hypothesis.

As far as I can determine, the only legitimate conclusion from this line of work is that (at least for the reports for which my analysis was possible) there is a significant tendency for participants to be inaccurate in making confidence calls during the pre-feedback period. Jackson et al. (1977) published essentially this conclusion long ago, and my own analyses, with corrected MCE, sustain it. Interpretation of this finding would have been easier had comparable information been available for Honorton's control conditions.

For the reason just indicated, the feedback work with confidence calls demonstrates nothing about discriminative learning of extrasensory cues. This caveat subsumes the effort (McCallam & Honorton, 1973) to show that participants' subjective descriptions of the bases of their confidence calls were related to pre- to post-feedback differences in confidence-call accuracy. The objective in these analyses apparently was to see whether subjects who attended to particular types of cues (or combinations of cues) were more successful in gaining insight as a result of feedback. To interpret such findings, we would need to know about the pre- to post-feedback ESP-task performance of subjects who reported specific types of cues as being associated with confidence calls. The problem, again, is that these authors' analysis ignored the effect of hit rate on confidence-call success.

Because of the wasted time and effort involved in doing these several studies, it is unfortunate that Honorton did not discern this problem in his statistical analyses. After R. Schechter et al. (1975) pointed out this fallacy in connection with his confidence-call analyses of data from high and low imagers, Honorton never again committed this error.

Training of EEG Alpha Rhythms

Honorton (1969b) observed, as had some earlier investigators (see his review), that forced-choice ESP-task performance correlated significantly with a measure of the percentage of time each subject showed occipital alpha rhythms during ESP testing (percent-time alpha). He showed, also, that significant psi-hitting was associated with high-alpha runs and that subjects above the median in alpha production scored significantly higher than those below the median. He felt that this supported the idea that a relaxed, somewhat passive mental state favored above-chance ESP-task performance. He also noted that the runs with a lower percent-time alpha showed an equally strong tendency toward psi-missing. Perhaps, he surmised, this was due to cognitive distortion because of the mental activity that desynchronized alpha. Honorton noted that psi researchers in other fields had recently demonstrated the possibility of training subjects to produce a higher abundance of alpha rhythms; the next step in the research therefore might profitably be to use feedback techniques to train alpha in the hope that this would enhance ESP-task performance. He also noted the desirability of using subjects' self-reports to assess alterations in awareness during the alpha training and ESP testing. Perhaps the relationship of alpha abundance to ESP-task performance would depend on the presence of an altered state of awareness.

His next study (Honorton & Carbone, 1971) involved an alpha-training paradigm and ESP testing. The results of this study must have been very disappointing: Alpha training was not successful, and all Honorton had to show that might be parapsychologically relevant was a significantly negative correlation between ESP-task performance and alpha during periods without alpha feedback. This was roughly comparable in magnitude, but opposite in direction, to the positive alpha-ESP correlation he had found (1969b) that had inspired this study. (Honorton and Carbone noted, though, that his earlier study had involved a between-subjects comparison, whereas their study had involved a within-subjects comparison.) Despite these disappointing outcomes, Honorton persevered with the biofeedback approach.

The subsequent alpha-feedback study (Honorton, Davidson, & Bindler, 1971) did much to redress the earlier failure and to move beyond it. Apart from its importance for parapsychology, this study made contributions to the emerging science of biofeedback and, more generally, to psychophysiology. These aspects were presented at the annual meeting of the Bio-Feedback Research Society, New Orleans, November 23, 1970. With this biofeedback-ESP work, Honorton made contributions to parapsychological and nonparapsychological science—the latter will not be reviewed here—and cultivated relationships with nonparapsychologists. Here is a model that other para psychologists could profitably emulate: Design studies so they can make contributions both to parapsychology and to areas of traditional psychology (or other sciences).

His earlier failure (Honorton & Carbone, 1971) to find evidence of successful alpha-feedback training had led Honorton to believe that his training regimen had been too lengthy. In the Honorton, Davidson, and Bindler (1971) study, subjects were selected who showed at least 10% alpha in an initial baseline period. (Rationale: How can you train a response that is not there to train?) They then were trained for alpha control in a single session. Honorton's interest in internal states and his conviction that physiological measures alone cannot adequately specify internal state caused him to incorporate state-report ratings into this study. Convergent operations were necessary, he believed, for the specification of state. He also included a postexperimental interview about internal experiences and feelings related to state. ESP testing, which was done on the day following alpha training, involved four ESP runs with attempted alpha generation and four with attempted alpha suppression. State reports were elicited at the end of each ESP run. They were also elicited during the alpha-training session at the end of both trial and rest periods.

Honorton et al. (1971) carefully documented (a) significant evidence of alpha training during the first session and (b) significantly more alpha during generation than during suppression periods at the time of ESP testing (with alpha feedback during each run). Also, there was evidence that state reports were related to percent-time alpha when results were pooled across generation and suppression periods (although the latter makes these results difficult to interpret). The guns seemed loaded for rabbit!

The Honorton et al. (1971) study was a well-conceived, sophisticated initial study in a difficult area, a study far ahead of anything previous in this area. The comments that follow are intended simply to show what would have to be done to clarify the interpretation of a study such as this and what would be needed to build effectively on the study's foundation.

Interpretation of the reported alpha-state relationship, including its relevance to ESP-task performance, is clouded by the fact that all participants, even during ESP testing, had external sensory feedback about alpha abundance. Judgments of state might have been influenced by the presence or absence of the alpha-feedback tone, instead of by inner experience and feelings. Judgments of state, as noted earlier, are attributional in character. Instructions emphasized their being made promptly, without reflection. It would be surprising if state reports were not influenced by the presence or absence of the alpha-feedback tone (perhaps in interaction with knowledge of the generate-suppress instructions). These considerations suggest the need for certain control groups if the data are to be interpreted clearly, but this is not the place to discuss the nature of those groups. The design that was used did not address the potentially serious problem of reactivity that inheres in state-report investigations. It also did not address the possibility that the parapsychological findings might have been mediated by expectancies generated by subjects' reflections on their state-related attributions (state reports), rather than by state per se.

Although ESP-task performance did not vary significantly as a function of the alpha suppression and generation instructions, it did, as hypothesized, vary as a joint function of the suppression-generation manipulation and whether participants, under those circumstances, reported themselves in a high or low state of internalization of attention. No formal test of the interaction was done, but there does appear to have been an interaction. Although the highest ESP-task performance was found, as anticipated, for subjects who experienced a high internalization level (high state) during alpha generation, the only statistically significant combination of these circumstances was when subjects tried to generate alpha but reported themselves as in a low level of internalized attention. Perhaps the poor ESP-task performance here occurred because the subject believed himself or herself to be in a state clearly contrary to the investigator's expectations and intentions but nonetheless had to do an ESP task. The psi-missing here might be due to negative expectations. One way to check on this would be to examine expectations generated by the various combinations of instructions (generate or suppress) and reported internal state (high or low).

A subsequent within-subjects analysis was based on a very different kind of breakdown. Honorton et al. (1971) compared within-subject performance for suppression and generation periods, but they did this analysis separately for three groups of subjects: those with (a) high state reports in both conditions, (b) low state reports in both conditions, and (c) high state reports in generation and low state reports in suppression. The mean ESP score farthest below MCE was that of participants who had low state reports under alpha-generation instructions (and who also happened to have had low state reports under suppression). ESP-task performance was significantly below MCE here (measured by *CR* based on trials). (No subjects gave low state reports under generation and high state reports under suppression.) The mean ESP score farthest above MCE was for participants who had high state reports under alpha-generation instructions (and who also happened to have had low state reports under suppression). ESP-task performance was significantly above MCE here (measured by *CR* based on trials). It is reasonable to suppose that expectations for ESP-task performance were very low for subjects in the former circumstance and maximal for those in the latter, given the demand characteristics of the situation. Whether state factors or expectancy factors (or some other factors or combination of factors) provide the best explanation of this pattern of outcomes cannot presently be determined.

Honorton et al. (1971) used postexperimental interview data to examine whether participants had had certain types of altered-states-related experiences (e.g., body-image changes, somatic effects, or quasi-hallucinatory experiences) during the study. They showed that participants with such experiences (apparently, during alpha generation) had significantly higher mean ESP-task performance under generation than under suppression. Although this group's alpha-generation ESP mean was above MCE and its alpha-suppression ESP mean was below MCE, both effects were of similar magnitude. If we assume that this group's odd experiences occurred during generation, as seems likely, the results fit nicely with the idea that expectancy might have meditated the effects.

The Honorton et al. (1971) study was at the forefront of research for the period and was well conceived. It brought together alpha biofeedback, EEG recording, state reports (during and after testing), and ESP testing. It was an ambitious project. Like many ground-breaking studies in diverse areas of behavioral science it raises more questions than it answers. No single study that is breaking new ground can be expected to resolve every potential ambiguity.

Partial Sensory Deprivation

As a study of ESP-task performance in a (partial) sensory-deprivation setting, the work of Honorton, Drucker, and Hermon (1973) was a direct predecessor of Honorton's later ganzfeld research. It must have encouraged him to move in that direction. It was also, empirically and conceptually, a follow-up of the Honorton et al. (1971) alpha-feedback study discussed in the preceding paragraph. Honorton et al. (1973), though, attempted to use sensory deprivation to produce an internal-attention state.

Honorton well knew that individuals would respond differently to this partial-sensory-deprivation situation, that some would tend much more strongly than others to enter an internally focused state. If entering such a state should be important to ESP-task performance, a measure of the internal direction of attention (or shift in direction) would be needed to predict such performance. Consequently, Honorton used the same state-report scale that he had successfully used in earlier work and had found to be related both to physiological measures and ESP-task performance (Honorton, 1972b; Honorton et al., 1971).

The blindfolded participant was strapped into a suspended metal cradle that was slowly rotated by the experimenter at the start of the session; thereafter, more subtle movement continued as a result of movements of the subject's body (largely unintentional ones). The telepathic agent, who was housed in another room, looked at the target picture only during the last ten minutes of the session. Apparently, this was done to give the participant time to enter an altered state before the agent began transmission. State reports were elicited every five minutes during the 30-minute session. The subject reported mentation only at the end of the procedure. Mentation was elicited, at session's end, through an interview of the participant by the experimenter. There were 30 participants, a substantial study.

The ESP-test procedure here left something to be desired in three respects: (a) A duplicate copy of the target was not used for judging. Fortunately, there was no contact between the target and the participant before judging; (b) although the target was chosen randomly, the seven foils or control pictures (to be judged, along with the target, for similarity to mentation) were not thus chosen. Honorton selected them, ad libitum at the end of each session, to be different from one another and from the target; (c) Honorton then shuffled the eight pictures himself (albeit face down). These features raise questions about the adequacy of the design as a study of ESP.

Judging was done by the participant, who, blind to the identity of the target, ranked the eight pictures for degree of correspondence with mentation. A hit was later scored if the participants gave any one of the top four (of eight) correspondence rankings to the target. The level of success across participants was not significant, but those with above-mean state reports showed significant psi-hitting, whereas those below that mean were slightly below MCE. Comparable results were found when subjects above and below the mean on state-report shift (from the first to the last ten minutes of the

session) were compared. Honorton did not report whether the high-
and low-state (or shift) groups scored significantly differently on the
ESP task, but with ESP-task hit or miss as the predictor variable,
mean-state shift was significantly different for hitters and missers.
The ESP results here are remarkably parallel to the state (and especially to the state-shift) results in earlier studies by Honorton and
colleagues (Honorton, 1972b; Honorton, Davidson, & Bindler,
1971).

The Honorton et al. (1973) findings relating state shift (and state
per se) to ESP-task performance are not easy to interpret. They
might reflect a true relationship between the degree of development
of an internal-attention state and ESP-task performance, just as
Honorton seemed to think. On the other hand, the proper interpretation of these findings remains in limbo. Having to give state
reports might be central to what was found here. In other words,
the effect might have been mediated by expectations, rather than by
state per se, and those expectations might themselves have been influenced by the attributional act required to give state reports. Honorton, through diverse replications of the state-related effects, has
posed an important agenda for future process-oriented work. Future empirical work might best be guided by process-oriented meta-
analysis of this domain.

Honorton did not tarry to sort out what might be happening
here. He moved ahead to developing and refining work in the ganzfeld. That work logically followed from the ideas guiding his earlier
work on internal-attention states and from its success. The ganzfeld
work did little to clarify the reason(s) for its own ESP success (with
the exception of the evidence, discussed earlier, about individual
differences and ESP-task performance). Instead, Honorton busied
himself with providing evidence for replicability within a paradigm
and for strengthening that evidence against nonparapsychological
interpretations. These facts say much, in my view, about the motivation that drove him to his great productivity. He was interested in
having rabbit stew and providing others with the necessary steps for
having it themselves. His not having resolved the interpretation of
his state-shift findings before moving to the ganzfeld paradigm suggests, not that he was unaware of the ambiguities in the state-shift
work, but that he probably was more interested in having rabbit
stew than in clarifying rabbit psychology.

Process-Relevant Work in Ganzfeld

Although the ganzfeld work of Honorton seemed directed more
at replicability within a paradigm than at understanding process,

some of the ganzfeld findings warrant consideration here because of their possible relevance to process.

Stimulation level. In Honorton's automated ganzfeld work the participant was allowed, at the beginning of the session, to set both the level of noise heard through the headset and the intensity of the light used to illuminate the acetate hemispheres over the eyes (see details in Honorton et al., 1990). Honorton et al. (1990) reported the point-biserial correlations between the levels of these variables that the subject set for a given session and whether the ESP outcome was a direct hit. These correlations did not differ significantly from zero, despite their being based on hundreds of sessions.

What this reveals about process is far from clear. First, the statistical model used was linear, and there might have been a nonlinear function relating these variables to ESP-task performance. Second, the noise-light aspects of stimulation level were set by the subject, not by experimental manipulation. Traits of participants (e.g., Geen, 1984, regarding Extraversion and preferred level of stimulation) might have influenced their preference for stimulation level. What resulted might have been an optimal level for that person in that setting. This alone might virtually have insured no relationship between stimulation level and success. Honorton et al. (1990) reported a very substantial and significant positive correlation between the noise and light settings. This is compatible with the suggestion above that participant trait(s) or individual differences affected choice of stimulation level. Wisely, Honorton and colleagues did not attempt to interpret these null correlations under these circumstances.

Allowing participants to select their own stimulation level—as Honorton did—might be important to ganzfeld ESP-task success. Each participant would thus be able to optimize his or her stimulation level for the setting at hand, and this might reduce the degree to which the individual differences would interact with the test situation (see Stanford, Frank, Kass, & Skoll, 1989, for discussion of this rationale). Consequently, subject choice of stimulation level should reduce error variance in the data. It is possible that this freedom to adjust stimulation level was important to the overall success of the ganzfeld paradigm, an overall success that Honorton did not have with some of the other paradigms (e.g., the partial-sensory-deprivation cradle; Honorton et al., 1973). Having said this much, it is well to note that the roles of the noise and light levels in ganzfeld-ESP work remain unclarified because these variables were not experimentally manipulated and then examined for their potential interaction with relevant individual differences. It is again clear that

Honorton was more interested in having rabbit stew than in studying rabbit psychology.

Dynamic versus static targets. The work contrasting dynamic and static targets may be one of Honorton's most important contributions to process-oriented parapsychology. Dynamic targets, in the ganzfeld work, consisted of short video segments; static targets were still pictures. In the automated ganzfeld work the former targets were associated with significant success at a high level; the latter, with nonsignificant performance (Honorton et al., 1990). Honorton et al. (1990) found a large and significant point-biserial correlation between series effect size and target type. They also noted what seemed to them a comparable effect in the earlier ganzfeld series, those included in Honorton's meta-analysis (1985). The contrast there was between stereoscopic *View Master* slide reels and single pictures or slides. The former presents several slides all centered on a common theme. Honorton et al. (1990) regarded the former as dynamic targets, the latter as static. Although they did not discuss the matter in this particular way, a basis for arguing the comparability of the truly dynamic (video) targets and the *View Master* reel targets is that both insure a temporally changing range of simulation for the agent. The dynamic targets, thus broadly defined, were associated with significantly larger effect sizes in both the automated ganzfeld series and in the meta-analysis database. Honorton et al. (1990) argued that this "evidence strongly indicates that dynamic targets are more accurately retrieved than static targets" (p. 129).

I am not sure whether the statement just quoted was intended to imply a theoretical interpretation of this finding (e.g., that the effect is due to greater extrasensory encodability for dynamic targets). In any event, the interpretation of this finding is decidedly ambiguous.

In some of the work involved in this contrast, either dynamic or static targets alone were used in a given series, and the experimenter (and conceivably the research participant) knew ahead of time which target type was being used. This might have provided opportunity for experimenter effects (expectations) to play a role, perhaps mediated by nonverbal or even verbal manifestations of enthusiasm and confidence that might have been communicated to the research participant. If subjects were informed about target type ahead of time, that, too, might have played a role. Even in series in which both types of targets were used, I have been unable to ascertain from published sources that both experimenter and subject were fully blind about the nature of the target, although my recollection (personal communication from Honorton) is that this was the case in some series. It is unfortunate that Honorton et al. (1990) did not adequately clarify these matters, given the emphasis on the target-type findings in their discussion. Meta-analysis might profitably have been used to show whether blindness affected the relationship between hitting and target type. Additional experimental work is warranted in which both experimenter and subject-expectancy effects are rigorously controlled.

A potential competing explanation for the superior performance with dynamic targets might involve active-agent telepathy. As noted above, both the video segments and the *View Master* reels provide for the agent a changing set of images. A possible factor in the greater success with dynamic targets might be that when a given image changes, the agent is no longer mentally focusing on the former one. There is suggestive (nonquantitative) evidence from older work relevant to telepathy that an image is more likely to be received by the percipient when it is not in the conscious focus of the agent, and there is even the suggestion that information that has recently left the focus of consciousness of the telepathic agent might be particularly effective (e.g., Warcollier, 1938, and various other sources as cited in Stanford, 1974). It is conceivable that dynamic targets gain some of their efficacy by allowing the agent to release conscious attention from target elements (without feeling intimidated by having done so). This possibility warrants investigation, though it is presently speculative and is based on nonexperimental, nonquantitative evidence.

Nonparapsychological work by Marcel (1980) involving backward-masked primes suggests that preconsciously presented verbal stimuli semantically prime *all* their related meanings, which is not true of verbal stimuli presented consciously as primes. If this result should hold for pictorial as well as verbal stimuli, this might explain why pictorial stimuli recently, but not presently, in the conscious focus of the agent seem to be effectively transmitted. (It might also suggest that stimuli presented "subliminally" to the agent would be particularly well retrieved; see later discussion of the work of Smith, Tremmel, & Honorton, 1976.) With the target being presented outside the constraints of focused attention, diverse associations may be activated in the agent, and this may increase the chance that a corresponding trace might be activated in the percipient. Perhaps this adds some credibility to the idea that the greater proficiency of dynamic targets lies in the domain of how they affect the agent. Dynamic targets serially stimulate the agent, perhaps encouraging this rich form of preconscious processing of the material that has recently disappeared (to be replaced by the next scene or phase of movement).

Another possibility is that dynamic targets are more interesting, involving, and motivating for the agent. Perhaps dynamic targets are more thoroughly processed by the agent.

There are several considerations that support the possibility of a percipient-based effect of such targets. On the basis of his telepathy work, Warcollier (1963) felt strongly that moving objects (albeit those depicted statically) made particularly good targets, and he discussed this matter at some length. If there is a percipient-based (as opposed to a telepathic-agent-based) efficacy to dynamic targets, might the efficacy of dynamic targets (or static targets suggesting dynamism) derive from their capacity to garner attention? This is one possibility, but there are others.

Motion has diverse functions in perception, including its importantance for perceptually differentiating figure and ground (Sekuler, Anstis, Braddick, Brandt, Movshon, & Orban, 1990). This feature of visual perception might itself be a reason for superiority of dynamic images, as in video images. It might make a moving figure stand out relative to the background.

Motion that differentiates figure from ground would not appear relevant to the success obtained with *View Master* reels. What might be important there is that figure and ground are especially distinct, as perceived by the agent, thanks to the stereoscopic nature of the image.

The superiority of dynamic targets also might be due to the judging process. One judgment-related possibility is that any enhancement of figure-ground discriminability might aid judging. Let us assume that ESP is occurring in the ganzfeld sessions, as seems reasonable (Honorton, 1985; Honorton et al., 1990). Discriminating the target from the foils (control pictures) might be easier with dynamic targets because the mentation-target (or mentation-foil) correspondences might be more detectable or noticeable when figures stand out from the ground (because of motion or stereoscopic properties). Even if the effect were mediated by some mechanism other than figure-ground relationships (e.g., by enhanced interest in the depicted materials), the consequences might be created during judging, instead of, or in addition to, any effects on psi-mediated encoding. Dynamic targets might, for example, more strongly interest and motivate judges. If ESP were occurring, this would lead to superiority for dynamic targets.

Honorton's exciting work on dynamic versus static targets cries out for follow-up and extension. It could lead to some of the most theoretically rich and interesting work ever undertaken in parapsychology. It might even provide conceptual links with findings in sensory-perceptual or cognitive psychology. If so, Honorton's abiding interest in forging links between parapsychology and psychology would have been realized in a highly meaningful way.

Work with direct relevance to the role of the telepathic agent. Smith, Tremmel, and Honorton (1976) compared information retrieval rates for ESP subjects in ganzfeld and for telepathic agents who sensorially viewed the target for only one millisecond. The targets here were drawn from the special target series developed by Honorton (1975a) to allow more objective determination of the rate of information retrieval than could be had in traditional free-response work. Each of the 1,024 targets in the series included each of 10 content categories, either present or absent, on a random-permutation basis. Thus, an ESP score could be developed for each participant, one ranging from 0 to 10 bits correct. This target system was used for a relatively brief time in Honorton's work, but he eventually seemed to become disenchanted with it, perhaps because of the artificiality of the stimuli involved. In the Smith et al. (1976) study it was found that the retrieval rates for ESP and for weak sensory stimulation were similar, with the latter only slightly higher.

An important feature of this study was a manipulation of whether the agent received the aforementioned weak stimulation from the target or viewed it normally for 10 minutes. The percipient was not told which agent-stimulation condition was being used. Weak sensory stimulation for the agent was associated with significant retrieval by the percipient. Retrieval by the percipient did not approach significance with 10-minute exposures for the agent. This set of findings is reminiscent of Warcollier's findings that information not in the conscious focus of the agent was particularly likely to be transmitted. Here was a very interesting manipulation that held potential for understanding the role of the agent. So far as I know, this set of findings was not followed up. Honorton was the last of the three authors of this report, and I do not know what role, if any, he played in the planning of this study.

Miscellaneous Process-Relevant Work

Social Factors

The meta-analysis of forced-choice precognition studies by Honorton and Ferrari (1989) hinted at a possible social-psychological effect. Studies that tested subjects in groups showed significantly smaller effect sizes than those that tested them individually. Perhaps testing persons in groups creates less of a sense of responsibility for the overall outcome—a "Let George (or Jill) do it" mentality—by analogy with the well-documented social-loafing phenomenon (e.g., Latané, Williams, & Harkins, 1979). Whether this type of social effect is present in this database cannot be determined from available data. This difference might be due to a selection factor whereby studies with individual testing involved more talented subjects. There might also be other confounds. This meta-analytic finding warrants follow-up studies with deliberate experimental manipulation of this variable.

One of Honorton's process-oriented studies was intended to illumine the problem of replicability in parapsychology. It addressed the question of whether the quality of social interaction between the experimenter and participants was a factor in ESP-task performance (Honorton, Ramsey, & Cabbibo, 1975). Specifically, Honorton and colleagues studied whether interaction with a *friendly, casual,* and *supportive* experimenter would favor higher ESP-task performance than with one who was *abrupt, formal,* and *unfriendly.* This quality-of-social-interaction variable was experimentally manipulated and the efficacy of the manipulation was checked by postexperimental questionnaire. The manipulation apparently did create the social impression that was intended (although the questionnaire used to assess this was not published), and the effects on ESP-task performance were also as expected.

The report of the study was submitted to *Science*, apparently in an effort to explain to nonparapsychological scientists some of the problems of replicability in parapsychology. It unsuccessfully went through two rounds of refereeing. In the process, it engendered some remarkable referees' comments (which were published in Honorton et al., 1975).

This study established a solid case for investigating how the quality of experimenter-subject social interaction affects ESP-task performance. It successfully used rigorous methodology to address an important hypothesis about the variability in outcomes in ESP research. The terse written report of this work, though, was deficient in that anyone wishing to try to replicate the study would have little indication of how to operationalize the independent variable.

Psi-Mediated Experimenter Effects

In considering why some investigators obtain the desired effect but others do not, Honorton (1991) pointed to the numerous objective, nonsocial differences in their superficially similar research paradigms and laboratory settings. He also asked experimenters to reflect on their styles of interacting with participants. Consideration of those factors would be more useful, he thought, than spinning yarns about experimenter psi. He decried the readiness of some parapsychologists to invoke experimenter psi for replication failures when there are many other, less far-fetched, explanations.

It was not that Honorton denied the possibility of experimenter-psi effects. Instead, he grew weary, in his last years, of the plethora of untested claims about this problem that threatened the credibility of parapsychology and discouraged investigators' careful reexamination of their own research practices, physical settings, and social milieux. He thought that experimenter-psi advocates should produce supportive data instead of supportive verbiage.

Notwithstanding Honorton's concerns about the overzealousness of some experimenter-psi advocates, near the conclusion of his Parapsychological Association Presidential Address (1975, published in 1976), he courageously detailed evidence that he had, in three of his own studies, exerted unconscious experimenter goal-relevant influences on random event generators (REGs). (See, also, Honorton & Barksdale, 1972). He ended his address by urging that investigators give serious consideration to experimenter-psi effects. This was one of Honorton's agendas that he was unable (or perhaps unready) to carry to fruition in his own laboratory.

This was probably unfortunate because target selection by REG was at the heart of his automated ganzfeld paradigm and because he, by his own admission (1976), was able to produce unconscious experimenter goal-relevant REG effects. Success in the ganzfeld paradigm might have occurred because of an REG effect related either to the experimenter or to the subject, in lieu of (or along with) extrasensory encoding of the target by the subject's mind. REG target selections might have been made inadvertently through unconscious experimenter (or subject) psi such that they would match subject mentation tendencies during ganzfeld. If this happened, it would greatly influence the scientific interpretation of this work and might affect cross-experimenter replicability. In any event, there is a simple remedy for this kind of problem (Stanford, 1981).

On a number of occasions I suggested to Honorton that he replace the REG target-selection paradigm with one less amenable to experimenter-psi influence, especially given his own preference for interpreting the outcomes as due to ESP by research participants and as due to psychophysical noise reduction. In conversations with me he never agreed to remove the REG from his ganzfeld paradigm. He did, though, agree—perhaps two years before his laboratory in Princeton closed—to try to implement in his ganzfeld design both REG and non-REG target selection (e.g., based on computerized sampling of a random number table) to allow a comparison of outcomes. He never got around to that before his laboratory closed. I mentioned this matter to him in our last meeting (August, 1992) before his untimely passing. He said he would consider implementing this comparison in at least some of his work at Edinburgh. His busy life was cut short before he was able to do this.

The Roles of Feedback and Temporal Interval in Precognition Studies

The meta-analysis of forced-choice precognition studies (Honorton & Ferrari, 1989) provided two tantalizing findings that deserve experimental follow-up. The quality of feedback that subjects got about their ESP performance showed a low, but significantly positive, correlation with effect size. Also, the time between the subject's response and target selection showed a low, but significantly negative, correlation with effect size. Honorton and Ferrari noted that this latter finding might not indicate an intrinsic boundary condition: It held only for unselected subjects, and there was a nonsignificant positive correlation of these variables for selected subjects. The findings on temporal interval suggest the need for experimental work with subjects and experimenters blind, at the time of testing, to the temporal interval.

These two sets of findings indicate what Honorton knew well: Meta-analysis can suggest hypotheses not examined in individual studies (Cooper & Lemke, 1991). This is because it allows comparison of effect sizes from studies with different characteristics. In this particular respect, it is a tool for fostering new research rather than a basis for conclusions. Any patterns thus discovered are essentially correlational rather than experimental in character, and cannot, therefore, legitimately be used for drawing conclusions about process. Their usefulness is in fostering research on questions that might not otherwise have arisen.

Process-Oriented Work with a Special Subject

Honorton (1987) showed that Malcolm Bessent, a subject who had done very well in earlier precognition work, scored significantly positively on precognition trials but nonsignificantly on real-time clairvoyance trials. Moreover, Bessent was blind to which trial involved which target mode. The difference of performance on the two modes was statistically significant. This was important and innovative work because target mode was automatically randomly selected just before each run and Bessent did not learn its nature until the end of each run. (The experimenter also remained blind to this selection.) In many ways, this target-mode phase of the study was a model of what process-oriented work with a talented subject should be.

Honorton had long been interested in the kinds of cues used by subjects in making their calls. Such cues might provide a basis on which the subject could discriminate psi cues from nonpsi information. In this report he discussed evidence that those calls for which Bessent based his response on impressions (i.e., images or verbal associations) were more accurate than those involving simply a feeling (i.e., he felt drawn to that choice) or a guess (i.e., he could not identify a basis for the choice). Honorton construed this as evidence for an ability to discriminate between cues related to hitting and missing. This suggestion is doubtful. Any judgment about whether impressions (as contrasted with feelings or guesses) have special efficacy must be based on comparing the hit rates for impression-based responses and feeling-based ones (or guess-based ones). The impression-based trials achieved a hit rate that did not differ significantly from that of feeling-based ones; $z = .57$, ns (my computation). Also, the contrast of hit rates for impressions and for feelings and guesses combined was not significant; $z = .64$, ns (my computation). Honorton's argument for a cognitive basis for discriminating hits and misses was not supported by these data.

A much more promising finding was that, for precognition trials, after the "pack" (choice options) had been presented on the computer monitor, Bessent took significantly longer to indicate a choice on hits than on misses. (This did not occur in the case of the clairvoyance trials.) This type of fine-grained response-based analysis could be important in understanding extrasensory function. It is another respect in which this study broke important ground.

Reflection

Honorton contributed many replicated findings in a variety of areas having relevance to process. Many of these findings came from his experimental work; several emerged from meta-analyses.

The proper interpretation of most of his findings remains unclear, but many of them may be among the most important clues presently available to researchers. To repeat just one example, his well-supported finding of superior performance for dynamic, as opposed to static, targets in ganzfeld poses a singularly important agenda for process-oriented work. This problem is amenable to experimental study, and it poses some intriguing theoretical questions.

It should not be surprising that his multifaceted research program produced a series of replicated findings that still challenge interpretation. The driving force behind his work seemed to be producing replicable evidence with a particular paradigm and getting others to do likewise. The objective was to find something that worked reliably, across investigators and laboratories. Honorton saw that understanding process would be much easier after finding a dependable way to lure the rabbit into the laboratory. In his view, replicability, even without scientific understanding, would force the scientific community to begin to address parapsychological claims. In the wake of this, understanding would come. In the interim, first things first.

Honorton appreciated the scientific importance of understanding process, but he was, in many ways, more a pragmatist than a theoretician. He understood the difference between finding something that works and knowing why it works.

In planning his research program he drew from scientific and nonscientific sources, such as the ancient *Yoga Aphorisms* of Patanjali and the personal insights of the people who came to his laboratory to share their experiences and to participate in his work. His concept of psychophysical noise reduction was strongly influenced by Patanjali's yoga treatise. Honorton was singularly open to any inputs that might provide useful hints about luring the rabbit. He used insights derived from several areas of psychology, from biofeedback, from folk and religious tradition, and from what practitioners told him. He was a careful listener, an avid reader, and a great borrower (always with full and proper credit). He was a syncretist and a bold pragmatist who succeeded famously in luring the rabbit into his laboratory and in showing others how it is done. In the process, he provided manifold clues to the behavior of this sometimes-elusive creature.

References

ARONSON, E., ELLSWORTH, P. C., CARLSMITH, J. M., & GONZALES, M. H. (1990). *Methods of research in social psychology* (2nd ed.). New York: McGraw-Hill.

BROUGHTON, R. S., KANTHAMANI, H., & KHILJI, A. (1990). Assessing the PRL success model on an independent ganzfeld database. In L. A. Henkel & J. Palmer (Eds.), *Research in parapsychology 1989* (pp. 32–35). Metuchen, NJ: Scarecrow.

COOPER, H. M., & LEMKE, K. M. (1991). On the role of meta-analysis in personality and social psychology. *Personality and Social Psychology Bulletin,* **17,** 245–251.

GEEN, R. G. (1984). Preferred stimulation levels in introverts and extraverts: Effects on arousal and performance. *Journal of Personality and Social Psychology,* **46,** 1303–1312.

GEORGE, L. (1981). A survey of research into the relationships between imagery and psi. *Journal of Parapsychology,* **45,** 121–146.

HONORTON, C. (1964). Separation of high- and low-scoring ESP subjects through hypnotic preparation. *Journal of Parapsychology,* **28,** 250–257.

HONORTON, C. (1965). The relationship of ESP and manifest anxiety level. *Proceedings of the Parapsychological Association,* **2,** 30–31.

HONORTON, C. (1966). A further separation of high- and low-scoring subjects through hypnotic preparation. *Journal of Parapsychology,* **30,** 172–183.

HONORTON, C. (1967). Creativity and precognition scoring level. *Journal of Parapsychology,* **31,** 29–42.

HONORTON, C. (1969a). A combination of techniques for the separation of high- and low-scoring subjects. Experiments with hypnotic and waking-imagination instructions. *Journal of the American Society for Psychical Research,* **63,** 69–82.

HONORTON, C. (1969b). Relationship between EEG alpha activity and ESP in card-guessing performance. *Journal of the American Society for Psychical Research,* **63,** 365–374.

HONORTON, C. (1970). Effects of feedback on discrimination between correct and incorrect ESP responses. *Journal of the American Society for Psychical Research,* **64,** 404–410.

HONORTON, C. (1971). Effects of feedback on discrimination between correct and incorrect ESP responses: A replication study. *Journal of the American Society for Psychical Research,* **65,** 155–161.

HONORTON, C. (1972a). Reported frequency of dream recall and ESP. *Journal of the American Society for Psychical Research,* **66,** 369–374.

HONORTON, C. (1972b). Significant factors in hypnotically-induced clairvoyant dreams. *Journal of the American Society for Psychical Research,* **66,** 86–102.

HONORTON, C. (1975a). Objective determination of information rate in psi tasks with pictorial stimuli. *Journal of the American Society for Psychical Research,* **69,** 353–359.

HONORTON, C. (1975b). Psi and mental imagery: Keeping score on the Betts scale. *Journal of the American Society for Psychical Research,* **69,** 327–332.

HONORTON, C. (1976). Has science developed the competence to confront claims of the paranormal? (Presidential Address, Parapsychological Association 18th Annual Convention, August 21-23, 1975.) In J. D. Morris, W. G. Roll, & R. L. Morris (Eds.), *Research in parapsychology 1975* (pp. 199–223). Metuchen, NJ: Scarecrow.

HONORTON, C. (1977). Psi and internal attention states. In B. B. Wolman (Ed.), *Handbook of parapsychology* (pp. 435–472). New York: Van Nostrand Reinhold.

HONORTON, C. (1985). Meta-analysis of psi ganzfeld research: A resposne to Hyman. *Journal of Parapsychology,* **49,** 51–91.

HONORTON, C. (1987). Precognition and real-time ESP performance in a computer task with an exceptional subject. *Journal of Parapsychology,* **51,** 291–320.

HONORTON, C. (1991). [Honorton's remarks in a panel discussion, "Increasing Psychic Reliability," presented at the 33rd Annual Convention of the Parapsychological Association, Chevy Chase, MD, August 16–20, 1990.] *Journal of Parapsychology,* **55,** 74–75.

HONORTON, C. (1992). The ganzfeld novice: Four predictors of initial ESP performance. In E. W. Cook (Ed.), *The Parapsychological Association 35th annual convention: Proceedings of presented papers* (pp. 51–58). Durham, NC: Parapsychological Association, Inc.

HONORTON, C., BARKER, P., VARVOGLIS, M., BERGER, R., & SCHECHTER, E. (1986). First-timers: An exploration of factors affecting initial psi ganzfeld performance. In D. H. Weiner & D. I. Radin (Eds.), *Research in parapsychology 1985* (pp. 28–32). Metuchen, NJ: Scarecrow.

HONORTON, C., & BARKSDALE, W. (1972). PK performance with waking suggestions for muscle tension versus relaxation. *Journal of the American Society for Psychical Research,* **66,** 208–214.

HONORTON, C., BERGER, R. E., VARVOGLIS, M. P., QUANT, M., DERR, P., SCHECHTER, E. I., & FERRARI, D. C. (1990). Psi communication in the ganzfeld: Experiments with an automated testing system and a comparison with a meta-analysis of earlier studies. *Journal of Parapsychology,* **54,** 99–139.

HONORTON, C., & CARBONE, M. (1971). A preliminary study of feedback-augmented EEG alpha activity and ESP card-guessing performance. *Journal of the American Society for Psychical Research,* **65,** 66–74.

HONORTON, C., DAVIDSON, R., & BINDLER, P. (1971). Feedback-augmented EEG alpha, shifts in subjective state, and ESP card-guessing performance. *Journal of the American Society for Psychical Research,* **65,** 308–323.

HONORTON, C., DRUCKER, S. A., & HERMON, H. C. (1973). Shifts in subjective state and ESP under conditions of partial sensory deprivation: A preliminary study. *Journal of the American Society for Psychical Research,* **67,** 191–196.

HONORTON, C., & FERRARI, D. C. (1989). "Future telling": A meta-analysis of forced-choice precognition experiments. *Journal of Parapsychology,* **53,** 281–308.

HONORTON, C., FERRARI, D. C., & BEM, D. J. (1992). Extraversion and ESP performance: A meta-analysis and a new confirmation. In L. A. Henkel & G. R. Schmeidler (Eds.), *Research in parapsychology 1990* (pp. 35–38). Metuchen, NJ: Scarecrow.

HONORTON, C., & KRIPPNER, S. (1969). Hypnosis and ESP performance: A review of the experimental literature. *Journal of the American Society for Psychical Research, 63*, 214–252.

HONORTON, C., & RAMSEY, M., & CABIBBO, C. (1975). Experimenter effects in extrasensory perception. *Journal of the American Society for Psychical Research, 69*, 135–149.

HONORTON, C., & SCHECHTER, E. I. (1987). Ganzfeld target retrieval with an automated testing system: A model for initial ganzfeld success. *Research in parapsychology 1986* (pp. 36–39). Metuchen, NJ: Scarecrow.

HONORTON, C., & STUMP, J. P. (1969). A preliminary study of hypnotically-induced clairvoyant dreams. *Journal of the American Society for Psychical Research, 63*, 175–184.

HONORTON, C., TIERNEY, L., & TORRES, D. (1974). The role of mental imagery in psi-mediation. *Journal of the American Society for Psychical Research, 68*, 385–394.

JACKSON, M., FRANZOI, S., & SCHMEIDLER, G. R. (1977). Effects of feedback on ESP: A curious partial replication. *Journal of the American Society for Psychical Research, 71*, 147–155.

JOHNSON, M. (1968). Relationship between dream recall and scoring direction. *Journal of Parapsychology, 32*, 56–57. (Abstract)

KENNEDY, J. E. (1979). Methodological problems in free-response ESP experiments. *Journal of the American Society for Psychical Research, 73*, 1–15.

KREIMAN, N., & IVNISKY, D. (1973). [Effects of feedback on ESP responses.] *Cuadernos de Parapsicología, 6*(2), 1–10. (Abstract in *Journal of Parapsychology, 37*, 369).

KRISHNA, S. R., & RAO, K. R. (1991). Effect of ESP feedback on subjects' responses to a personality questionnaire. *Journal of Parapsychology, 55*, 147–158.

LATANÉ, B., WILLIAMS, K., & HARKINS, S. (1979). Many hands make light the work: The causes and consequences of social loafing. *Journal of Personality and Social Psychology, 37*, 822–832.

MARCEL, A. J. (1980). Conscious and preconscious recognition of polysemous words: Locating the selective effects of prior verbal context. In R. S. Nickerson (Ed.), *Attention and performance VIII* (pp. 435–457). Hillsdale, NJ: Lawrence Erlbaum Associates.

McCALLAM, E., & HONORTON, C. (1973). Effects of feedback on discrimination between correct and incorrect ESP responses: A further replication and extension. *Journal of the American Society for Psychical Research, 67*, 77–85. (Note: The April 1973 number of the *Journal of the American*

Society for Psychical Research, Vol. 67, carried a correction, on page 196, of the spelling of the surname "McCallam." It should have appeared as "McCollam." The originally published spelling was used in this paper to facilitate bibliographic searches).

PALMER, J. (1978). Extrasensory perception: Research findings. In S. Krippner (Ed.), *Advances in parapsychological research 2. Extrasensory perception* (pp. 59–243). New York: Plenum.

PALMER, J. (1982). ESP research findings: 1976–1978. In S. Krippner (Ed.), *Advances in parapsychological research 3* (pp. 41–82). New York: Plenum.

ROSENTHAL, R. (1991). *Meta-analytic procedures for social research* (rev. ed.). Newbury Park, CA: Sage.

SCHECHTER, R., SOLFVIN, G., & McCOLLUM, R. (1975). Psi and mental imagery. *Journal of the American Society for Psychical Research,* **69,** 321–326.

SCHLITZ, M., & HONORTON, C. (1992). Ganzfeld psi performance within an artistically gifted population. *Journal of the American Society for Psychical Research,* **86,** 83–98.

SEKULER, R., ANSTIS, S., BRADDICK, O. J., BRANDT, T., MOVSHON, J. A., & ORBAN, G. (1990). The perception of motion. In L. Spillman & J. S. Werner (Eds.), *Visual perception: The neurophysiological foundations* (pp. 205–230). New York: Academic Press.

SMITH, M., TREMMEL, L., & HONORTON, C. (1976). A comparison of psi and weak sensory influences on ganzfeld mentation. In J. D. Morris, W. G. Roll, & R. L. Morris (Eds.)., *Research in parapsychology 1975* (pp. 191–194). Metuchen NJ: Scarecrow.

SPENCE, K. W., FARBER, I. E., & McFANN, H. H. (1956). The relation of anxiety (drive) level to performance in competitional paired-associates learning. *Journal of Experimental Psychology,* **52,** 296–305.

STANFORD, R. G. (1972). Suggestibility and success at augury—Divination from "chance" outcomes. *Journal of the American Society for Psychical Research,* **66,** 42–62.

STANFORD, R. G. (1974). An experimentally testable model for spontaneous psi events: II. Psychokinetic events. *Journal of the American Society for Psychical Research,* **68,** 321–356.

STANFORD, R. G. (1981). Are we shamans or scientists? *Journal of the American Society for Psychical Research,* **75,** 61–70.

STANFORD, R. G. (1988, October). *ESP research and internal attention states: Sharpening the tools of the trade.* Paper presented at the 1988 Annual International Conference of the Parapsychology Foundation, Durham, NC.

STANFORD, R. G., FRANK, S., KASS, G., & SKOLL, S. (1989). Ganzfeld as an ESP-favorable setting: Part I. Assessment of spontaneity, arousal, and internal attention state through verbal transcript analysis. *Journal of Parapsychology,* **53,** 1–42.

TYRRELL, G. N. M. (1946). The "modus operandi" of paranormal cognition. *Proceedings of the Society for Psychical Research,* **48,** 65–120.

WARCOLLIER, R. (1938). *Experimental telepathy* (J. B. Gridley, Trans.). Boston: Boston Society for Psychic Research.

WARCOLLIER, R. (1963). *Mind to mind.* New York: Collier.

WHITE, R. A. (1964). A comparison of old and new methods of response to targets in ESP experiments. *Journal of the American Society for Psychical Research,* **58,** 21–56.

THE PSI CONTROVERSY

By John Palmer

Although the great majority of Charles Honorton's intellectual contributions to parapsychology were the reports of his consistently successful and well-designed experiments, he was keenly aware of the relevance of psi research to controversial questions about the nature of humanity. Because of his commitment to science, he believed, along with many other parapsychologists past and present, that these issues can be and should be addressed by the scientific method. Yet he came to realize very early in his career that most scientists, through their embrace of materialism, were convinced that science already possessed the answers to the fundamental aspects of these questions and that for this reason they could ignore or condemn the parapsychological data that seemed to suggest otherwise. It was inevitable that Honorton would occasionally cross swords with those individuals who have propagated such attitudes in defense of scientific orthodoxy.

It is important to recognize, however, that Honorton was conservative when it came to drawing metaphysical conclusions from the mere reality of psi. I remember from conversations with him in the 1960s that he was critical of J. B. Rhine for proclaiming that psi, and hence the mind, must be nonphysical (Rhine, 1947). Honorton believed that such conclusions were premature and needlessly antagonistic to other scientists. What bothered him was that the great majority of these other scientists refused to take the data of parapsychology seriously as even raising questions about the contemporary worldview. His intense frustration on this point came to the surface in his 1975 Presidential Address to the Parapsychological Association, when in the midst of discussing promising data from selected subareas of psi research, he burst forth with the following heart-felt polemic:

> We must not continue merely bemoaning the fact that parapsychology is not accepted by establishment science; we ought not to feel that, despite the fact that we know our literature and what we are doing in our laboratories, there must be something wrong with the work since it is not accepted; we should not continue to play the game that eventually,

after all, science is objective and our findings will eventually become accepted on their merit. I do not believe this. We have been struggling against irrational prejudice for a long time. Patience goes only so far and I think that if the situation is going to change, we are going to have to change it. Our findings deserve better than they have received from the scientific establishment. If our work is faulty, it should be criticized, but the criticism must be substantive, not *a priori*. The scientific community has an obligation to assess, without prejudice, the serious research in this area. The only way in which this can be done is through dissemination of research reports to a wide scientific audience. As the *Nature* editors suggested, this would have the effect, not of providing an endorsement of any claims, but rather of stimulating critical discussion and further replication. I can see no basis of justification for the refusal of journals such as *Science* to accept research reports of good quality. (Honorton, 1976, p. 215)

The Honorton-Hansel Exchanges

Honorton's interest in the psi controversy can be traced back at least as far as his days as an undergraduate student at the University of Minnesota, which at that time had among its faculty several experts on the mind/body problem. Among these notables whom Honorton had contact with were the psychologist Paul Meehl and the philosopher Herbert Feigl. He found Feigl particularly receptive to parapsychology and ended up taking his philosophy of science course.

Honorton's first published contribution to the psi controversy was a trenchant response to Fraser Nicol's (1964) review of a lecture on parapsychology by the philosopher C. D. Broad. Nicol used this occasion to disparage the experimental card-guessing research of the preceding thirty years as essentially worthless, in contrast to the earlier qualitative studies that he favored. Among other things, Honorton (1965) accused Nicol of appealing to "hearsay and innuendo" by not citing references for certain critical remarks about the experimental research. For instance, Nicol (1964) wrote that "in recent years some long-unpublished facts concerning [the Pearce-Pratt, Soal-Shackleton, and Soal-Stewart experiments] have come to light, leading inevitably to a reduction of confidence in the reports and in their authors" (p. 266).

It shortly became apparent that this piece of unseemly gossip referred at least in part to points subsequently raised in a caustic attack on parapsychology by the British psychologist C. E. M. Hansel

(1966). Taking his cue from a letter published a decade earlier in the journal *Science* by a research chemist named George Price (1955)—to which letter Meehl had coauthored a critical response (Meehl & Scriven, 1956)—Hansel argued that the best ESP experiments up to that time could be interpreted as fraud on the part of the subject or one or more of the experimenters. He concluded that because ESP was so improbable on a priori grounds, these fraud interpretations should be preferred, irrespective of their complexity or the lack of any hard evidence for them; in other words, the experiments did not provide conclusive evidence for ESP.

Rhine gave Honorton (1967) the task of reviewing Hansel's book, *ESP: A Scientific Evaluation* (1966), for the *Journal of Parapsychology*. Honorton began by quoting the highly respected physicist P. W. Bridgman, who, in the course of defining operationism, wrote that "[the physicist] recognizes no a priori principles which determine or limit the possibilities of new experience" (p. 78). After pointing out some logical inconsistencies in Hansel's reasoning, Honorton zeroed in on Hansel's critique of the famous Pearce-Pratt clairvoyance experiment. This experiment was noteworthy at the time as being a methodological advance because the subject and the experimenter (who had the ESP target cards in his possession) were located in different buildings. Hansel had hypothesized that the unsupervised subject (Pearce) could have sneaked into the building where Pratt was located, situated himself in a room across the hall from the experimenter's (Pratt's) room, observed the targets on Pratt's desk by looking through the transoms, and returned to his own room to fill out his response sheet. The rebuttal was that Hansel's hypothesis rested on a "not-to-scale" diagram of the layout of rooms in the building occupied by Pratt. The correct diagram revealed that there was no direct line of sight from the room across the hall onto Pratt's desk, as required by Hansel's hypothesis.

Honorton also chided Hansel for various misrepresentations and omissions in the latter's all-too-brief discussion of less "conclusive" psi research. These included failure to acknowledge such facts as successful replications of the sheep-goat effect, significant psi-missing in an allegedly chance experiment conducted by Beloff with the subject Stepanek, and successful precognition experiments that by definition precluded sensory cues. Hansel never replied to Honorton's review.

A decade later, the *Journal of The American Society for Psychical Research* gave Honorton (1981) an opportunity to review an updated version of Hansel's book (Hansel, 1980). Honorton reiterated many of his criticisms of the earlier book and added some new ones, such as the violation of the parsimony principle by Hansel's elaborate fraud scenarios. This second review was heavily influenced by Honorton's recent acquaintance with the newly developed meta-analytic techniques discussed elsewhere in this issue of the *Journal of Parapsychology*. He stressed the point that systematic lines of research must be evaluated collectively, in contrast to Hansel's approach of debunking isolated experiments individually. The impact of methodological "flaws," Honorton maintained, should be dealt with empirically (for example, by comparing the outcomes of "flawed" and "unflawed" studies) rather than speculatively. As a concrete example, he observed that one experiment that Hansel extolled—an unsuccessful random event generator (REG) experiment with the VERITAC machine—suffered from many of the same alleged flaws as the ones found in another set of REG experiments that Hansel attacked—those of Helmut Schmidt. Finally, Honorton once again criticized Hansel for failing to acknowledge the successful replications of various prominent experimental findings and for failing to correct the errors and omissions that Honorton had pointed out in his review of the earlier book.

This time Hansel did reply. At the end of the most recent update of his book, Hansel (1989) reproduced several critical reviews by parapsychologists of the 1980 version, each followed by his rebuttal. Because Honorton never replied to Hansel's rebuttal of his review, I will take the liberty to do so here, using arguments similar to what I suspect Honorton might have used.

Hansel defended his claim of the a priori improbability of psi on the grounds that it conflicts with the rest of scientific knowledge, in particular with what we know about ordinary perception and the brain. This is debatable, but in any event the a priori principle at issue is not the validity of perceptual psychology, but whether these ordinary perceptual processes preclude "extraordinary" ones. As Honorton has repeatedly pointed out, the fact that scientists in the past have had to confess that their knowledge of what can occur in nature is less complete than they had previously thought renders such a priori criticisms very hazardous.

Hansel argued that Honorton's charge of unparsimoniousness is irrelevant to Hansel's fraud scenarios because the parsimony principle refers to scientific theories rather than to empirical observations. Apparently, Hansel thought that ESP falls in the latter category, but Honorton was obviously using the term in a theoretical sense to account for the covariance between sets of targets and responses. I have noted elsewhere (Palmer, 1986) that using the same terms (for example, *ESP*) both for events and for a possible explanation of those events creates conceptual confusion. This is a good case in point.

As for the Pearce-Pratt experiment, Hansel criticized Honorton for claiming that he (Hansel) had said that the room from which Pearce had allegedly observed the targets was "directly opposite" Pratt's room; Hansel in fact had stated that the room was "on the opposite side farther down the corridor." But Honorton's exact words were that the room was "across the hall," which does not necessarily imply *directly* across the hall. The crucial point, which Hansel ignored in his linguistic smokescreen, is that the correct diagram revealed there was no direct line of sight to the targets from the room in question, wherever that room was deemed precisely to be located. Ironically, Hansel introduced this discussion with the statement that "the case of Hubert Pearce is surely of little further interest" (Hansel, 1989, p. 300); if that is so, why did he include a chapter on it in the latest incarnation of his book?

Hansel attempted to defend his focus on "individual experiments" with the argument that this focus "was necessary if those experiments were to be examined that were considered by parapsychologists to be 'conclusive' " (Hansel, 1989, p. 299). This is not a defense of his position but merely a restatement of it. Also, what Honorton was telling him in his reply was that at least one parapsychologist (Honorton himself) did *not* believe that any of these individual experiments were "conclusive," and there were and are many other parapsychologists who share Honorton's opinion.

Later on, Hansel turned to the replication issue. He stated that "any ESP experiment in which the result is assessed in terms of the odds against chance of the result will be replicable in [the sense used by Honorton]," because "it is a simple matter to increase the number of observations required in an experiment that is to provide the repeatable demonstration" (Hansel, 1989, p. 300). The first statement is false, and it is also untrue that successful replication attempts in parapsychology use much larger sample sizes than the studies they replicate. The section including these quotes seems to suggest that Hansel would reject the outcome of any psi experiment that is based on statistics. If that is really what he means to say, his position is more radical than any of us had previously thought, and it is totally inconsistent with most of the rest of psychology, which depends heavily on statistical evaluation. How many babies is Hansel prepared to throw out with the bath water?

Hansel concluded his reply by asking what "systematic lines of research" critics should focus on. If he had been doing his homework, he would not need to ask this question. His repeated failures to accurately represent the degree of replication that does exist in parapsychology or to respond to Honorton's criticisms in this regard suggest that he does not really care about the matter.

The Honorton-Kennedy Exchange

Because Honorton was a skillful and careful researcher, his own experiments have rarely been criticized in the literature. An exception occurred when James Kennedy (1979a) published a major critique of methodology in free-response ESP experiments. Kennedy was a parapsychologist who worked for several years at the Institute for Parapsychology, and thus he was not in the same category as Hansel, who is classified as an outside, or external, critic. Parapsychologists generally agree that the most incisive criticisms usually come from internal critics like Kennedy, who tend to have a better familiarity with and understanding of psi research than do the external critics.

Honorton (1979) wrote a lengthy and respectful reply to Kennedy's critique, expressing agreement with some of his criticisms and disagreement with others. Areas of agreement included the lack of statistical independence in the analyses of some free-response ESP data, the failure to correct for multiple statistical analyses, and the inadequacy of a statistic called the *psi quotient* as a measure of the information content of target-response matches.

Areas of disagreement understandably focused on criticisms that were applicable to Honorton's own research, particularly one of two ganzfeld experiments reported by Terry and Honorton (1976). Kennedy noted that the authors used a more liberal criterion for a hit in this experiment than in other ganzfeld experiments by Honorton. The implication was left that this more liberal criterion might have been selected post hoc. While acknowledging that the issue should have been addressed in the research report, Honorton explained that the decision was not post hoc and that he chose the more liberal criterion because the subjects were less experienced than those in the other studies. Kennedy also criticized the experiment because data from four subjects who dropped out before they completed the prespecified 10 sessions were excluded. Honorton responded that the success rate for the remaining subjects was consistent across the 10 sessions. Kennedy (1979b) replied that whereas this secondary finding was favorable to the ESP hypothesis, it would have been better to show that the excluded data manifested a hit rate comparable to that of the included data.

Kennedy (1979a) also criticized an evaluation by Honorton (1977) of ESP experiments involving internal attention states. Honorton had concluded that a greater proportion of these experiments were significant at $p < .05$ than chance would predict. Kennedy complained that this conclusion might be invalid if some of the studies used multiple analyses of the same effect and the most significant of these analyses were then selected for the evaluation. Honorton (1979) replied by noting that the .05 criterion was conservative. Although I don't think this response successfully addressed Kennedy's point, Honorton obviously took the criticism to heart. When the external critic Ray Hyman (1985) made the same point regarding the meta-analysis of ESP-ganzfeld research, Honorton (1985) demonstrated a highly significant success rate when the evaluation was based on a uniform ESP measure.

Honorton used his reply to Kennedy to stress once again his point that disputes about the seriousness of flaws should be resolved empirically. A good example is Kennedy's criticism that in some free-response ESP experiments subjects may have been exposed to subtle sensory cues, as in cases when the target picture handled by the sender was included in the judging packet. Although stressing that such "subliminal cues" should be avoided, Honorton reported that studies susceptible to these cues were no more successful than studies that controlled for them, and he cited other research showing that subjects do not take advantage of such cues when they are available. This line of argument also played a role in the subsequent ganzfeld debate.

Finally, Honorton made the point that many of the faults Kennedy cited were not as widespread as Kennedy implied, and that in general they were less of a problem in free-response experiments than in forced-choice experiments.

Some General Papers

Honorton published several other important papers relevant to the psi controversy. I will treat these more briefly than I have done for his replies to Hansel and Kennedy, because many of the points he raised in these papers are available in his own words in his article

"Rhetoric over Substance: The Impoverished State of Skepticism" (this issue of the *JP*), the last paper he wrote before his death. It was submitted as part of a written exchange between parapsychologists and their critics that was sponsored by the Italian equivalent of the American-based Committee for the Scientific Investigation of Claims of the Paranormal, an organization dedicated to debunking psychic claims. Written in response to critiques by Ray Hyman, James Alcock, and James Randi, it provides an excellent short overview of Honorton's perspective on the psi controversy.

Many of the points Honorton makes in the first half of "Rhetoric over Substance" were first introduced in two articles he wrote in the mid-1970s. The first was a contribution to a set of articles on various aspects of parapsychology that was published in the *Journal of Communication*, a non-parapsychological journal (Honorton, 1975). It had the catchy title "Error Some Place!," a redefinition of the acronym ESP coined by an unnamed "skeptical psychologist." (Honorton began the article by saying, "I believe he was right, but for the wrong reasons.") The second paper was his Presidential Address to the Parapsychological Association in 1975, the one year in which he received this well-deserved honor. The title was "Has Science Developed the Competence to Confront Claims of the Paranormal?" (Honorton, 1976). It was basically a comparison of how well establishment science and parapsychology, respectively, have addressed the issues raised by the psi controversy.

I will limit myself to a brief discussion of two important themes in these two articles, both of which were carried over into "Rhetoric over Substance." The first is Honorton's repeated references to the double standard applied to psi research and research in conventional scientific disciplines. He points out that in orthodox science, as well as in parapsychology, fundamental questions about subject matter have yet to be resolved. The replication rate is no worse in parapsychology than it is in many areas of psychology, and parapsychologists are more conscientious than orthodox psychologists both in attempting to replicate previous findings and in publishing the results irrespective of their statistical significance. Finally, several major findings and theories in the traditional sciences, especially physics, are as counterintuitive or "mind boggling" as psi is.

Although Honorton to my knowledge has never stated so explicitly, I suspect that he might agree with me in rejecting for parapsychology the common skeptical refrain that "extraordinary claims require extraordinary proof." First, I think he would reject the premise that psi claims are extraordinary; he believed strongly in the normalization of psi and wanted to replace the term *paranormal* with *psychophysical* (Honorton, 1976). Second, I think he would agree that to the extent possible, science should be governed by one uniform (and rigorous) set of standards, lest its results be biased in favor of "a priori probable" viewpoints (Palmer, 1987).

The second major theme I would draw attention to in this series of papers is Honorton's historical perspective on the psi controversy. He saw this history in terms of three or four distinct periods. The first was the 1930s, when the controversy centered around the card-guessing paradigm of Rhine. Honorton believed that it was during this period that "the major *substantive methodological issues* were raised and to a large extent consensually resolved" (Honorton, 1975, p. 113, italics in original). The period from 1940 to 1955 he considered a period of stagnation in which psi was simply ignored by established science. The period from 1955 to 1980 was a period of "speculative," and in Honorton's opinion, unfruitful criticism. This was the era dominated by Hansel's fraud scenarios. Finally, he felt that 1980 heralded a new period of substantive and fruitful criticism, represented most clearly by the writings of psychologist Ray Hyman.

The Hyman-Honorton Exchanges

This brings us to the main topic of the second half of "Rhetoric over Substance," the ESP-ganzfeld controversy. The controversy was launched when Hyman decided to "accept the parapsychologists' challenge to examine carefully the best evidence for the reality of psi" (Hyman, 1983, p. 21). He chose for this purpose a collection of 42 ESP experiments that incorporated the ganzfeld, a short-term perceptual deprivation procedure designed to facilitate free-response ESP by creating an internal attention state. Honorton, a pioneer in ESP-ganzfeld research, had previously reviewed these studies and claimed that they had a success rate of 55%, a conclusion that Hyman challenged. What followed was a personal but professional interaction between Honorton and Hyman that lasted several years. During this time, they attempted to use meta-analytic techniques to determine whether the ganzfeld research indeed provided evidence for psi. The most difficult issues for them to resolve were how to classify experiments as successful or unsuccessful, and what flaws, if any, should be assigned to them.

The debate first surfaced at a symposium held at the 1982 Parapsychological Association convention at Cambridge University (Honorton, 1983; Hyman, 1983). This convention was also noteworthy as the celebration of the 100th anniversary of the founding of the (British) Society for Psychical Research and the 25th anniversary of the Parapsychological Association. The debate resumed in separate articles by Hyman (1985) and Honorton (1985) in the *Journal of Parapsychology*, and in response to which several other parapsychologists and a critic wrote short commentaries. It culminated in a "Joint Communiqué" in which the main protagonists summarized their agreements and disagreements and offered a set of methodological recommendations for future ganzfeld research (Hyman & Honorton, 1986). This article has been widely praised as a model for constructive cooperation between parapsychologists and their critics (e.g., Benassi, 1987; Krippner, 1987).

Unfortunately, this spirit of cooperation was compromised by the publication of a critical evaluation of parapsychology and other purported techniques for "enhancing human performance." The evaluation was requested by the U.S. Army and was conducted by the National Research Council (NRC) of the National Academy of Sciences (Druckman & Swets, 1988). The NRC selected Hyman to chair the subcommittee on parapsychology, and he clearly was the principal, if not the sole, author of its report. Although the report did countenance some additional psi research—in the unlikely event that the Army would still be interested in sponsoring it after reading the report—its tone and content were more uniformly negative. The punch line, widely quoted in the media, stated: "The Committee finds no scientific justification from research conducted over a period of 130 years for the existence of parapsychological phenomena" (Druckman & Swets, 1988, p. 22).

The Board of Directors of the Parapsychological Association quickly authorized and then published a response to the NRC report (Palmer, Honorton, & Utts, 1988). Although I was selected as first author, Honorton's contributions to the reply were at least as great as mine. We expressed our outrage at the biased composition of the parapsychology subcommittee, and in particular at the attempt by the chairman of the umbrella committee to suppress a favorable evaluation of ESP ganzfeld research contained in a background paper the committee had solicited from the prominent psychologist Robert Rosenthal. Our main substantive point was directed at the subcommittee's concession that they could find no plausible alternative explanations for the better psi experiments. We asserted that their condemnation of such experiments, based as it was on the presence of alleged flaws that they in effect admitted were inconsequential, was illogical as well as incompatible with the committee's own published standards of evaluation.

Honorton's most telling response to Hyman was to conduct a highly automated series of ganzfeld experiments that followed the prescriptions they had agreed to in the "Joint Communiqué" (Honorton et al., 1990). Hyman (1991) could find no fault with these experiments but wanted to withhold final judgment until they were replicated by other investigators. One such replicator may be Daryl Bem, another prominent psychologist whom Honorton had interested in the ganzfeld research and who has reported some initial success with the ganzfeld procedure (Bem, 1992). Shortly after Honorton's death, we learned that a joint paper by Bem and Honorton, covering Honorton's automated ganzfeld experiments as well as his meta-analysis of previous ganzfeld studies, has been accepted for publication in *Psychological Bulletin,* a prominent mainstream psychology journal (Bem & Honorton, in press). This achievement, which Honorton regrettably could not live to see, fulfilled the plea he so eloquently voiced in his 1975 Presidential Address to the Parapsychological Association, which I quoted at the beginning of this paper.

Conclusion

There is no doubt that Charles Honorton was a skillful and articulate defender of parapsychology against attacks by its critics. As effective as his written replies were, I found him even more effective in oral debates, even though he was sometimes reluctant to participate in them. Like most of us, he would rather have spent all his time doing research, but his understanding and appreciation of the role of the psi controversy in the advancement both of parapsychology and of science as a whole compelled him to come forward when necessary. Answering the critics is yet another dimension of parapsychology where Honorton's intellect and tenacity will be sorely missed.

REFERENCES

BEM, D. J. (1992, August). *Musings (and data) from a beginner.* Paper presented at the meeting of the Parapsychological Association, Las Vegas, NV.

BEM, D. J., & HONORTON, C. (in press). Does psi exist? Replicable evidence for an anomalous process of information transfer. *Psychological Bulletin.*

BENASSI, V. A. (1987). Believers, nonbelievers, and the parapsychology debate. *Behavioral & Brain Sciences,* **10,** 570–571.

DRUCKMAN, D., & SWETS, J. A. (Eds.). (1988). *Enhancing human performance: Issues, theories, and techniques.* Washington, DC: National Academy Press.

HANSEL, C. E. M. (1966). *ESP: A scientific evaluation.* New York: Scribners.

HANSEL, C. E. M. (1980). *ESP and parapsychology: A critical re-evaluation.* Buffalo: Prometheus.

HANSEL, C. E. M. (1989). *The search for psychic power: ESP and parapsychology revisited.* Buffalo: Prometheus.

HONORTON, C. (1965). [Letter to the editor]. *International Journal of Parapsychology,* **7,** 110–112.

HONORTON, C. (1967). [Review of *ESP: A scientific evaluation*]: *Journal of Parapsychology,* **31,** 76–82.

HONORTON, C. (1975). Error some place! *Journal of Communication,* **25,** 103–116.

HONORTON, C. (1976). Has science developed the competence to confront claims of the paranormal? In J. D. Morris, W. G. Roll, & R. L. Morris (Eds.), *Research in parapsychology 1975* (pp. 199–223). Metuchen, NJ: Scarecrow Press.

HONORTON, C. (1977). Internal attention states. In B. Wolman (Ed.), *Handbook of parapsychology* (pp. 435–472). New York: Van Nostrand Reinhold.

HONORTON, C. (1979). Methodological issues in free-response psi experiments. *Journal of the American Society for Psychical Research,* **73,** 381–394.

HONORTON, C. (1981). Beyond the reach of sense: Some comments on C. E. M. Hansel's *ESP and parapsychology: A critical re-evaluation. Journal of the American Society for Psychical Research,* **75,** 155–166.

HONORTON, C. (1983). Response to Hyman's critique of psi ganzfeld studies. In W. G. Roll, J. Beloff, & R. W. White (Eds.), *Research in parapsychology 1982* (pp. 23–26). Metuchen, NJ: Scarecrow Press.

HONORTON, C. (1985). Meta-analysis of psi ganzfeld research: A response to Hyman. *Journal of Parapsychology,* **49,** 51–91.

HONORTON, C., BERGER, R. E., VARVOGLIS, M. P., QUANT, M., DERR, P., SCHECHTER, E. I., & FERRARI, D. C. (1990). Psi communication in the ganzfeld: Experiments with an automated testing system and a comparison with a meta-analysis of earlier studies. *Journal of Parapsychology,* **54,** 100–139.

HYMAN, R. (1983). Does the ganzfeld experiment answer the critics' objections? In W. G. Roll, J. Beloff, & R. A. White (Eds.), *Research in parapsychology 1982* (pp. 21–23). Metuchen, NJ: Scarecrow Press.

HYMAN, R. (1985). The ganzfeld psi experiment: A critical appraisal. *Journal of Parapsychology,* **49,** 3–49.

HYMAN, R. (1991). Comment. *Statistical Science,* **6,** 389–392.

HYMAN, R., & HONORTON, C. (1986). A joint communiqué: The psi ganzfeld controversy. *Journal of Parapsychology,* **50,** 351–364.

KENNEDY, J. E. (1979a) Methodological problems in free-response ESP experiments. *Journal of the American Society for Psychical Research,* **73,** 1–15.

KENNEDY, J. E. (1979b). More on methodological issues in free-response psi experiments. *Journal of the American Society for Psychical Research,* **73,** 395–401.

KRIPPNER, S. (1987). Never say never again: Rapproachment may be nearer than you think! *Behavioral & Brain Sciences,* **10,** 595–596.

MEEHL, P. E., & SCRIVEN, M. (1956). Compatibility of science and ESP. *Science,* **123,** 14–15.

NICOL, J. F. (1964). C. D. Broad on psychical research. *International Journal of Parapsychology,* **6,** 261–288.

PALMER, J. (1986). Terminological poverty in parapsychology: Two examples. In D. H. Weiner & D. I. Radin (Eds.), *Research in parapsychology 1985* (pp. 138–141). Metuchen, NJ: Scarecrow Press.

PALMER, J. (1987). Dulling Occam's razor: The role of coherence in assessing scientific knowledge claims. *European Journal of Parapsychology,* **7,** 73–82.

PALMER, J. A., HONORTON, C., & UTTS, J. (1988). *Reply to the National Research Council study on parapsychology.* Research Triangle Park, NC: Parapsychological Association.

PRICE, G. R. (1955). Science and the supernatural. *Science,* **122,** 359–367.

RHINE, J. B. (1947). *The reach of the mind.* New York: William Sloane.

TERRY, J. C., and HONORTON, C. (1976). Psi information retrieval in the ganzfeld: Two confirmatory studies. *Journal of the American Society for Psychical Research,* **70,** 207–217.

RHETORIC OVER SUBSTANCE: THE IMPOVERISHED STATE OF SKEPTICISM

By Charles Honorton

Few of us can afford to take time to familiarize ourselves with the detailed and often technical arguments underlying new knowledge claims that would enable us to evaluate properly the merits of such claims for ourselves. Most of the time we have to rely on "experts" to do this for us. We are poorly served when only one side of a controversy is presented and benefit most when all perspectives are vigorously debated by knowledgeable protagonists. The Comitato Italiano per il Controllo delle Aftermazioni sul Paranormale has provided an invaluable service by presenting a balanced forum for discussing the status of parapsychology by six leading researchers and critics. CICAP's initiative in this regard is probably unique and one that its American counterpart, the Committee for the Scientific Investigation of Claims of the Paranormal, would do well to emulate. To fill out this innovative format, CICAP asked a skeptical parapsychologist, Susan Blackmore, to critique the contributions of the parapsychologists, and I have been asked to comment on the critics' contributions.

1. What the Critics No Longer Claim

Before examining the current arguments made by Hyman, Alcock, and Randi, it is important to understand what they are *not now* claiming but *have* claimed in the past. First, they no longer claim that the results of the major lines of experimental psi research are consistent with the null hypothesis (mere chance fluctuation). They now concede that at least some parapsychological effects are, to use Hyman's words, "astronomically significant." This concession is important because it shifts the focus of the debate from the *existence* of effects to their *interpretation*. Second, they no longer claim to have

This article originally appeared in *Scienza & Paranormale*, Vol. 1, No. 3, June 1993, and is reprinted here with permission of the publishers.

192

demonstrated a relationship between methodological flaws and study outcomes. These concessions, which are documented in Section 3, did not come quickly or easily and the critics are obviously not eager to advertise them. Over the past decade Hyman and other critics tried very hard to show that psi effects are either not really significant or that their significance is systematically related to the presence of flaws in the experiments. Having failed on both counts, the critics now face a serious dilemma: they have been forced to admit parapsychology has demonstrated anomalous effects that need to be explained and they have run out of plausible conventional explanations.

2. What the Critics Now Claim

A Century of Failure?

Instead, they offer a caricature of the history of parapsychology and present polemical arguments designed to convince us that there is really nothing in parapsychology that warrants scientific interest, except, perhaps, for the motivations of those who persist in studying it. Hyman's use of absolutist language to characterize parapsychologists' data claims seems designed to turn off scientists. Unlike the formal sciences such as mathematics, empirical science does not deal with "irrefutable proof" or "foolproof evidence." Empirical evidence is always a matter of degree and remains subject to later reinterpretation. It is in this sense that science represents a unique self-correcting approach to knowledge. Scientific truth always carries the caveat, "until further notice."

At the core of the critics' current arguments is the rhetorical claim that 100 years of research has failed to provide convincing evidence for parapsychological phenomena. When parapsychologists have not been given an opportunity to respond, they have claimed that *130* years of research has produced *no* evidence for psi (e.g., Druckman & Swets, 1988). An English critic, who was recently appointed to a four-year £100,000 psychical research fellowship at Darwin College, Cambridge, to write a book about why people believe impossible things, has been quoted in *The New Scientists* as saying that after *150* years of psychical research "there is no evidence at all of there being any phenomena" (Bown, 1992). Such statements are themselves extraordinary claims inasmuch as psychical research did not exist until 1882 and systematic laboratory research using quantitative methods did not begin until the early 1930s. Throughout its history, research in parapsychology has been sustained through extremely meager resources. Utrecht University psychologist Sybo Schouten (in press) compared funding patterns in parapsychology with those of American psychology; he found that the total human and financial resources devoted to parapsychology since 1882 might, at best, equal the expenditures for *two months* of conventional psychological research in the United States in the year 1983!

Is psychology a "failed" science? If we were to apply the "century of failure" arguments of Hyman and Alcock to academic psychology, we might well conclude that psychology has failed in its mission: after a hundred years of relatively well-funded research, vigorous controversies continue over such basic phenomena as memory, learning, and perception. The simple act of human facial recognition, for example, remains a mystery and is currently a hot research topic in cognitive psychology. And while it is widely assumed that consciousness is a by-product of brain activity, neither psychology nor physiology has produced, over the past 100 years, even an intelligible model of how biochemical processes could be transformed into conscious experience. Are psychology and physiology failed sciences? Of course not. The most successful sciences such as physics deal with relatively simple and invariant processes: electrons, for example, are interchangeable; they do not have individual personalities, intentions, emotional states, or motivations. The behavioral sciences must contend with extremely complex and variable biological systems that possess these and many other individual attributes. Nevertheless, these sciences have produced many achievements, and so has parapsychology, even though it has been forced to exist on the outskirts of established science with marginal resources. The papers by Broughton, Krippner, and Morris summarize some of parapsychology's accomplishments.

The lack of research by critics and its consequences. There is, however, one important difference between the psi controversy and more conventional scientific disputes. Controversies in science normally occur between groups of *researchers* who formulate hypotheses, develop research methods, and collect empirical data to test their hypotheses. When disputes arise over the interpretation of experimental findings, or when critics suspect that the findings were caused by artifacts, they design new experiments to test alternative explanations or the impact of suspected artifacts. It is through this process

that scientific controversies are resolved. In contrast, the psi controversy is largely characterized by disputes between a group of researchers, the parapsychologists, and a group of critics who do not
do experimental research to test psi claims or the viability of their
counterhypotheses. Psi critics argue the plausibility of various alternative hypotheses (or the implausibility of the psi hypothesis) but
they rarely feel obliged to test them. This has been especially true
of the current generation of psi critics, most of whom have made
no original research contributions. Exceptions like Susan Blackmore
and David Marks prove the rule. The lack of research by critics may
surprise you, especially if your primary source of information about
parapsychology has come from the skeptical literature where you
may have encountered statements such as the following by the well-
known American skeptic Martin Gardner (1983).

> How can the public know that for fifty years skeptical psychologists have
> been trying their best to replicate classic psi experiments, and with not-
> able unsuccess? It is this fact more than any other that has led to para-
> psychology's perpetual stagnation. Positive evidence keeps coming from
> a tiny group of enthusiasts, while *negative evidence keeps coming from a
> much larger group of skeptics.* (p. 60, my emphasis)

Gardner does not attempt to document this assertion, nor could
he. It is pure fiction. Look for the skeptics' experiments and see
what you find. (To his credit, Gardner did get one thing right: half
a century is a more accurate time-frame than 100, 130, or 150
years.) The lack of research by critics serves to perpetuate the psi
controversy by enabling them to shift continually from one line of
criticism to another as each is successively answered through new
research conducted by parapsychologists. It is clear from their statements that Hyman, Alcock, and Randi expect the controversy to extend into the indefinite future. Whatever time-frame one chooses to
adopt, I think we can all agree on two points: the psi controversy
has gone on for a long time, and its lack of resolution represents a
very unsatisfactory state of affairs.

Lack of Cumulativeness?

How can we reconcile the "century of failure" argument with the
critics' admission that there are "astronomically significant" effects
and their failure to demonstrate even plausible alternative explanations for those effects? The answer, they say, is that parapsychology

lacks "cumulativeness." "Every science, except parapsychology," Hyman says, "builds upon its previous data. The data base continually expands with each new generation but the original investigations are still included. In parapsychology, the data base expands very little because previous experiments are continually discarded and new ones take their place." The "astronomically significant" effects for which they have no plausible alternative explanations are, Hyman says, based upon "retrospective" meta-analyses of many similar experiments. Truly skeptical readers should be alarmed by the logical contradiction in this argument: if parapsychology is "noncumulative," and if each new generation of parapsychologists discards the findings of earlier generations, how could there be "astronomically significant" effects in meta-analyses that are, by definition, the cumulation of findings from many earlier studies? Hyman refers only to meta-analyses of two relatively recent research areas, the ganzfeld and random number generator experiments (Honorton, 1985; Hyman, 1985; Radin & Nelson, 1989). He overlooks other meta-analyses, such as those discussed by Broughton and Morris involving precognition experiments (Honorton & Ferrari, 1989) and psychokinesis research with dice (Radin & Ferrari, 1991), both of which involve the cumulation of research findings going back to the 1930s. In Section 3, I present a detailed example of a line of parapsychological research that has systematically built upon earlier research. There are other inconsistencies in Hyman's historical analysis that are also self-documenting:

In 1940 J. B. Rhine and his colleagues published a book entitled *Extra-Sensory Perception After Sixty Years* which summarized all quantitative ESP studies since the founding of the Society for Psychical Research in 1882 (Pratt, Rhine, Smith, Stuart, & Greenwood, 1940/ 1966). Known within the field as *ESP-60*, this book is the central classic of experimental parapsychology. How can we reconcile *ESP-60* with Hyman's claim that each successive generation of parapsychologists claims evidence for psi *"without any reference to the data used by the preceding generation"* (Hyman's emphasis)?

"By the 1940s," Hyman claims, "even parapsychologists admitted that Rhine's experiments possessed too many flaws to qualify as foolproof evidence for psi." How can we reconcile this statement with the fact that as late as 1980 the English critic C. E. M. Hansel was still trying to account for the results of these experiments on the basis of speculative and elaborate fraud scenarios (Hansel, 1966/ 1980)?

3. Historical Overview of the Psi Controversy

I will now summarize an alternative view of the history of the psi controversy that suggests a very different conclusion, namely, that over the past 60 years of active experimental research by parapsychologists, critics have consistently failed to demonstrate plausible alternative explanations of psi effects. In examining the psi controversy, it is useful to note the order in which various types of criticism have occurred. During each major phase of the controversy, the criticisms have followed this pattern:

- *Statistical criticisms seeking to demonstrate that the claimed effects are not really significant.* This type of criticism has usually been championed by psychologists and refuted by statisticians. If critics could sustain their case at this point, the controversy would end here.

- *Methodological criticisms asserting that the effects are caused by procedural flaws.* As I have already stated, advocates of flaw hypotheses have seldom subjected their flaw hypotheses to empirical test, but have tended instead to argue for their plausibility. In response, parapsychologists have conducted new experiments that eliminate the suspected flaws.

- *Speculative criticisms based on* a priori *and* ad hominem *arguments.* This form of criticism has usually been founded on the assumption that the existence of psi phenomena is incompatible with fundamental scientific principles, but the proponents of *a priori* arguments have never successfully demonstrated the nature of such incompatibilities.

The ESP Controversy of the 1930s

The first major phase of the psi controversy occurred between 1934 and 1939, and was stimulated by publication of the ESP card-guessing experiments initiated by J. B. Rhine and his colleagues at Duke University (Rhine, 1934/1964). During this period, approximately 60 critical articles appeared, primarily in the American psychological literature. Elsewhere (Honorton, 1975) I have presented a more detailed review of this controversy with references to most of the critical papers. Figure 1 summarizes the major issues raised during this phase of the psi controversy.

In most of the early card-guessing experiments, subjects were asked to guess the order of concealed decks of 25 randomized cards containing five each of five geometrical symbols. Since subjects usually did not receive feedback of the actual target order until after one or more runs of 25 trials, statistical analysis of the card exper-

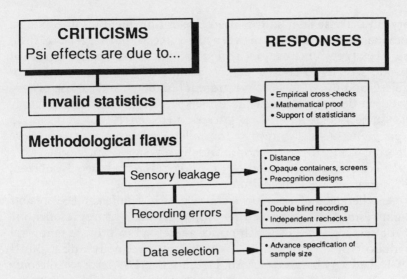

Figure 1. The ESP card-guessing controversy of the 1930s.

iments assumed that the probability of success on each trial was 1/5. The first major criticism of Rhine's work questioned the validity of this assumption. This issue was resolved by mathematical proof and through empirical "cross-checks," a type of control series in which subjects' guesses were deliberately compared with target orders for which they were not intended. For example, the guesses intended for target cards in run 1 were compared with the targets for run 2, and so on. Empirical cross-checks were reported for 24 separate experimental series and while the actual experimental run scores (i.e., guesses for Run 1 compared to targets for Run 1) were highly significant (average: 7.23/25), the control cross-check results were in all cases nonsignificant (average: 5.04/25). (See Pratt et al., 1940/1966.) Other technical statistical issues were raised and eventually abandoned. In a 1938 article, E. V. Huntington asked, "If mathematics has successfully disposed of the hypothesis of chance, what has psychology to say about the hypothesis of ESP?"

By far the most serious methodological criticism of the early card-guessing experiments concerned the possibility of sensory cues. It is clear that some of the early studies reported in Rhine's 1934 monograph did not adequately control against possible sensory leakage. Rhine did not base any major conclusions on these early studies, but their inclusion in his monograph provided a basis for legitimate criticism and sidetracked discussion away from the better controlled studies which were not susceptible to explanation by sensory cues. These later studies used one of four methods to eliminate potential sensory contact between the subjects and target cards: (a) use of targets enclosed in sealed opaque envelopes, (b) use of opaque screens to conceal targets from subjects, (c) separation of subjects and use of targets in different buildings, and (d) use of pre-cognition designs in which the targets were randomly selected only *after* subjects registered their guesses. Between 1934 and 1939, 33 experiments involving nearly one million experimental trials were reported using these methods, and highly significant results were obtained with each method. (For study references, see Honorton, 1975; Pratt et al., 1940/1966).

Another line of criticism suggested that significant ESP results might result from motivated recording errors. This represents one of the few instances in which critics attempted to provide empirical evidence for an alternative explanation. Kennedy and Uphoff (1939) had 28 observers record 11,125 mock ESP trials. While only 1.13 percent were misrecorded overall, both "believers" and "skeptics" systematically erred in the direction of their biases: 71.5 percent of the errors by observers favorable to ESP spuriously increased the ESP scores, and 100 percent of the errors by those unfavorable to ESP decreased the ESP scores. Many years later, Robert Rosenthal (1978) summarized 27 different recording error studies in the behavioral sciences and again found the average error rate to be about 1 percent. An error-rate of this magnitude could not explain the results of the ESP card-guessing experiments, but investigators quickly adopted controls against recording errors. By the end of the 1930s, double-blind data recording and checking had become routine. The results were still "astronomically significant." (See Pratt et al., 1940/1966, Table 9, p. 102.)

The final major issue to arise during this period concerned the possibility of improper data selection. By convention, the criterion of significance for statistical tests is usually set at $p = .05$. When the outcome of a study reaches this criterion it means that the odds are 20:1 against the likelihood that the observed result arose purely by chance. This, of course, does happen. If an investigator conducts 100 experiments, we would on the average expect five to yield spuriously significant results. When chance alone is operating, these pseudosignificant results will be cancelled out by the other experiments. Now consider an extreme case of data selection where the investigator discards the 95 "unsuccessful" experiments and attempts to draw conclusions only from the "successful" ones. This would be highly improper and the investigator's conclusions would be meaningless. As we shall see later, there are various other ways in which data selection problems could compromise research findings. In the 1930s, the issue was addressed by parapsychology researchers through studies which specified the number of trials in advance or explicitly stated that all of the data collected was used in the analysis. (See Pratt et al., 1940/1966, pp. 118–124, for an extensive discussion of data selection issues in the 1930s.)

By the end of the decade, there was general agreement that the various methodological counterhypotheses raised by critics during this period could not explain the outcomes of the more rigorously controlled experiments. (See comments by leading critics of the day in Pratt et al., 1940/1966, chap. 8.) One final point is in order concerning this phase of the psi controversy. It is still widely believed that most of the successful ESP card-guessing experiments came from Rhine and his Duke University group while most of the independent replications were unsuccessful. This is not true. Independent investigators contributed 33 of the 50 studies published during this period, and 61 percent of these studies reported significant ESP effects. Moreover, the difference in success rate between Duke and other investigators was not significant (Honorton, 1975, Table 2).

An Era of Speculative Criticism (1950–1980)

Virtually no new substantive criticisms appeared between 1950 and 1980. This phase of the psi controversy centered instead on two speculative claims. Figure 2 summarizes the issues raised during this period. The first line of speculative attack, championed by Spencer Brown (1953, 1957), was that the card-guessing experiments provided evidence not for ESP, but rather that there were fundamental defects in probability theory. Spencer Brown's arguments, based upon irregularities in early random number tables, were refuted by Scott (1958). This approach never attracted serious support, and it requires little imagination to see why. Much of modern science relies upon probability theory, and acceptance of Spencer Brown's claims would have far greater consequences for science than would ESP. In any case, his arguments do not explain the ESP results. They do not explain the empirical cross-check controls I summarized in the preceding section, and they are incapable of explaining systematic variations in performance such as "sheep/goat" experiments where psi believers consistently score higher than psi skeptics, studies showing correlations between psi performance and personality var-

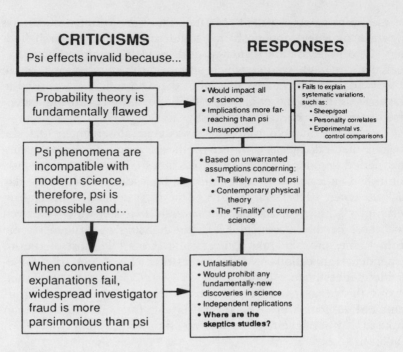

Figure 2. An era of speculative criticism.

iables such as extraversion, or those in which psi performance systematically varies in relation to different experimental conditions as when subjects are instructed to alternate producing high versus low scores.

The second line of attack during this period centers on the hypothesis of widespread investigator fraud. It was most forcefully presented in a lead article in *Science*, entitled "Science and the Supernatural," by Price (1955), who began with the following observations:

> Believers in psychic phenomena... appear to have won a decisive victory and virtually silenced opposition.... This victory is the result of an impressive amount of careful experimentation and intelligent argumentation.... Against all this evidence, almost the only defense remaining to the skeptical scientist is ignorance, ignorance concerning the work itself and concerning its implications. The typical scientist contents himself with retaining... some criticism that at most applies to a small fraction of the published studies. But these findings (which challenge our very concepts of space and time) are—if valid—of enormous importance... so they ought not to be ignored. (p. 359)

Price then went on to assert that ESP is "incompatible with current scientific theory," and that it is therefore more parsimonious to believe that parapsychologists cheat than that ESP is a real phenomenon. He based this argument on philosopher David Hume's essay on miracles. Hume argued that since we know people lie but have no independent evidence of miracles it is more reasonable to believe that claims of miracles are based on lies than that miracles actually occur. Price concluded, "My opinion concerning the findings of the parapsychologists is that many of them are dependent on clerical and statistical errors and unintentional use of sensory clues, *and that all extrachance results not so explicable are dependent on deliberate fraud or mildly abnormal mental condition*" (p. 360). Since it was given such prominence in one of the scientific world's leading interdisciplinary journals, this remarkable critique was widely reviewed. Responses came not only from parapsychologists but also from other scientists as well. One of the most effective responses was a joint paper by psychologist Paul Meehl and philosopher of science Michael Scriven (1956), who pointed out that Price's argument rests on two highly questionable assumptions: that contemporary scientific knowledge is complete and that ESP necessarily conflicts with it.

The most prominent critic of this period was the English psychologist C. E. M. Hansel (1966/1980). Hansel pursued the line of attack initiated by Price.[1] "It is wise," Hansel wrote, "to adopt initially the assumption that ESP is impossible, since there is a great weight of knowledge supporting this point of view" (Hansel, 1980, p. 22). He provided no documentation whatsoever for this assumption. Neither Hansel, nor any other critic has ever, to the best of my knowledge, shown that the existence of psi phenomena necessarily conflicts with established knowledge. Consider, for example, the following comment by physicist Gerald Feinberg (1975), concerning what is probably the most intuitively distressing parapsychological phenomenon—precognition:

> Instead of forbidding precognition from happening, [accepted physical] theories typically have sufficient symmetry (between past and future) to suggest that phenomena akin to precognition should occur.... Indeed, phenomena involving a reversed time order of cause and effect are generally excluded from consideration on the ground that they have not been observed, rather than because the theory forbids them. This exclusion itself introduces an element of asymmetry into the physical theories, which some physicists have felt was improper or required further

---

[1] Citation to Hansel in this section are to Hansel's (1980) revision.

explanation.... Thus, if such phenomena indeed occur, *no change in the fundamental equations of physics would be needed to describe them.* (pp. 54– 55, emphasis added)

Asserting that psi is *a priori* extremely unlikely has permitted Hansel and other psi critics extraordinary latitude in the types of alternative explanations they allow themselves to entertain: "A possible explanation other than [ESP], provided it involves only well-established processes," he said, "should not be rejected on the grounds of its complexity" (p. 21). "If the result *could have arisen through a trick,* the experiment must be considered unsatisfactory proof of ESP, *whether or not it is finally decided that such a trick was, in fact, used*" (p. 21, my emphasis). Hansel admitted that "no single experiment can be conclusive," and that replications of "an ESP experiment by independent investigators could render the possibility of deception or error extremely unlikely... if the original result is repeatedly confirmed,... ESP becomes increasingly likely" (p. 21). Hansel then proceeded to examine the evidence in a manner that was logically inconsistent with these statements. His critique, which focused on a small number of the classic card-guessing experiments, consisted of showing how each individual experiment could be dismissed if one were willing to adopt complex and elaborate fraud scenarios. He succeeded only in reaffirming his initial proposition that no single experiment should be regarded as conclusive.

There have been two documented cases of investigator fraud in parapsychology (Markwick, 1978; Rhine, 1974), and the scientific community has, in recent years, been forced to confront the unpleasant fact that scientific fraud is more common than we earlier believed (Broad & Wade, 1982; Kohn, 1988). Surely the most effective solution to this problem is, as Hansel says, to require independent replication of studies believed to have important practical or theoretical consequences before their findings are accepted. Unsubstantiated fraud accusations are not merely unethical, they are incompatible with scientific progress. New discoveries in science would be impossible if scientists rejected unexpected findings on the ground that "if the result could have arisen through a trick, the experiment must be considered unsatisfactory evidence of X, *whether or not it is finally decided that such a trick was, in fact, used.*"

Unfortunately, replication research is neither strongly encouraged nor highly valued in mainstream science. A recent study of social and behavioral science journal editors' attitudes toward publication of replication studies found a strong bias against publishing replications (Neuliep & Crandall, 1991). Other studies of behavioral science publication practices show similar biases against publication of studies that do not produce statistically significant results (Bozarth & Roberts, 1972; Sterling, 1959). In their survey of 1,334 articles from psychological journals, Bozarth and Roberts found that while 94 percent of the articles using statistical tests reported significant results, less than one percent involved replications. In contract, parapsychologists have long recognized the importance of replications and of reporting nonsignificant results. The Parapsychological Association (PA) has had an official policy against selective reporting of "positive" results since 1975. The PA is, to the best of my knowledge, the *only* professional scientific organization that has adopted such a policy. If you examine the PA-affiliated journals and conference proceedings, you will find many replication attempts, both successful and unsuccessful

The "Ganzfeld Debate" of the 1980s

The ESP ganzfeld paradigm provides an excellent counter to Hyman's central theme, that parapsychology lacks cumulativeness. I will precede discussion of the psi ganzfeld controversy with a brief account of the background and rationale underlying psi ganzfeld research to show how it has systematically built upon earlier research. (See Figure 3.)

Historically, apparent psi effects have been frequently associated with dreaming, hypnosis, meditation, and other naturally occurring or deliberately induced internal attention states. This generalization is based on converging evidence from spontaneous case studies, claims associated with various cultural practices, clinical observations, and experimental studies. I have presented this background material in detail elsewhere (Honorton, 1977). To recapitulate:

Dreaming. Cross-cultural surveys of spontaneous cases indicate that approximately 2 out of 3 reported "real-life" psi interactions are mediated through dreams rather than waking experiences (Green, 1960; Prasad & Stevenson, 1968; L. E. Rhine, 1962; Sannwald, 1959). Of course spontaneous cases are anecdotal and no conclusions should be based upon them; but they can (and should) serve as the basis of hypotheses to be tested experimentally. Experimental evidence supporting these spontaneous case trends was first provided by the ESP dream studies at Maimonides Medical Center in New York (Child, 1985; Ullman & Krippner with Vaughan, 1973). Using electrophysiological sleep-monitoring techniques to de-

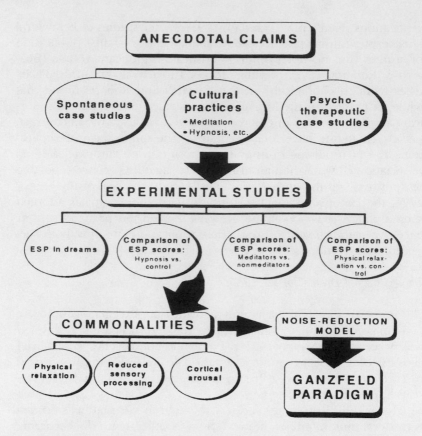

Figure 3. Origins of the ESP ganzfeld paradigm.

tect dream (REM) periods, investigators awoke physically remote senders who concentrated on randomly selected target pictures while the subjects dreamed. The subject was awakened and a dream report was recorded after each dream period. Following an experimental series, outside judges read transcripts of each night's dream reports and attempted, on a blind basis, to match them to the actual target picture used that night. The judges successfully matched the dream reports to their correct targets to a highly significant degree.

Hypnosis. The association between hypnosis and ostensible psi effects dates back to the claims of "travelling clairvoyance" and "community of sensation" in early mesmerism (Dingwall, 1968). Experimental support for a relationship between hypnosis and ESP comes from a variety of experimental studies, perhaps most persuasively from modern experimental studies comparing the effects of hypnotic induction versus nonhypnotic control conditions on ESP card-guessing performance (Schechter, 1984; Van de Castle, 1969). Schechter, for example, reported a meta-analysis of 25 experiments carried out between 1945-1981 by investigators in 10 different laboratories. ESP scores in the hypnotic induction condition were consistently (and significantly) higher than in the control condition of these experiments.

Meditation/relaxation. Claims of ostensible psychic phenomena occurring during the practice of meditation occur in most of the classical texts on meditation. A variety of modern experimental studies have indicated that meditation and relaxation exercises facilitate ESP test performance relative to control conditions (e.g., Braud & Braud, 1973, 1974; Dukhan & Rao, 1973; Stanford & Mayer, 1974).

Commonalities and a provisional model. The psi ganzfeld paradigm emerged as an attempt to explain the apparent psi-conduciveness of these and similar conditions. The question was asked: "What do dreaming, hypnosis, and meditation have in common that would lead each of them to facilitate ESP test performance?" While differing in many ways, each of these states involves physical relaxation, a reduction in ordinary perceptual processing (sensory deprivation), and a sufficient level of cortical arousal to sustain conscious awareness. This led to the development of a low-level descriptive model of ESP functioning, according to which internal attention states facilitate psi detection by reducing sensory and somatic stimuli that normally mask weaker psi input. This "noise-reduction" model thus identified sensory deprivation as a key to the frequent association between ostensible psi communication and internal states, and the ESP ganzfeld procedure was specifically developed to test the impact of perceptual isolation on psi performance. Thus we can see that the ganzfeld paradigm systematically built upon a diverse range of evidence including four different lines of experimental findings.

The ganzfeld debate consisted of a set of exchanges between Hyman (1983, 1985) and myself (Honorton, 1983, 1985), involving meta-analyses of 42 ganzfeld studies reported between 1974 and 1981. This phase of the psi controversy is unique because it resulted in a joint collaboration between critics and researchers who agreed upon specific methodological guidelines for future research that would be mutually acceptable (Hyman & Honorton, 1986). The various issues are summarized in Figure 4.

As in earlier phases of the psi controversy, the first issue concerned whether there was any effect requiring explanation. Initial estimates of ganzfeld replication rates suggested that around 50 per-

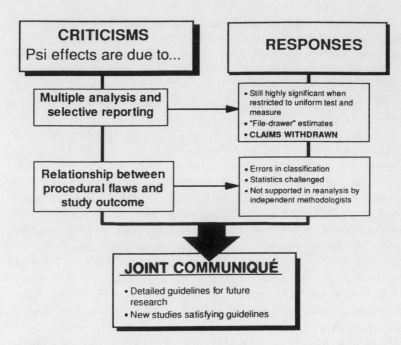

Figure 4. The ganzfeld debate of the 1980s.

cent of the reported ganzfeld studies yielded significant results compared to the expected chance rate of 5 percent. These estimates were challenged by Hyman. He pointed out that a number of the ganzfeld investigators had either applied multiple statistical tests or multiple measures of success to the results of their studies, creating a multiple analysis problem that *could* have inflated the estimates of significance; in fact, Hyman argued that the effects of multiple analysis were such as to increase the chance rate from 5 percent to 25 percent. He also argued that biased reporting of positive results (the "file-drawer" problem) might have exaggerated the significance of the known studies. In response, I restricted my analysis to 28 of the 42 studies examined by Hyman for which a uniform measure (direct hits) and test could be applied. The results were still "astronomically significant," with odds against chance of a billion to one, and would require 15 unknown studies averaging chance results for every known study in order to reduce the overall results to nonsignificance. Hyman subsequently agreed that the significance of the ganzfeld studies could not be explained through multiple analysis or selective reporting:

Although we probably still differ on the magnitude of the biases contributed by multiple testing, retrospective experiments, and the file-drawer problem, we agree that the overall significance observed in these studies cannot reasonably be explained by these selective factors. Something beyond selective reporting or inflated significance levels seems to be producing nonchance outcomes. Moreover, we agree that the significant outcomes have been produced by a number of different investigators. (Hyman & Honorton, 1986, p. 352)

The next line of criticism concerned the effects of procedural flaws on the study outcomes. In our meta-analyses of the ganzfeld studies, Hyman and I independently coded each study's procedures with respect to potential flaws involving sensory cues, randomization method, security, and so on. Here Hyman and I did not agree: my analysis showed no significant relationship between these variables and study success, while Hyman claimed that some of the flaw variables, such as the type of randomization, did correlate with results. In his initial assessment, Hyman claimed there was a nearly perfect linear correlation between the number of flaws in a study and its success (Hyman, 1982); this analysis contained a large number of errors that Hyman later attributed to typing errors (communication to Honorton, November 29, 1982). Later, Hyman (1985) claimed a significant relationship between study flaws and outcomes based on a complex multivariate analysis. However, an independent psychological statistician described this analysis as "meaningless" (Saunders, 1985). Finally, Hyman agreed that "the present data base does not support any firm conclusion about the relationship between flaws and study outcome" (Hyman & Honorton, 1986, p. 353). Were our differences in flaw assessment simply reflections of our respective biases? Perhaps, but independent examination of the issue by non-parapsychologists has unanimously failed to support Hyman's conclusions (Atkinson, Atkinson, Smith, & Bem, 1990; Harris & Rosenthal, 1988a, 1988b; Saunders, 1985; Utts, 1991). In an independent analysis using Hyman's own flaw codings, two behavioral science methodologists concluded, "Our analysis of the effects of flaws on study outcome lends no support to the hypothesis that Ganzfeld research results are a significant function of the set of flaw variables" (Harris & Rosenthal, 1988b, p. 3).

Rather than continue the debate, Hyman and I collaborated on a "joint communiqué" in which we agreed that:

the best way to resolve the controversy between us is to await the outcome of future ganzfeld psi experiments. These experiments, ideally, will be carried out in such a way as to circumvent the file-drawer problem, problems of multiple analysis, and the various defects in randomization, statistical application, and documentation pointed out by Hyman. If a variety of parapsychologists and other investigators continue to obtain significant results under these conditions, then the existence of a genuine communications anomaly will have been demonstrated. (Hyman & Honorton, 1986, pp. 353–354)

The joint communiqué presented detailed methodological guidelines for the conduct and reporting of future ganzfeld experiments. Four years later, my colleagues and I reported an extensive series of ganzfeld experiments using an automated methodology that satisfied these guidelines (Honorton et al., 1990). These experiments are discussed from several different perspectives in the contributions by Broughton, Krippner, and Morris, but are curiously omitted from the contributions of Alcock, Hyman, and Randi. Elsewhere, however, Hyman has commented on these studies:

Honorton's experiments have produced intriguing results. If, as Utts suggests, independent laboratories can produce similar results with the same relationships and with the same attention to rigorous methodology, then parapsychology may indeed have finally captured its elusive quarry. (Hyman, 1991, p. 392)

In this paper I have focused at length on Hyman's contribution because he more than the other skeptical contributors to this series has taken the trouble to familiarize himself with the material he is criticizing and has been willing, in the face of contrary evidence, to modify his position. His critical evaluations of various areas of psi research have been hard-hitting and I believe they have often been mistaken. But his involvement has contributed to a more accurate appraisal of the status of the areas in question and, most importantly, to the development of better experiments. It is therefore disappointing that he does not, in the spirit of our joint communiqué, actively encourage replication attempts by a broader range of scientists outside of parapsychology. Instead, here as in his other recent writings, Hyman appears to discourage replication efforts by scientists outside of parapsychology.

The automated ganzfeld experiments provide further evidence of cumulativeness in addition to confirmation of an overall effect consistent with the earlier studies. As Morris points out in his contribution, several additional hypotheses derived from trends in the previous meta-analysis were tested and supported, including superior performance in trials using dynamic rather than static targets and the use of senders who were friends of the subjects rather than relative strangers. It is important to draw attention to the fact that for each of the above hypotheses—overall success rate, impact of target type, and sender type—the actual *magnitudes* of the effects were consistent with the meta-analytic estimates. This was also true of another hypothesis based on a meta-analysis of the relationship between ESP performance and the psychological trait extraversion (Honorton, Ferrari, & Bem, in press); the magnitude of the correlation between psi performance and extraversion in the automated ganzfeld studies was significant and very close to the estimate from that meta-analysis. Findings such as these are important because they indicate the operation of a systematic process, not just an anomalous departure from a chance baseline, and they demonstrate that it is possible to build systematically upon earlier findings. They validate the meta-analytic estimates and provide the kind of "prospective evidence" Hyman calls for.

4. Other Issues

Parapsychology's Hidden Agenda?

Alcock's contribution does not address the scientific issues and therefore provides little basis for substantive comment. As in his earlier writings (e.g., Alcock, 1981; 1987), Alcock continues to focus on what he perceives to be a hidden agenda of religious or philosophical belief among parapsychologists—the desire to justify some form of spiritual belief. Most parapsychologists are motivated by a desire to increase fundamental understanding of human nature, but so too are most other scientists. Parapsychology is a scientific problem area, not a belief system. There are parapsychologists who believe that the findings of psi research will ultimately require accepting some form of mind-body dualism. Others believe the findings can be accommodated within a monistic framework. And there are still others—I suspect the majority of the contemporary researchers—who believe that a satisfactory scientific understanding of the psi data must await theoretical developments in other areas, especially physics and neurophysiology. Contrast this with the sort of appeals to religious belief that one sees in the popular writings of certain modern cosmologists and even prominent skeptics. Consider, for example, the final paragraph of Stephen Hawking's widely-acclaimed book, *A Brief History of Time*:

However, if we do discover a complete theory, it should in time be understandable in broad principle by everyone.... Then we shall all, philosophers, scientists, and just ordinary people, be able to take part in the discussion of the question of why it is that we and the universe exist. If we find the answer to that, it would be the ultimate triumph of human reason—for then we would know the mind of God. (Hawking, 1988, p. 175)

And what would Alcock say of the "hidden agenda" of psi-skeptic Martin Gardner?

As for empirical tests of the power of God to answer prayer, I am among those theists who, in the spirit of Jesus' remark that only the faithless look for signs, consider such tests both futile and blasphemous. (Gardner, 1983, p. 239)

Should the sentiments expressed in these and similar statements cast doubt on Hawking's physics or Gardner's skeptical acumen? I think not. They are entitled to their personal beliefs. Such beliefs should be considered irrelevant to the assessment of their scientific accomplishments unless there is ample reason to suspect that their science has been compromised by those beliefs.

Randi as Methodologist and Statistician

Randi's contribution is pure polemic and fails to deal in any substantive way with the scientific issues underlying the psi controversy. His disparaging comments about meta-analysis suggest that he does not understand meta-analysis and is unaware of its widespread use in medicine and the behavioral sciences. Randi's skill as a magician is well-known; but despite well-publicized claims to methodological expertise, his ability to design scientifically adequate psi experiments is not at all apparent from an examination of his public efforts. Serious methodological weaknesses and statistical errors occur, for example, in his book on testing ESP and in his televised tests of psychics (e.g., Morris, 1992; Rao, 1984).

5. Skepticism, Science, and the "Paranormal"

I believe the concept of the "paranormal" is an anachronism and should be abandoned. The term is usually used to imply that psi interactions must necessarily, if real, represent an order of reality outside the natural realm. The term emerged within the context of Newtonian physics and has, in my view, clearly outlived whatever usefulness it ever had. It has not served to guide the development of constructive research programs; indeed, its primary effect has been to create an artificial schism between psi researchers and the broader scientific community. A more empirically fruitful conceptualization is that parapsychology involves the study of currently anomalous communication and energetic processes. This approach guides the efforts of most of the parapsychological researchers I know, who work on the assumption that they are dealing with unexplained—anomalous, but not unexplainable—natural processes.

I believe in science, and I am confident that a science that can boldly contemplate the origin of the universe, the nature of physical reality 10^{-33} seconds after the Big Bang, anthropic principles, quantum nonlocality, and parallel universes, can come to terms with the implications of parapsychological findings—whatever they may turn out to be. There is no danger for science in honestly confronting these issues; it can only be enriched by doing so. But there is a danger for science in encouraging self-appointed protectors who engage in polemical campaigns that distort and misrepresent serious research efforts. Such campaigns are not only counterproductive, they threaten to corrupt the spirit and function of science and raise doubts about its credibility. The distorted history, logical contradictions, and factual omissions exhibited in the arguments of the three critics represent neither scholarly criticism nor skepticism, but rather counteradvocacy masquerading as skepticism. True skepticism involves the suspension of belief, not disbelief. In this context, we would do well to recall the words of the great nineteenth century naturalist and skeptic, Thomas Huxley: "Sit down before fact like a little child, be prepared to give up every preconceived notion, follow humbly to wherever and to whatever abysses nature leads or you shall learn nothing."

REFERENCES

ALCOCK, J. E. (1981). *Parapsychology: Science or magic?* Oxford: Pergamon Press.

ALCOCK, J. E. (1987). Parapsychology: Science of the anomalous or search for the soul? *Behavioral and Brain Sciences*, **10**, 553–565.

ATKINSON, R. L., ATKINSON, R. C., SMITH, E. E., & BEM, D. J. (1990). *Introduction to psychology* (10th ed.). New York: Harcourt Brace Jovanovich.

BOWN, W. (1992). Unholy row rages over Trinity's ghostbuster. *New Scientist*, **135** (No. 1831), 9.

BOZARTH, J. D., & ROBERTS, R. R. (1972). Signifying significant significance. *American Psychologist*, **27**, 774–775.

212

BRAUD, L. W., & BRAUD, W. G. (1974). Further studies of relaxation as a psi-conducive state. *Journal of the American Society for Psychical Research,* **68,** 229–245.

BRAUD, W. G., & BRAUD, L. W. (1973). Preliminary explorations of psi-conducive states. Progressive muscular relaxation. *Journal of the American Society for Psychical Research,* **67,** 27–46.

BROAD, W., & WADE, N. (1982). *Betrayers of the truth: Fraud and deceit in the halls of science.* New York: Simon & Shuster.

CHILD, I. L. (1985). Psychology and anomalous observations: The question of ESP in dreams. *American Psychologist,* **40,** 1219–1230.

DINGWALL, E. J. (Ed.). (1968). *Abnormal hypnotic phenomena* (4 vols.). London: Churchill.

DRUCKMAN, D., & SWETS, J. A. (Eds.). (1988). *Enhancing human performance: Issues, theories, and techniques.* Washington, DC: National Academy Press.

DUKHAN, H., & RAO, K. R. (1973). Meditation and ESP scoring. In W. G. Roll, R. L. Morris, & J. D. Morris (Eds.) *Research in parapsychology 1972* (pp. 148–151). Metuchen, NJ: Scarecrow Pres.

FEINBERG, G. (1975). Precognition—a memory of things future. In L. Oteri (Ed.), *Quantum physics and parapsychology* (pp. 54–73). New York: Parapsychology Foundation.

GARDNER, M. (1983). *The whys of a philosophical scrivener.* New York: Quill.

GREEN, C. E. (1960). Analysis of spontaneous cases. *Proceedings of the Society for Psychical Research,* **53,** 97–161.

HAWKING, S. W. (1988). *A brief history of time.* New York: Bantam.

HANSEL, C. E. M. (1966/1980). *ESP and parapsychology: A critical re-evaluation.* Buffalo, NY: Prometheus.

HARRIS, M. J., & ROSENTHAL, R. (1988a). *Interpersonal expectancy effects and human performance research.* Washington, DC: National Academy Press.

HARRIS, M. J., & ROSENTHAL, R. (1988b). *Postscript to interpersonal expectancy effects and human performance research.* Washington, DC: National Academy Press.

HONORTON, C. (1975). "Error some place!" *Journal of Communication,* **25,** 103–116.

HONORTON, C. (1977). Psi and internal attention states. In B. B. Wolman (Ed.), *Handbook of parapsychology* (pp. 435–472). New York: Van Nostrand Reinhold.

HONORTON, C. (1983). Response to Hyman's critique of psi ganzfeld studies. In W. G. Roll, J. Beloff, & R. A. White (Eds.), *Research in parapsychology 1982* (pp. 23–26). Metuchen, NJ: Scarecrow Press.

HONORTON, C. (1985). Meta-analysis of psi ganzfeld research: A response to Hyman. *Journal of Parapsychology,* **49,** 51–91.

HONORTON, C., BERGER, R. E., VARVOGLIS, M. P., QUANT, M., DERR, P., SCHECHTER, E. I., & FERRARI, D. C. (1990). Psi communication in the ganzfeld: Experiments with an automated testing system and a comparison with a meta-analysis of earlier studies. *Journal of Parapsychology,* **54,** 99–139.

HONORTON, C., & FERRARI, D. C. (1989). "Future telling": A meta-analysis of forced-choice precognition experiments, 1935–1987. *Journal of Parapsychology*, **53**, 281–308.

HONORTON, C., FERRARI, D. C., & BEM, D. J. (in press). Extraversion and ESP performance: Meta-analysis and a new confirmation. In *Research in parapsychology 1990*. Metuchen, NJ: Scarecrow Press.

HUNTINGTON, E. V. (1938). Is it chance or ESP? *American Scholar*, **7**, 201–210.

HYMAN, R. (1982). Hyman's tally of flaws in ganzfeld/psi experiments. Written communication to C. Honorton, July 29, 1982.

HYMAN, R. (1983). Does the ganzfeld experiment answer the critics' objections? In W. G. Roll, J. Beloff, & R. A. White (Eds.), *Research in parapsychology 1982* (pp. 21–23). Metuchen, NJ: Scarecrow Press.

HYMAN, R. (1985). The ganzfeld psi experiment: A critical appraisal. *Journal of Parapsychology*, **49**, 3–49.

HYMAN, R. (1991). Comment. *Statistical Science*, **6**, 389–392.

HYMAN, R., & HONORTON, C. (1986). A joint communiqué: The psi ganzfeld controversy. *Journal of Parapsychology*, **50**, 351–364.

KENNEDY, J. L., & UPHOFF, H. F. (1939). Experiments on the nature of extrasensory perception: III. The recording error criticism of extra-chance results. *Journal of Parapsychology*, **3**, 226–245.

KOHN, A. (1988). *False prophets: Fraud and error in science and medicine*. Oxford: Blackwell.

MARKWICK, B. (1978). The Soal-Goldney experiments with Basil Shackleton; New evidence of data manipulation. *Proceedings of the Society for Psychical Research*, **56**, 250–281.

MEEHL, P. E., & SCRIVEN, M. (1956). Compatibility of science and ESP. *Science*, **123**, 14–15.

MORRIS, R. L. (1992). Reply to Randi. *The Psi Researcher*, No. 5, 16–18.

NEULIEP, J. W., & CRANDALL, R. (1991). Editorial bias against replication research. In J. W. Neuliep (Ed.), *Replication research in the social sciences* (pp. 85–90). Newbury Park, CA: Sage.

PRASAD, J., & STEVENSON, I. (1968). A survey of spontaneous psychical experiences in school children of Uttar Pradesh, India. *International Journal of Parapsychology*, **10**, 241–261.

PRATT, J. G., RHINE, J. B., SMITH, B. M., STUART, C. E., & GREENWOOD, J. A. (1940/1966). *Extra-sensory perception after sixty years*. Boston: Bruce Humphries.

PRICE, G. R. (1955). Science and the supernatural. *Science*, **122**, 359–367.

RADIN, D. I., & FERRARI, D. C. (1991). Effects of consciousness on the fall of dice: A meta-analysis. *Journal of Scientific Exploration*, 61–83.

RADIN, D. I., & NELSON, R. D. (1989). Evidence for consciousness-related anomalies in random physical systems. *Foundation of Physics*, **19**, 1499–1514.

RAO, K. R. (1984). Review of *Test your ESP potential: A complete kit with instructions, scorecards, and apparatus* by James Randi. *Journal of Parapsychology*, **48**, 356–358.

214

RHINE, J. B. (1934/1964). *Extra-sensory perception.* Boston: Bruce Humphries.

RHINE, J. B. (1974). Comments: A new case of experimenter unreliability. *Journal of Parapsychology,* **38,** 215–225.

RHINE, L. E. (1962). Psychological processes in ESP experiences: I. Waking experiences. *Journal of Parapsychology,* **26,** 88–111.

ROSENTHAL, R. (1978). How often are our numbers wrong? *American Psychologist,* **33,** 1005–1008.

SANNWALD, G. (1959). Statistische untersuchungen an Spontanphänomene. *Zeitschrift für Parapsychologie und Grenzgebiete der Psychologie,* **3,** 59–71.

SAUNDERS, D. R. (1985). On Hyman's factor analyses. *Journal of Parapsychology,* **49,** 86–88.

SCHECHTER, E. I. (1984). Hypnotic induction vs. control conditions: Illustrating an approach to the evaluation of replicability in parapsychology. *Journal of the American Society for Psychical Research,* **78,** 1–27.

SCHOUTEN, S. A. (in press). Are we making progress? In *Psi research methodology: A re-examination* (37th Annual International Conference of the Parapsychology Foundation). New York: Parapsychology Foundation, Inc.

SCOTT, C. (1958). G. Spencer Brown and probability: A critique. *Journal of the Society for Psychical Research,* **39,** 217–234.

SPENCER BROWN, G. (1953). Statistical significance in psychical research. *Nature,* **172,** 154–156.

SPENCER BROWN, G. (1957). *Probability and scientific inference,* NY: Longmans.

STANFORD, R. G., & MAYER, B. (1974). Relaxation as a psi-conducive state: A replication and exploration of parameters. *Journal of the American Society for Psychical Research,* **68,** 182–191.

STERLING, T. C. (1959). Publication decisions and their possible effects on inference drawn from tests of significance—or vice versa. *Journal of the American Statistical Association,* **54,** 30–34.

ULLMAN, M., KRIPPNER, S., & VAUGHAN, A. (1973). *Dream telepathy: Experiments in noctural ESP.* New York: Macmillan.

UTTS, J. M. (1991). Replication and meta-analysis in parapsychology. *Statistical Science,* **6,** 363–403.

VAN DE CASTLE, R. L. (1969). The facilitation of ESP through hypnosis. *American Journal of Clinical Hypnosis,* **12,** 37–56.

BIBLIOGRAPHY OF THE PUBLISHED WORKS OF CHARLES HONORTON

COMPILED BY CARLOS S. ALVARADO, RHEA A. WHITE, AND
NANCY L. ZINGRONE

This bibliography of Honorton's published works includes a variety of material, such as experimental reports, literature reviews, and book reviews. Our efforts have been facilitated by having access to Honorton's own list of publications in his curriculum vitae. Nonetheless we have added some publications not included in his list, as well as a few works now in press. Overall, however, we have not listed unpublished works such as conference presentations or annual reports. When published papers have also appeared in abstract form (for instance, research presented at a conference), we have listed the full paper rather than the abstract, but some overlap may still be present (e.g., dreams studies). In citing conference presentations that have not been published, we have listed abstracts in *Research in Parapsychology* (*RIP*) rather than the Parapsychological Association's conference proceedings circulated at the meetings. We have done this because *RIP* is more widely available than conference proceedings and is more frequently found in college libraries. We hope that this list of publications may serve as a memorial for one of the most creative members of the contemporary parapsychological community.

1964

Separation of high- and low-scoring ESP subjects through hypnotic preparation. *Journal of Parapsychology*, **28**, 250–257.

1965

(With Morris, R., second author). A critique of Sprinthall's article "ESP: Some attitudinal factors relating to ability." *Journal of Parapsychology*, **29**, 200–203.

Editorial: Student contributions to psi research. *MSPR Newsletter*, **1**(1), 5.

We wish to thank James C. Carpenter, who gave us some references of Honorton's early publications in difficult-to-find newsletters.

How uncontrollable is psi? *Psi Worker's Newsletter,* No. 1, 1–2.

The relationship between ESP and manifest anxiety level. *Journal of Parapsychology,* **29,** 291–292. (Abstract)

The transition from Duke to FRNM. *MSPR Newsletter,* 1(2), 7–8.

1966

Emotional arousal in a long-distance ESP experiment. *Psi Worker's Newsletter,* No. 3, 13–14.

A further separation of high- and low-scoring ESP subjects through hypnotic preparation. *Journal of Parapsychology,* **30,** 172–183.

The Macalester College series. *Psi Worker's Newsletter,* No. 3, 14–15.

A year of research. *MSPR Newsletter,* 1(3), 1.

Creativity and precognition scoring level. *Journal of Parapsychology,* **31,** 29–42.

(With Stump, J., first author). Position effects in restricted calling tests. *Journal of Parapsychology,* **31,** 329–330. (Abstract)

Review of *ESP: A scientific evaluation* by C. E. M. Hansel. *Journal of Parapsychology,* **31,** 76–82.

The role of assocative habits in ESP performance. *Journal of Parapsychology,* **31,** 326–327. (Abstract)

1968

(With Carlson, T., second author, & Tietze, T., third author). Combined methods in subject selection. In J. B. Rhine & R. Brier (Eds.), *Parapsychology today* (pp. 138–145). New York: Citadel.

(With Ullman, M., first author, & Krippner, S., second author). A confirmatory study of the telepathic dream with EEG-REM monitoring. *Psychophysiology,* **5,** 218. (Abstract)

(With White, R. A., first author, Krippner, S., second author, & Ullman, M., third author). Experimentally-induced telepathic dreams with EEG-REM monitoring: Some manifest content variables related to psi operation. *Proceedings of the Parapsychological Association,* No. 5, 85–87.

Review of *The hypnotic investigation of dreams* by C. S. Moss. *International Journal of Parapsychology,* **10,** 420–423.

1969

A combination of techniques for the separation of high- and low-scoring ESP subjects: Experiments with hypnotic and waking-imagination instructions. *Journal of the American Society for Psychical Research,* **68,** 69–82.

(With Ullman, M., first author, & Krippner, S., second author). Electrophysiological studies of ESP in dreams: An investigation into the nature of psi-processing in dreams. *Proceedings of the Parapsychological Association,* No. 6, 62–63. (Abstract)

(With Krippner, S., second author). Hypnosis and ESP performance: A review of the experimental literature. *Journal of the American Society for Psychical Research,* **63,** 214–252.

(With Stump, J. P., second author). A preliminary study of hypnotically-induced clairvoyant dreams. *Journal of the American Society for Psychical Research,* **3,** 175–184.

Relationship between EEG alpha activity and ESP card-guessing performance. *Journal of the American Society for Psychical Research,* **63,** 365–374.

Review of *Experimenter effects in behavioral research* by R. Rosenthal. *Journal of the American Society for Psychical Research,* **63,** 303–307.

Review of *The founders of psychical research* by A. Gauld. *Journal of the American Society for Psychical Research,* **63,** 203–205.

Review of *Trances* by S. Wavell, A. Butt, & N. Epton. *Theta,* No. 24, 4.

Some current perspectives on the hypnotic dream. *Journal of the American Society for Psychosomatic Dentistry and Medicine,* **16**(3), 88–92.

1970

Effects of feedback on discrimination between correct and incorrect ESP responses. *Journal of the American Society for Psychical Research,* **64,** 404–410.

(With Krippner, S., first author, Ullman, M., second author, Hughes, W., fourth author, Goodman, G., fifth author, & Harris, R., sixth author). An eight-night study of precognitive dreams using EEG-EOG techniques. *Proceedings of the Parapsychological Association,* No. 7, 27–28.

A post-mortem on mesmerism and the paranormal: Comments on *Abnormal hypnotic phenomena. Journal of the American Society for Psychical Research,* **64,** 104–110.

(With Ullman, M., first author, & Krippner, S., second author). A review of the Maimonides dream ESP experiments: 1964–1969. *Psychophysiology,* **7,** 352–353. (Abstract)

Review of *Mind over matter* by L. E. Rhine. *Psychic,* **2**(3), 36.

Symposium: EEG studies of ESP. *Proceedings of the Parapsychological Association,* No. 7, 77.

Tracing ESP through altered states of consciousness. *Psychic,* 2(2), 18–22.

1971

Automated forced-choice precognition tests with a "sensitive." *Journal of the American Society for Psychical Research,* **65,** 476–481.

Effects of feedback on discrimination between correct and incorrect ESP responses: A replication study. *Journal of the American Society for Psychical Research,* **65,** 155–161.

(With Davidson, R., second author, & Bindler, P., third author). Feedback-augmented EEG alpha, shifts in subjective state, and ESP card-guessing performance. *Journal of the American Society for Psychical Research,* **65,** 308–323.

Honorton's reply to Elguin. *Journal of Parapsychology,* **35,** 140–141.

Identification and augmentation of ESP favorable states at both the physiological and behavioral level. In J. Mihalasky (Ed.), *Techniques and status of modern parapsychology: First symposium presented at the 137th annual meeting of the American Association for the Advancement of Science* (pp. 6.1–6.7). [Newark: Psi Communications Project].

(With Krippner, S., first author, Ullman, M., third author, Masters, R., fourth author, & Houston, J., fifth author). A long-distance "sensory bombardment" study of ESP in dreams *Journal of the American Society for Psychical Research,* **65,** 468–475.

(With Krippner, S., first author, & Ullman, M., second author). A precognitive dream study with a single subject. *Journal of the American Society for Psychical Research,* **65,** 192–203.

(With Carbone, M., second author). A preliminary study of feedback-augmented EEG alpha activity and ESP card-guessing performance. *Journal of the American Society for Psychical Research,* **65,** 66–74.

Review of *LSD, marihuana, yoga and hypnosis* by T. X. Barber. *Journal of the American Society for Psychical Research,* **65,** 488–492.

Review of *Parapsychology—A scientific approach* by M. Ryzl. *Journal of the American Society for Psychical Research,* **65,** 227–229.

(With Rubin, L., first author). Separating the Yins from the Yangs: An experiment with the I Ching. *Proceedings of the Parapsychology Association,* No. 8, 6–7. (Abstract)

1972

The Edinburgh P.A. convention. *ASPR Newsletter,* No. 15, 2.

(With Krippner, S., first author, & Ullman, M., third author). A long-distance ESP dream study with the "Grateful Dead." *Journal of the American Society for Psychosomatic Dentistry and Medicine,* **20,** 9–17.

(With Foulkes, D., first author, Belvedere, E., second author, Masters, R. E. L., third author, Houston, J., fourth author, Krippner, S., fifth author, & Ullman, M., seventh author). Long-distance "sensory bombardment" ESP in dreams: A failure to replicate. *Perceptual and Motor Skills,* **35,** 731–734.

Parapsychology and education—circa 1972: An appreciation of R. A. McConnell's *ESP curriculum guide. Journal of the American Society for Psychical Research,* **66,** 408–414.

(With Barksdale, W., second author). PK performance with waking suggestions for muscle tension versus relaxation. *Journal of the American Society for Psychical Research,* **66,** 208–214.

Reported frequency of dream recall and ESP. *Journal of the American Society for Psychical Research,* **66,** 369–374.

(With Krippner, S., first author, & Ullman, M., third author). A second precognitive dream study with Malcolm Bessent. *Journal of the American Society for Psychical Research,* **66,** 269–279.

(With Davidson, R., second author, & Bindler, P., third author). Shifts in subjective state associated with feedback-augmented EEG alpha. *Psychophysiology,* **9,** 269–270. (Abstract)

Significant factors in hypnotically-induced clairvoyant dreams. *Journal of the American Society for Psychical Research,* **66,** 86–102.

(With Krippner, S., first author, & Ullman, M., third author). A sixteen-night study of pre-experience and post-experience dreams. *Psychophysiology,* **9,** 114. (Abstract)

(With Krippner, S., second author, & Ullman, M., third author). A study of telepathically-influenced dream content under two conditions. *Psychophysiology,* **9,** 115. (Abstract)

(With Krippner, S., second author, & Ullman, M., third author). Telepathic transmission of art prints in sleep under two conditions.

220

Proceedings of the 80th Annual Convention of the American Psychological Association, 7, 319–320.

"Tuning up" for psi. *ASPR Newsletter,* No. 12, 2–3.

1973

(With McCallam, E., first author). Effects of feedback on discrimination between correct and incorrect ESP responses: A further replication and extension. *Journal of the American Society for Psychical Research,* **67,** 77–85.

Introduction. In T. R. Tietze, *Margery* (pp. xv–xviii). New York: Harper & Row.

Parapsychology and consciousness. In W. G. Roll, R. L. Morris, & J. D. Morris (Eds.), *Research in parapsychology 1972* (pp. 118–120). Metuchen, NJ: Scarecrow Press. (Abstract). (Also published in *Theta,* 1974, **42,** 4–5)

Review of *Biofeedback and self-control,* edited by J. Kamiya and others, and of *Biofeedback and self-control 1970,* edited by T. X. Barber and others. *Journal of the American Society for Psychical Research,* **67,** 211–215.

(With Drucker, S. A., second author, & Hermon, H. C., third author). Shifts in subjective state and ESP under conditions of partial sensory deprivation: A preliminary study. *Journal of the American Society for Psychical Research,* **67,** 191–196.

1974

Apparent psychokinesis on static objects by a "gifted" subject. In W. G. Roll, R. L. Morris, & J. D. Morris (Eds.), *Research in parapsychology 1973* (pp. 128–131). Metuchen, NJ: Scarecrow Press. (Abstract)

ESP and altered states of consciousness. In J. Beloff (Ed.), *New directions in parapsychology* (pp. 38–59). London: Elek Science.

Psi-conducive states of awareness. In J. White (Ed.), *Psychic exploration: A challenge for science* (pp. 616–638). New York: G. P. Putnam's Sons.

(With Harper, S., second author). Psi-mediated imagery and ideation in an experimental procedure for regulating perceptual input. *Journal of the American Society for Psychical Research,* **68,** 156–168.

(With Tierney, L., second author, & Torres, D., third author). The role of mental imagery in psi-mediation. *Journal of the American Society for Psychical Research,* **68,** 385–394.

State of awareness factors in psi activation. *Journal of the American Society for Psychical Research*, **68**, 246–256.

1975

(With Ullman, M., second author, & Krippner, S., third author). Comparison of extrasensory and presleep influences on dreams: A preliminary report. In J. D. Morris, W. G. Roll, & R. L. Morris (Eds.), *Research in parapsychology 1974* (pp. 82–84). Metuchen, NJ: Scarecrow Press. (Abstract)

Error some place! *Journal of Communication*, **25**, 103–116.

(With Ramsey, M., second author, & Cabibbo, C., third author). Experimenter effects in extrasensory perception. *Journal of the American Society for Psychical Research*, **69**, 135–149.

Objective determination of information rate in psi tasks with pictorial stimuli. *Journal of the American Society for Psychical Research*, **69**, 353–359.

Psi and mental imagery: Keeping score on the Betts scale. *Journal of the American Society for Psychical Research*, **69**, 327–332.

1976

(With Smith, M., first author, & Tremmel, L., second author). A comparison of psi and weak sensory influences on Ganzfeld mentation. In J. D. Morris, W. G. Roll, & R. L. Morris (Eds.), *Research in parapsychology 1975* (pp. 191–194). Metuchen, NJ: Scarecrow Press. (Abstract)

(With May, E. C., first author). A dynamic PK experiment with Ingo Swan. In J. D. Morris, W. G. Roll, & R. L. Morris (Eds.), *Research in parapsychology 1975* (pp. 88–89). Metuchen, NJ: Scarecrow Press. (Abstract)

Has science developed the competence to confront claims of the paranormal? In J. D. Morris, W. G. Roll, & R. L. Morris (Eds.), *Research in parapsychology 1975* (pp. 199–223). Metuchen, NJ: Scarecrow Press.

Length of isolation and degree of arousal as probable factors influencing information retrieval in the Ganzfeld. In J. D. Morris, W. G. Roll, & R. L. Morris (Eds.), *Research in parapsychology 1975* (pp. 184–186). Metuchen, NJ: Scarecrow Press. (Abstract)

(With Barker, P. L., second author). Locating hidden coordinates. In J. D. Morris, W. G. Roll, & R. L. Morris (Eds.), *Research in parapsychology 1975* (pp. 32–33). Metuchen, NJ: Scarecrow Press. (Abstract)

(With Terry, J., first author). Psi information retrieval in the Ganzfeld: Two confirmatory studies. *Journal of the American Society for Psychical Research*, **70**, 207–217.

Review of *The roots of consciousness* by J. Mishlove. *Journal of the American Society for Psychical Research*, **70**, 325–326.

(With May, E. C., second author). Volitional control in a psychokinetic task with auditory and visual feedback. In J. D. Morris, W. G. Roll, & R. L. Morris (Eds.), *Research in parapsychology 1975* (pp. 90–91). Metuchen, NJ: Scarecrow Press. (Abstract)

1977

A comment. *Psychoenergetic Systems*, **2**, 89–90.

Effects of meditation and feedback on psychokinetic performance: A pilot study with an instructor of transcendental meditation. In J. D. Morris, W. G. Roll, & R. L. Morris (Eds.), *Research in parapsychology 1976* (pp. 95–97). Metuchen, NJ: Scarecrow Press. (Abstract)

(With Winnett, R., first author). Effects of meditation and feedback on psychokinetic performances: Results with practitioners of Ajapa Yoga. In J. D. Morris, W. G. Roll, & R. L. Morris (Eds.), *Research in parapsychology 1976* (pp. 97–98). Metuchen, NJ: Scarecrow Press. (Abstract)

Optimizing receivers for remote perception using sensory noise reduction techniques. In T. Berger & R. Blahut (Eds.), *Abstracts of papers of the 1977 IEEE international symposium on information theory*. New York: Institute of Electrical and Electronics Engineers. (Abstract)

Psi and internal attention states. In B. B. Wolman (Ed.), *Handbook of parapsychology* (pp. 435–472). New York: Van Nostrand Reinhold.

1978

Are there especially psi-conducive internal states? In W. G. Roll (Ed.), *Research in parapsychology 1977* (pp. 15–16). Metuchen, NJ: Scarecrow Press. (Abstract)

[Discussion remarks]. In B. Shapin & L. Coly (Eds.), *Psi and states of awareness* (pp. 36, 41, 53, 54, 77, 91, 92–93, 94–95, 96, 98, 99, 100, 149, 162, 165–166, 177–178, 231–232, 235, 237, 245, 257–258, 262, 264, 267, 269–270, 273, 274, 275–276, 277). New York: Parapsychology Foundation.

Psi and internal attention states: Information retrieval in the ganzfeld. In B. Shapin & L. Coly (Eds.), *Psi and states of awareness* (pp. 79–90). New York: Parapsychology Foundation.

1979

(With Tremmel, L., first author). Directional PK effects with a computer-based random generator system: A preliminary study. In W. G. Roll (Ed.), *Research in parapsychology 1979* (pp. 69–71). Metuchen, NJ: Scarecrow Press. (Abstract)

[Discussion remarks]. In B. Shapin & L. Coly (Eds.), *Brain/mind and parapsychology* (pp. 34, 44–45, 46–48, 50, 51, 92, 109–110, 114, 138–139, 173, 200–201, 219, 231, 232, 250, 251). New York: Parapsychology Foundation.

Methodological issues in free-response psi experiments. *Journal of the American Society for Psychical Research*, **73**, 381–394.

A parapsychological test of Eccles' "neurophysiological hypothesis" of psychophysical interaction. In B. Shapin & L. Coly (Eds.), *Brain/mind and parapsychology* (pp. 35–43). New York: Parapsychology Foundation.

(With Tremmel, L., second author). Psi correlates of volition: A preliminary test of Eccles' "neurophysiological hypothesis" of mindbrain interaction. In W. G. Roll (Ed.), *Research in parapsychology 1978* (pp. 36–38). Metuchen, NJ: Scarecrow Press. (Abstract)

1980

(With Child, I. L., first author, Kelly, E. F., third author, Morris, R. L., fourth author, & Stanford, R. G., fifth author). Merging of humanistic and laboratory traditions in parapsychology. *Parapsychology Review*, **11**(2), 1–13.

(With Tremmel, L., second author). Psitrek: A preliminary effort toward development of psi-conducive computer software. In W. G. Roll (Ed.), *Research in parapsychology 1979* (pp. 159–161). Metuchen: NJ: Scarecrow Press. (Abstract)

1981

Beyond the reach of sense: Some comments on C. E. M. Hansel's *ESP and parapsychology: A critical re-evaluation. Journal of the American Society for Psychical Research*, **75**, 155–166.

[Discussion remarks]. In B. Shapin & L. Coly (Eds.), *Concepts and theories in parapsychology* (pp. 61–62, 63, 64–65, 66–67, 68, 89, 90, 103–104, 110–111). New York: Parapsychology Foundation.

224

Parapsychology and the mind-body problem. In R. A. McConnell (Ed.), *Encounters with parapsychology* (pp. 145–154). Pittsburgh: Author.

Psi, internal attention states and the Yoga Sutras of Patanjali. In B. Shapin & L. Coly (Eds.), *Concepts and theories in parapsychology* (pp. 55–60). New York: Parapsychology Foundation.

Psychophysical interaction. In R. G. Jahn (Ed.), *The role of consciousness in the physical world (AAAS Selected Symposium 57)* (pp. 19–36). Boulder, CO: Westview Press for the American Association for the Advancement of Science.

1983

(With Barker, P., second author, & Sondow, N., third author). Feedback and participant-selection parameters in a computer RNG study. In W. G. Roll, J. Beloff, & R. A. White (Eds.), *Research in parapsychology 1982* (pp. 157–159). Metuchen, NJ: Scarecrow Press. (Abstract)

1984

(With Schechter, E. I., first author, Barker, P., third author, & Varvoglis, M. P., fourth author). Relationships between participant traits and scores on two computer-controlled RNG-PK games. In R. A. White & R. S. Broughton (Eds.), *Research in parapsychology 1983* (pp. 32–33). Metuchen, NJ: Scarecrow Press. (Abstract)

1985

[Discussion remarks]. In B. Shapin & L. Coly (Eds.), *The repeatability problem in parapsychology* (pp. 16–18, 19–20, 38–39, 41, 45, 49, 67–68, 94, 96, 135, 136, 141, 142, 176, 179–180, 202–203, 207–208, 228–229, 235–236, 237, 256, 257–258, 259, 261, 262). New York: Parapsychology Foundation.

How to evaluate and improve the replicability of parapsychological effects. In B. Shapin and L. Coly (Eds.), *The repeatability problem in parapsychology* (pp. 238–249). New York: Parapsychology Foundation.

Meta-analysis of psi ganzfeld research: A response to Hyman. *Journal of Parapsychology,* **49,** 51–92.

Programmatic research assessment. In R. A. White & J. Solfvin (Eds.), *Research in parapsychology 1984* (pp. 115–116). Metuchen, NJ: Scarecrow Press.

(With Berger, R. E., first author). Psilab *II*: A standardized psi-testing system. In R. A. White & J. Solfvin (Eds.), *Research in parapsy-*

225

chology 1984 (pp. 68–71). Metuchen, NJ: Scarecrow Press. (Abstract)

1986

(With Berger, R. E., first author). An automated psi Ganzfeld testing system. In D. H. Weiner & D. I. Radin (Eds.), *Research in parapsychology 1985* (pp. 85–88). Metuchen, NJ: Scarecrow Press. (Abstract)

(With Barker, P., second author, Varvoglis, M., third author, Berger, R., fourth author, & Schechter, E., fifth author). First-timers: An exploration of factors affecting initial psi Ganzfeld performance. In D. H. Weiner & D. I. Radin (Eds.), *Research in parapsychology 1985* (pp. 28–32). Metuchen, NJ: Scarecrow Press. (Abstract)

(With Hyman, R., second author). A joint communiqué: The psi Ganzfeld controversy. *Journal of Parapsychology,* **50,** 351–364.

(With Berger, R. E., first author, & Schechter, E. I., second author). A preliminary review of performance across three computer psi games. In D. H. Weiner & D. I. Radin (Eds.), *Research in parapsychology 1985* (pp. 1–3). Metuchen, NJ: Scarecrow Press. (Abstract)

1987

(With Schechter, E. I., second author). Ganzfeld target retrieval with an automated testing system: A model for initial Ganzfeld success. In D. H. Weiner & R. D. Nelson (Eds.), *Research in parapsychology 1986* (pp. 36–39). Metuchen, NJ: Scarecrow Press. (Abstract)

Precognition and real-time ESP performance in a computer task with an exceptional subject. *Journal of Parapsychology,* **51,** 291–320.

1988

(With Palmer, J., first author, & Utts, J., third author). *Reply to the National Research Council study on parapsychology.* Research Triangle Park, NC: Parapsychological Association. (Also in the *Journal of the American Society for Psychical Research,* 1989, **83,** 31–49)

1989

(With Ferrari, D. C., second author). "Future telling": A meta-analysis of forced-choice precognition experiments, 1935–1987. *Journal of Parapsychology,* **53,** 281–308.

1990

(With Berger, R. E., second author, Varvoglis, M. P., third author, Quant, M., fourth author, Derr, P., fifth author, Schechter, E. I.,

226

sixth author, & Ferrari, D. C., seventh author). Psi communication in the ganzfeld: Experiments with an automated testing system and a comparison with a meta-analysis of earlier studies. *Journal of Parapsychology*, **54**, 99–139.

1991

(With Targ, R., first author, Braud, W., second author, Stanford, R., third author, & Schlitz, M., fourth author). Increasing psychic reliability: A panel discussion presented at the 33rd annual conference of the Parapsychological Association, Chevy Chase, MD, August 16–20, 1990. *Journal of Parapsychology*, **55**, 59–83.

1992

(With Ferrari, D. C., second author, & Bem, D. J., third author). Extraversion and ESP performance: A meta-analysis and a new confirmation. In L. A. Henkel & G. R. Schmeidler (Eds.), *Research in parapsychology 1990* (pp. 35–38). Metuchen, NJ: Scarecrow Press. (Abstract)

The ganzfeld novice: Four predictors of initial ESP performance. *The Parapsychological Association 35th annual convention: Proceedings of presented papers* (pp. 51–58). [Research Triangle Park, NC]: Parapsychological Association.

(With Schlitz, M. J., first author). Ganzfeld psi performance within an artistically gifted population. *Journal of the American Society for Psychical Research*, **86**, 83–98.

In Press

(With Bem, D. J., first author). Does psi exist? Replicable evidence for an anomalous process of information transfer. *Psychological Bulletin*.

Summarizing research findings: Meta-analytic methods and their use in parapsychology. In L. Coly (Ed.), *Psi research methodology: A re-examination*. New York: Parapsychology Foundation.

INDEX